A VICTORIAN MASTER

DRAWINGS BY FREDERIC, LORD LEIGHTON

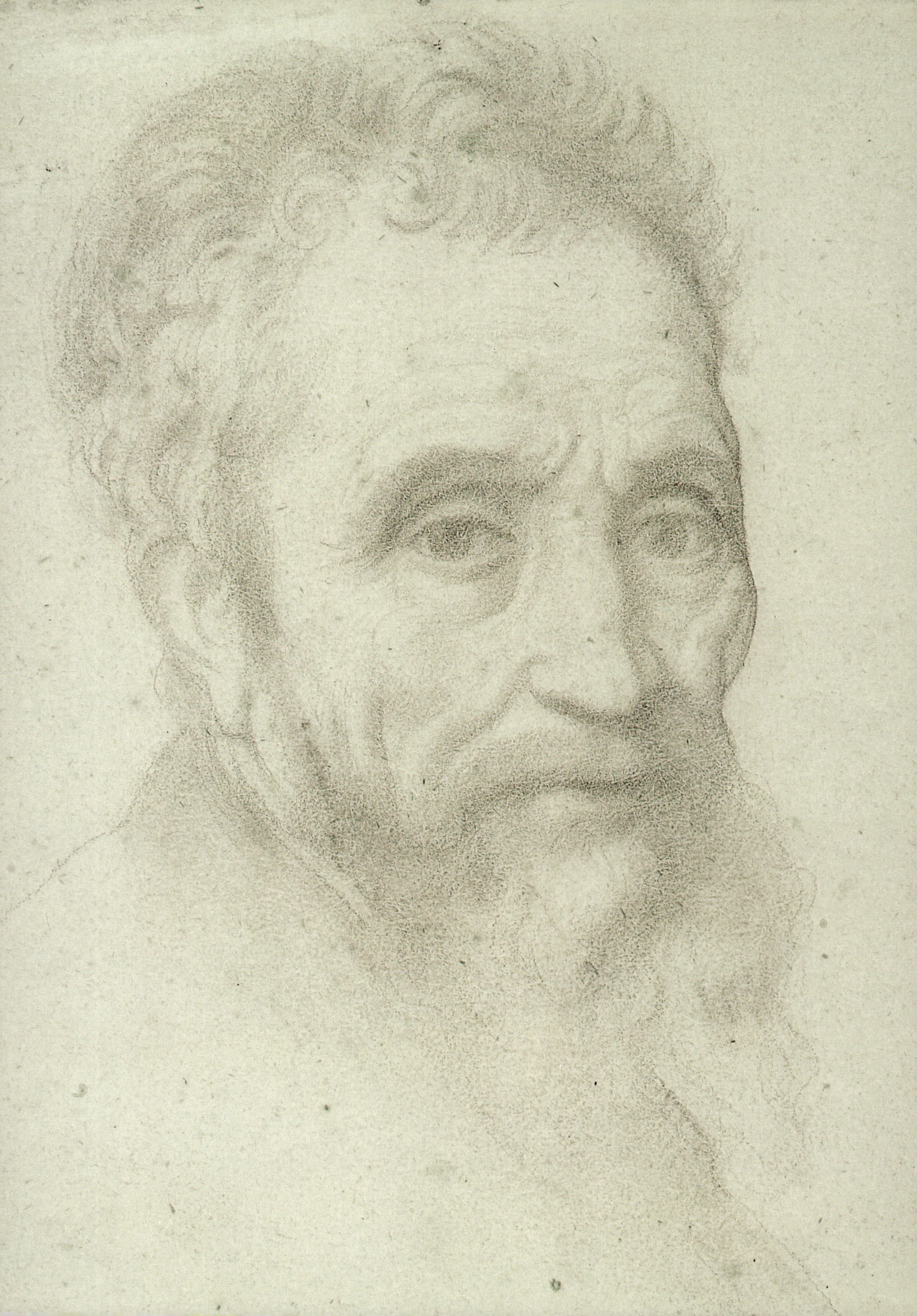

A VICTORIAN MASTER
DRAWINGS BY FREDERIC, LORD LEIGHTON

Essays by Philippa Martin and Alison Smith

Catalogue entries by Charlotte Gere, Philippa Martin, Christopher Newall, Daniel Robbins and Reena Suleman

Includes a full listing of the Leighton Drawings Collection held at Leighton House Museum.

A fully illustrated catalogue of this collection was created with the support of the Heritage Lottery Fund, and is available on-line at: www.rbkc.gov.uk/leightonhousemuseum/drawings.

The website also includes records for Leighton drawings in other public collections, created with the support of the Paul Mellon Centre for Studies in British Art.

Contributors

Charlotte Gere is a specialist in nineteenth-century decorative arts, particularly in jewellery, design and historic interiors, and a freelance exhibition curator.

Philippa Martin was a curatorial assistant at the RIBA Drawings Collection, before undertaking a series of contracts based at Leighton House Museum, most recently as Project Manager of the Leighton Drawings Project.

Christopher Newall is an independent writer and art historian. He was one of the organisers of the Royal Academy exhibition which marked the centenary of Leighton's death, in 1996, and was co-curator (with Allen Staley) of the exhibition *Pre-Raphaelite Vision: Truth to Nature* at Tate Britain in 2004.

Daniel Robbins is Senior Curator, Museums with the Royal Borough of Kensington & Chelsea, responsible for Leighton House Museum and Linley Sambourne House.

Alison Smith is a curator specialising in nineteenth-century British art at Tate Britain.

Reena Suleman is Curator of Collections and Research for Leighton House Museum and Linley Sambourne House.

Acknowledgments

Leighton House Museum and the authors would like to thank: Graham Bignell, Luisa Bockmeulen, Peter Bower, Barbara Bryant, Caroline Dakers, Alison Fawcitt, Veronica Franklin Gould, Lara Goodband, Elizabeth Gow, Gary Haines, Genevieve Hawkins, Dr Barbara Lester, Kathy Mclaughlan, Lisa Nash, Leonée and Richard Ormond, Carol Plazzotta, Kasey Schnormeier, Nicholas Tromans, Maria Grazia Vaccari, Malcolm Warner, Annette Wickham, Katharina Wippermann, Anne Young.

Photographic Credits

CONTENTS

FOREWORD

The collection of drawings by Frederic, Lord Leighton held at his former studio-house, now Leighton House Museum, is by some measure the largest and most significant body of his work in any museum worldwide. Representing the entire span of his career and including drawings relating to virtually all his major paintings, it provides an unrivalled insight into the working method of one of the most eminent British artists of the nineteenth century.

Leighton House Museum was established as a memorial to Leighton in the years immediately following his death in 1896, and the drawings collection was incorporated shortly after as a means of giving the new Museum a significant and unique body of the artist's work. The history of this collection is therefore closely bound up with the history of the Museum itself. However, the drawings have remained in need of attention for many years.

The Leighton Drawings Project, that culminates in this touring exhibition and catalogue, began in 2005 and has sought to address many of these issues. The drawings have all been conserved and re-catalogued, and the entire collection can now be viewed and researched on-line. Numerous educational activities and events have been arranged alongside this exhibition and, in the future, far greater access and enjoyment of this wonderful collection will be available at the Museum itself.

None of this would have been possible without the generous support of the Heritage Lottery Fund, whose grant award has allowed the project to proceed. In addition, we are grateful to the Paul Mellon Centre for Studies in British Art, whose award of a curatorial research grant allowed work to be undertaken to identify other public collections around the world holding examples of Leighton's drawings, so that these too could be included in the on-line catalogue. Further generous support has been received from Christopher Forbes, Shirley Nicholson and Nina Lobanov-Rostofsky in memory of Stephen Jones, curator of Leighton House Museum from 1982 to 1989.

Finally, I would like to take this opportunity to thank the staff of Leighton House Museum who have all contributed to the project in different ways, and particularly to Philippa Martin, who has researched and catalogued the drawings, and Rebecca Whamond, who has worked as the project assistant. Both posts were funded by the Heritage Lottery Fund. On behalf of the museum and the Royal Borough of Kensington & Chelsea I would also like to offer our gratitude to the private individuals and public institutions who have lent works to the exhibition, and the many others who have given their time and support to different aspect of this project over the last two years. Our thanks go to them all.

Councillor Nicholas Paget-Brown
Cabinet Member with responsibility for the Arts

THE ROYAL BOROUGH OF
KENSINGTON
AND CHELSEA

THE CREATION OF THE LEIGHTON DRAWINGS COLLECTION

Philippa Martin

At 5am on Thursday 23 January 1896, Frederic Leighton woke with agonising chest pains. Anxious not to disturb his valet, Sandercock, he waited two hours before calling for assistance. The artist had been troubled by a heart condition for several years. As early as 1889 he had complained of being short of breath: 'While ladies make with comfort and ease delightful ascents to neighbouring peaks, I humbly pant up an anthill or two'.[1] However, in the latter months of 1895 he had shown a dramatic decline, with up to 15 attacks of angina each day. Weary, and confined to his bed, Leighton knew that time was running out. On the afternoon of 23 January his two sisters, Augusta and Alexandra, were sent for. Leighton gave them verbal instructions on how to distribute his estate after his death. Two days later he spoke to his sisters in German and made a brief and hurried will, which read: 'This is the last will and testament of Frederic Leighton. I bequeath to my sisters, Alexandra Orr and Augusta Neunberg Matthews, the whole estate unconditionally. Fred Leighton.'[2] He died later that day, in the knowledge that his final wishes and all his possessions were safe in the hands of the two people he most trusted.

Leighton died in the modest bedroom of his substantial purpose-built studio-house, No. 2 (now 12) Holland Park Road in Kensington. His studio remained just as he had left it three days earlier, when last at work. His painting of *Clytie* (*c.*1895–96, Private Collection) with her arms out-stretched to Apollo the sun god, stood on an easel with unfinished areas of under-painting awaiting the artist's brush. A drawing in chalk of a female model drawing a bow, a study for one of four decorative panels he had recently been commissioned to paint, was on his drawing board.[3] Drawers, folios and cases in the studio held Leighton's drawings, sketchbooks and notebooks.[4] In fact, 'with very few exceptions, every sketch, study and drawing that Leighton ever made from his boyhood to his death was to be found preserved in portfolios or on the walls of his studio'.[5]

How these drawings, numbering some 1,650 in total, left the house to be disseminated, and how almost two thirds of them returned in the years immediately following, is a crucial part of the transformation of No. 2 Holland Park Road into Leighton House Museum. It also indicates how highly regarded Leighton was as an artist and, in particular, as a draughtsman.

Shortly after Leighton's death, the London based art dealers, the Fine Art Society, offered his sisters £1000 for the entire collection of drawings. By June 1896, the offer had been accepted and the Society announced plans to hold a selling exhibition the following December. The process of preparing the collection for sale then began. Each drawing was stamped with the monograph 'LLC' (Lord Leighton's Collection) in the lower left corner 'as a certificate that it is one of the drawings left by him'.[6] Someone with knowledge of Leighton's work – possibly his artist neighbour, Valentine Prinsep, or a knowledgeable member of staff from the Fine Art Society – gave each drawing a title along the lower edge of the sheet. Many could not be identified, and these were simply given the title 'Project'. The drawings were sorted into subjects, and a reference number written on the back of each. They were then individually priced, ranging from five shillings to 15 guineas, and this amount was also written on the reverse. Once this task was completed, an invitation to view the collection and have first refusal was sent to selected museums including the South Kensington Museum (now the Victoria and Albert Museum) and the British Museum.

Caspar Purdon Clarke, who had assisted Leighton in collecting tiles from Damascus for his Arab Hall and was now the Director of the South Kensington Museum, received a letter from the Fine Art Society on 7 November 1896. However, it was another old friend of Leighton's, Thomas Armstrong from the Department of Science and Art, who was sent to select drawings. Armstrong initially chose 40 examples, which he considered to 'represent [Leighton's] methods of working'. This initial selection was sent to South Kensington where it was whittled down to just 25 and the rejected drawings returned. However, a further selection of 30 was later made and with the addition of a compositional study entitled *The Plague in Florence* (1851, ref. no. 425–1897; acquired at the Fine Art Society's exhibition in February 1897) the South Kensington Museum's total collection amounted to 56 studies, purchased for approximately £194. Armstrong's intention was that the drawings would 'be framed at once to send into circulation immediately'.[7] Presumably they were to be lent to museums and colleges to be displayed or used as teaching aids. However, this may never have come to pass as prints of the drawings were later distributed 'for Camberwell' and 'for the Royal College of Art'. Following the selection, some drawings were loaned back to the Fine Art Society for inclusion in their forthcoming exhibition at Bond Street. Twenty of the South Kensington Museum's drawings were also exhibited at Leighton's Memorial Exhibition, held as the Royal Academy's Winter Exhibition of 1896–97.

Just before both exhibitions opened in December 1896, Walter Armstrong, Director of the National Gallery of Ireland in Dublin, travelled to London and selected just five drawings from the Fine Art Society. Rather than making a varied selection to represent highlights of Leighton's career he chose an impressive, large drapery study for the painting *Captive Andromache* (*c.*1888, Manchester Art Gallery); a nude figure study for the painting *And the Sea Gave Up the Dead Which Were in It* (*c.*1891–92, Tate Britain); and three studies for Leighton's lesser known designs for a medal (to be cast in bronze) in commemoration of Queen Victoria's Jubilee and for the decoration of the Royal Academy's Jubilee Address to the Queen, both of 1887. The drawings are recorded in the National Gallery's minute book as having been finally purchased in April 1897 for £57.10.0 – a considerable sum for just five drawings. One was included in the Memorial Exhibition at the Royal Academy.

As early as 5 May 1896, the Keeper of Prints and Drawings at the British Museum, Sidney Colvin, reported to his Trustees that Leighton's collection of Old Master drawings, and drawings by Leighton himself, were likely to be on the market soon, and that they would be 'very desirable to acquire for the British Museum'. Colvin instigated the purchase of a single drawing, a study of the head of Giotto for the painting *Cimabue's Celebrated Madonna is Carried in Procession through the Streets of Florence* (1852–55, Royal Collection) from a private collection in January 1897. He later made his selection from the Fine Art Society's drawings at Bond Street and those on loan to the Royal Academy. The 31 drawings chosen were delivered to the British Museum for final approval on 1 April 1897. They were accompanied by a note apologising for the late delivery, explaining that the Society 'waited until the closure of the RA [exhibition] before sending as some of the studies were on exhibition there'. The drawings were not actually purchased until after May 1897. Colvin's report to the Trustees, requesting £300 for the purchase, explains how the group were selected:

> [They] have been carefully chosen to represent all periods and styles of the artist's work from 1852 to 1895. They include a proportion of his early architectural and natural

fig. 1. Photograph of Emilie Isabel Barrington (1844–1933).

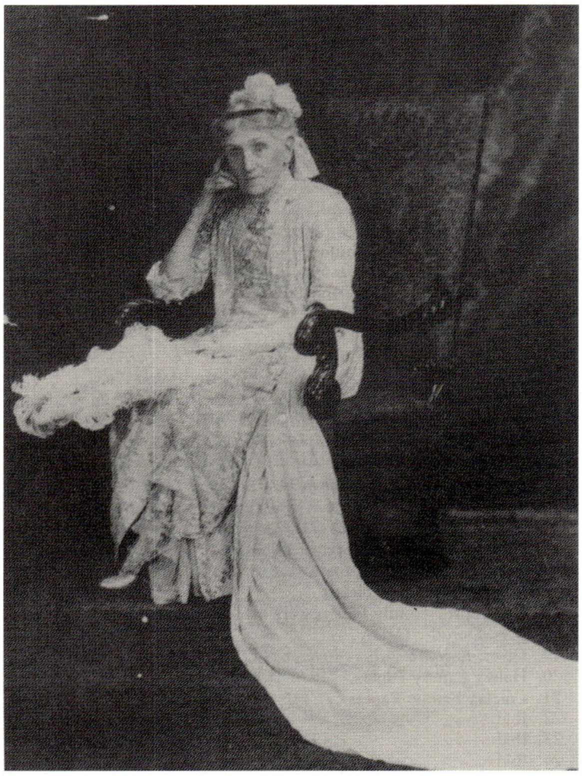

1.

history studies, which are of the finest possible quality, as well as studies for portraits, and for figures in many of his chief pictorial compositions from the earliest ('The Death of Brunellesco' [sic]) to the latest ('Clytie').

Whilst these national institutions secured significant collections of Leighton's drawings, by far the biggest single acquisition was negotiated by a smaller, newly established body. A brief article in *The Times*, written to mark the opening of the Fine Art Society exhibition, refers to this group in warning that 'many of the best [drawings] have been purchased already by the British and South Kensington Museums and by the friends who are hoping to re-adorn [Leighton's former] house'.[8] The 'friends' were the Leighton House Committee. From very shortly after Leighton's death, his sisters had supported pressure from his friends and fellow artists to preserve the house as a museum. They initially offered the house and its entire contents for sale for the bargain sum of £25,000, and expressed their support of a fundraising scheme to purchase it as a museum. However, when the scheme failed, the contents were sold separately through Christie's. The Christie's sale alone raised about £35,000, and the sisters decided to sign the lease of the house over to representatives of the Leighton House Committee.[9]

The Committee's principal ambition was to purchase as many of Leighton's drawings as possible from the Fine Art Society, to form a comprehensive collection of 'the best examples of the work executed in every period of Lord Leighton's life'.[10] In a letter to *The Times*, the artist Walter Crane emphasised the importance of seeing the drawings in Leighton's former home: 'To be able to see these records of an artistic life in their true relation to the surroundings of that life would be not the least part of their value.'[11]

The driving force behind the Committee was Emilie Barrington (fig. 1) a neighbour of Leighton's who had been a friend and regular visitor to his studio, as well as to the studio of his close friend George Frederic Watts. She was an amateur painter, and had persuaded both artists to give her advice and tuition. Following Leighton's death she wrote a two-volume biography of his life and work, which was published in 1906. Barrington's friendship with Leighton's sister, Alexandra, continued after the artist's death, helping to place her at the forefront of the scheme to preserve the house and establish the collection of drawings. Although the sisters did not become members of the Committee, they voiced their approval of its aims and gave a great deal of financial support.

On 9 December 1896, Emilie Barrington, together with two other representatives of the Leighton House Committee – the sculptor Hamo Thornycroft and the artist Frank Dicksee – went to the Fine Art Society to make an initial selection. Between them they selected 'a thousand pounds' worth of drawings which amounted to 'about 180' in total. Thornycroft would later recall: 'It was not [an] unpleasant bit of work and very conclusive of the energy of the man and painstaking student of nature wh[ich] Leighton was throughout his life.'[12] The exhibition opened to the public a week later. Included were 250 drawings, spanning Leighton's entire career and arranged in a loosely chronological order around three rooms of the Bond Street premises. The drawings represented the cream of the collection and included Leighton's fine detailed pencil drawing known as the *Byzantine Well-Head* (1852, Private Collection), admired by John Ruskin, and the beautiful pencil study of the head of Romeo for the painting *The Reconciliation of the Montagues and Capulets over the Dead Bodies of Romeo and Juliet* (1852–55, Private Collection) now at Birmingham Museums and Art Gallery.[13]

Such was the quantity of drawings held by the Fine Art Society that a second exhibition opened at Bond Street in August 1897, just four months after the closure of the first.[14] This time 133 drawings were displayed. A number were those that had remained unsold from the earlier exhibition, but most were from the Society's reserve stocks and were on display for the first time. When all the drawings were sold, the Society made a total income of £3,742.

The first catalogue of the Leighton House collection was published by March 1897, and includes 348 drawings purchased through the Leighton House Committee's 'Leighton Purchase Fund'. The Committee must therefore have continued to select and acquire further drawings after the initial group of 180 works chosen by Barrington, Thornycroft and Dicksee. The drawings had been mounted and framed, and were already on display at the house (fig. 2, page 11). Each drawing was listed with its individual price. The total amount spent on the drawings was £1,110, and the intention behind this first exhibition was to reimburse the Committee's funds through encouraging retrospective private sponsorship of the drawings. Also listed are drawings that were presented directly to the house by friends and admirers, including 19 given by Leighton's sisters, eight by Barrington, and three presented by the architect Alfred Waterhouse. The total number of drawings included in the catalogue was 439. Whilst the scheme to encourage sponsorship continued, additional drawings were also purchased by private individuals directly from the Fine Art Society and presented to the house.

On 22 March 1897, Emilie Barrington wrote a letter to *The Times* requesting support for the scheme.[15] At this time only £400 – £500 had been raised, of which £50 had been donated by the Fine Art Society. Donations could be sent directly to Henry Percy Horne, treasurer of the Leighton House Committee. Alternatively, Barrington could be contacted at her home just behind Leighton House, in Melbury Road, and a private viewing of the drawings arranged (as the house was only open by appointment).

At the time the drawings were first exhibited, the Leighton Memorial Fund was also established – to raise money for a memorial to the artist, to be placed in St Paul's Cathedral. The memorial was designed by sculptor Thomas Brock, and the public were called on to offer financial support to the scheme through appeals printed in *The Times*.[16] It was also in 1897 that the Committee began to struggle to meet the running costs of the house, and so established the Leighton House Endowment Fund in order to provide an income. The greatest contribution to this Fund was the bequest of Leighton's sister, Alexandra, who left £700 in her will – considerably more than the next largest contributions of £100 each from Leopold de Rothschild and 'a well wisher'. Despite these contributions, support for the Endowment Fund was sought through a further public appeal.[17] These appeals, requesting financial contributions for causes related to the memory of Frederic Leighton, were undoubtedly competing with the campaign to purchase drawings for the Leighton House Collection. However, the extent of their impact is difficult to establish.

A further factor that may have affected the success of the campaign was a rumour started by Leighton's friend, fellow artist and direct neighbour, Valentine Prinsep. Writing a letter to the vestry of Kensington on 8 October 1900, Prinsep asserted that, after leaving Leighton's side on the day he died, the sisters had informed him that their brother expressed a desire for everything to be sold after his death, including the house and its contents. The reply from the Leighton House Committee, sent to the editor of *The Times*, assured the public that the sisters 'alone received their brother's latest instructions and last wishes on his death bed, and from them alone can any knowledge of those wishes be obtained'.[18] It would be reasonable to assume that both parties were speaking truthfully, and the question was over the interpretation of Leighton's wishes. Undoubtedly Leighton did encourage the sisters to sell the house and contents, but his motive was probably to avoid leaving them a financial burden in fulfilling his numerous bequests. It seems unlikely that, having gone to some lengths to allow public access to his home and its contents during his lifetime, he would have raised any objection to public access after his death.[19]

In June 1898 *The Times* announced that Leighton's sisters had made the extraordinary decision to buy 'more than 500' of his drawings for Leighton House, more than doubling the size of the collection.[20] This is somewhat ironic as his sisters had sold the drawings to the Fine Art Society in the first place. They had also already presented the Leighton House Committee with 19 of their own drawings, presumably given to them by their brother during his lifetime. Their motive may have been to boost a failing public campaign, or perhaps embarrassment over the surplus money they were left with after the very successful sale of the contents of the house by Christie's in July 1896. These new drawings were first exhibited when the house formally opened to the public in April 1900, and a new catalogue of the collection was published (fig. 3).

With the addition of these 500 drawings, it would be reasonable to assume that a decade after Leighton's death the collection would number in excess of 1000 works. This figure is supported by contemporary accounts. A statement by the Leighton House Committee of 1905 reads: 'The house contains over a thousand drawings and sketches by Lord Leighton'[21] and a biography of Leighton, published the following year, states:

> The collection of original works – studies, drawings, sketches, etc., at Leighton House, number some 1120 items. Upwards of 600 are framed and hung upon the walls, whilst several hundreds are still uncatalogued and unframed, and not usually accessible to the public. As funds permit, the latter will be framed and circulated throughout the principal Schools of Art in the United Kingdom.[22]

This figure of 1120 may include some oil sketches and paintings. Today, however, the collection of drawings at Leighton House Museum numbers 665 loose drawings, an album of drawings and four sketchbooks. Of these, just 20 drawings have been purchased or donated to the collection in the last 80 years. Even if there were once more than the 69 oil paintings and sketches in the house today, it would seem that about 400 of the drawings present in 1905–06 are now unaccounted for. The first catalogue of the drawings, printed in 1897, includes several which can be positively identified as works in the Leighton Drawings Collection today. However, a large number of those listed are certainly not now part of the collection. For example, titles such as *Masqueraders Arriving at an Entertainment – Lord Leighton Receiving*, or *Study of a Sword in Watercolour* can no longer be linked to any known Leighton drawing. These, and many other drawings in the catalogue, are not only missing from Leighton House Museum but they are not known to survive at all. One explanation is that some were indeed 'circulated throughout the principal Schools of Art in the United Kingdom', or were sent for exhibition to 'the poorer parts of London and in the Provinces' as the Leighton House Committee had intended, and that due to poor record keeping, changes in the administration of the Museum or the impact of two world wars, they were never returned.[23] Another, perhaps more likely explanation is that at some point in the history of the Museum – when appreciation of Leighton's work and Victorian art generally was at a low ebb – unframed drawings and the entire collection of photographs of Leighton's work (also now missing) were disposed of as a result of being damaged beyond repair, or simply because they were considered insignificant.

Another intriguing aspect of the history of the collection is the role that Emilie Barrington may have played in the destiny of some of the drawings. As the Leighton House Committee struggled to meet the running expenses of the house, Leighton's sisters offered to present the property to the Borough of Kensington. An appeal for the council to acquire the house, made during a public meeting at Kensington Town Hall in 1901, was passed unanimously, and it seemed the transfer would be straightforward. However, Barrington was averse to the proposal, later claiming that objections to the transfer by local ratepayers concerned about the cost of maintaining the building had lead to her reservations. When the sisters subsequently withdrew their offer to present the house to the Borough, Barrington was held solely responsible, and her reluctance to relinquish power was blamed. Anger towards her lingered and was most publicly expressed in a newspaper article published in 1902 by an unknown author, criticising her involvement in the affair.[24] It is not easy to ascertain whether this dispute affected her support of Leighton House and its collections, but the extreme generosity she had once shown in helping to form the drawings collection, and in donating her own drawings to the collection, had certainly come to an end.

In 1909 Barrington presented the Hugh Lane Gallery in Dublin with a chalk study by Leighton for the painting *Antique Juggling Girl* (*c.*1873, Private Collection). Then, just before the

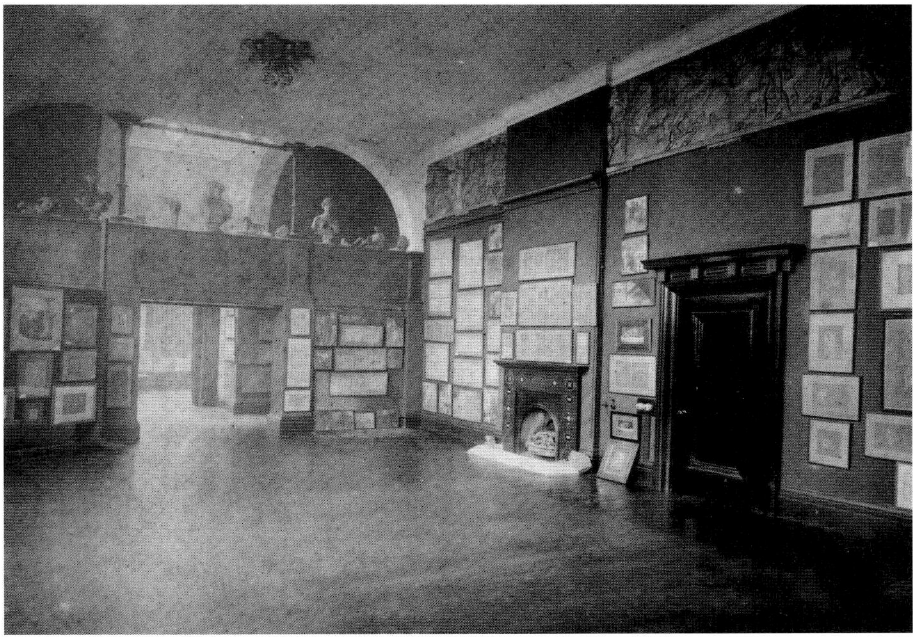

2.

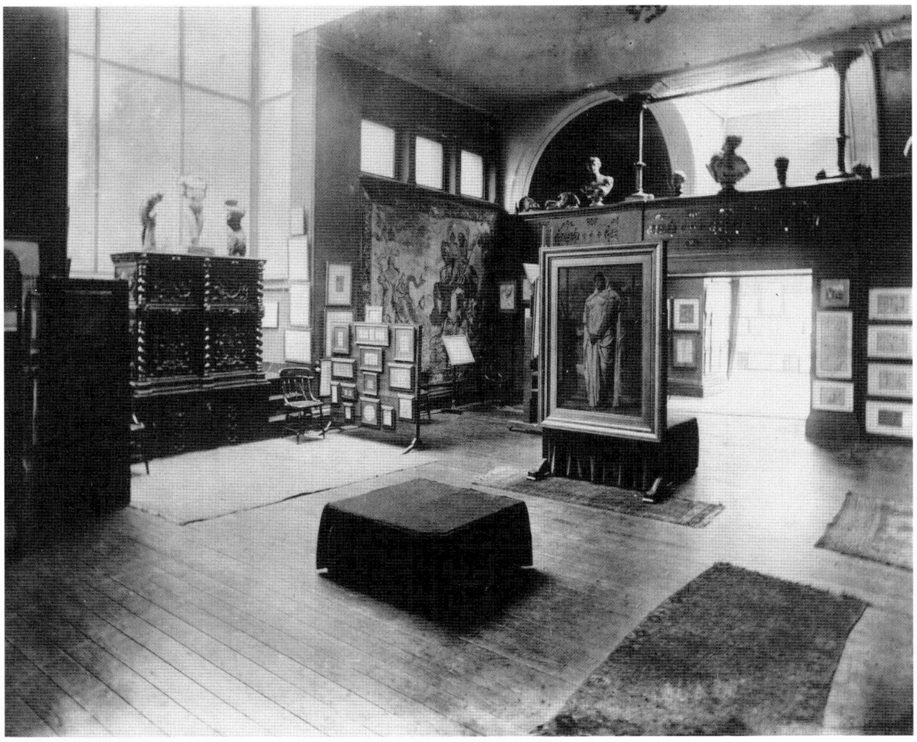

3.

fig. **2.** Photograph of the studio at Leighton House Museum in *c.*1897, showing the first exhibition, open by appointment only, of the newly formed Drawings Collection.

fig. **3.** Photograph of the studio at Leighton House Museum in *c.*1900, showing the second exhibition of the newly formed Drawings Collection and including many of the *c.*500 drawings presented to the Leighton House Committee by Leighton's sisters. The house opened six days per week from 9 April 1900, and was dressed with a few pieces of furniture and rugs that were deemed appropriate to the setting.

transfer of the house to the Borough of Kensington in 1926, Barrington drew up a list of items that she considered her own personal property and intended to remove. Amongst these was Leighton's watercolour view of the Ca' D'Oro in Venice, which her daughter-in-law returned to the house after her death. An inventory of 1926 also notes that there were '24 sketches and photographs framed' in the secretary's room (probably Leighton's former bedroom) and that 'Mrs. Barrington reserves the right to retain certain of these'.[25] However, whether or not these drawings were by Leighton is unclear. At her death Barrington was in possession of several Leighton drawings, which were left to her son, Guy. Some of these are now in public collections, and at least two examples seem to be drawings that were purchased by the Leighton House Committee and included in their catalogue of 1897. Curiously, Leighton House was not entirely forgotten in her will, which included £10 left to a steward of the Museum.

Photographs, together with early descriptions of the Museum and Barrington's catalogue of the items exhibited from 1900, give a clear picture of how the drawings were once displayed. When the house first formally opened as a museum, the drawings were mounted, framed and arranged on almost every wall, alongside photographic prints or engravings of the finished works they relate to. The display began in the Dining Room, continuing up the main staircase, around the Silk Room, through the main studio and ending in the Winter Studio (or Glass Studio). The Arab Hall and Narcissus Hall could not be used to display drawings because of their precious tiled walls, and Leighton's bedroom was probably the room used by Barrington as an office, but why the Drawing Room was unused is not clear.

From the time the Museum first opened until it was handed over to the Borough of Kensington, there was a varied programme of temporary exhibitions in the house, which appear to have run alongside the permanent display of drawings. A flyer advertising a 1901 loan exhibition of Leighton's paintings maintains that the 'permanent collection of sketches is also on view'.[26] Space for these exhibitions was made in the Winter Studio. When the house and contents were presented to the Borough in 1926, a list of the contents was drawn up. This room-by-room inventory lists almost no drawings, although at the end of each room-list is a reference to 'other pictures as per catalogue', almost certainly referring to Barrington's catalogue of 1900. In 1933, 376 drawings by Leighton were listed as 'framed and unhung' at the Museum. Presumably the vast majority of the drawings were still in frames and displayed on the walls.[27] Three years later, two screens were purchased for the display of the 'unhung' drawings, 'which it is not possible to display permanently owing to limited accommodation'.[28] This suggests that even in 1936 the majority of the drawings were still occupying the available wall space and that the collection had remained exactly as described in the catalogue of 1900. This long period of exposure would explain why some drawings are so dramatically bleached as a result of light damage. As the number of 'unhung' drawings is given as almost 400, this may be the quantity now missing, which was part of the collection in 1905–06. Some time after the Second World War, the drawings collection was taken down from the walls and the house redecorated.

Leighton House Museum has continued to acquire drawings since the collection was first established. In 1958, two early Leighton drawings (one depicting a dog and mule and the other a male nude) were presented to the museum by T.C. Sandercock. He was the son of Leighton's last valet, nicknamed 'Sanders' or 'Cockeye' by Leighton. After both Leighton and Sandercock had died, a group of Leighton's works was presented to Sandercock's widow by Leighton's sisters. Her son later returned the works to Leighton House Museum. Two of the most spectacular drawings in the collection are both studies for heads for the painting *Cimabue's Celebrated Madonna is Carried in Procession through the Streets of Florence* (1852–55). These were bequeathed to the Museum in 2003 by an American private collector, coincidentally just in time for an exhibition focusing on the painting at the house (cat. nos 1.3, 1.4).

Most recently, a drawing for the composition of the painting *Music* (*c.*1883–85, Leighton House Museum) designed as a frieze for the home of one of Leighton's foremost patrons James Stewart Hodgson, has been purchased in celebration of the 2006 exhibition (cat. no. 5.4). This drawing was one of a group that Leighton framed and placed on display under the north window of the main studio. He would frequently direct visitors to view this display of his studies (fig. 4).

The foreword of the 1897 catalogue of the drawings at Leighton House states 'Lord Leighton himself expressed a hope that these [drawings] would, if kept together, help art students who were in no position to travel...'. Almost certainly written by Emilie Barrington, this suggests that Leighton entertained the idea that his drawings would be preserved as a collection. Barrington also recalled that, after framing a drawing on her advice that was then borrowed and not returned, Leighton incessantly referred to it as 'that sketch you lost for me'. He had carefully preserved all of his studies for paintings and almost every drawing he made, forming a virtually complete record of his working methods and interests. Leighton used the collection as an archive, referring back to earlier drawings for inspiration, but he may also have preserved them with the idea that the collection might remain intact as a record of his life and work after his death. Details of his account with Roberson's, suppliers of art materials, indicate that between 1869 and 1890 he frequently purchased apparatus to fix chalk to paper, including blowing flasks, fixing liquid and glass tubes in order to better preserve his drawings.

There is further evidence of a desire to retain all his drawings in two letters in the Leighton House Archive. In March 1893 he wrote to the art critic Harry Quilter, 'I have for many years constantly declined to sell sketches or drawings, but shall be happy to lend you for reproduction the original study (from life) of one of my pictures'.[29] Similarly, in response to a request for drawings to be included in an exhibition in 1895, Leighton was most concerned as to whether the intention was to sell them. 'And I ask this not out of pettiness,

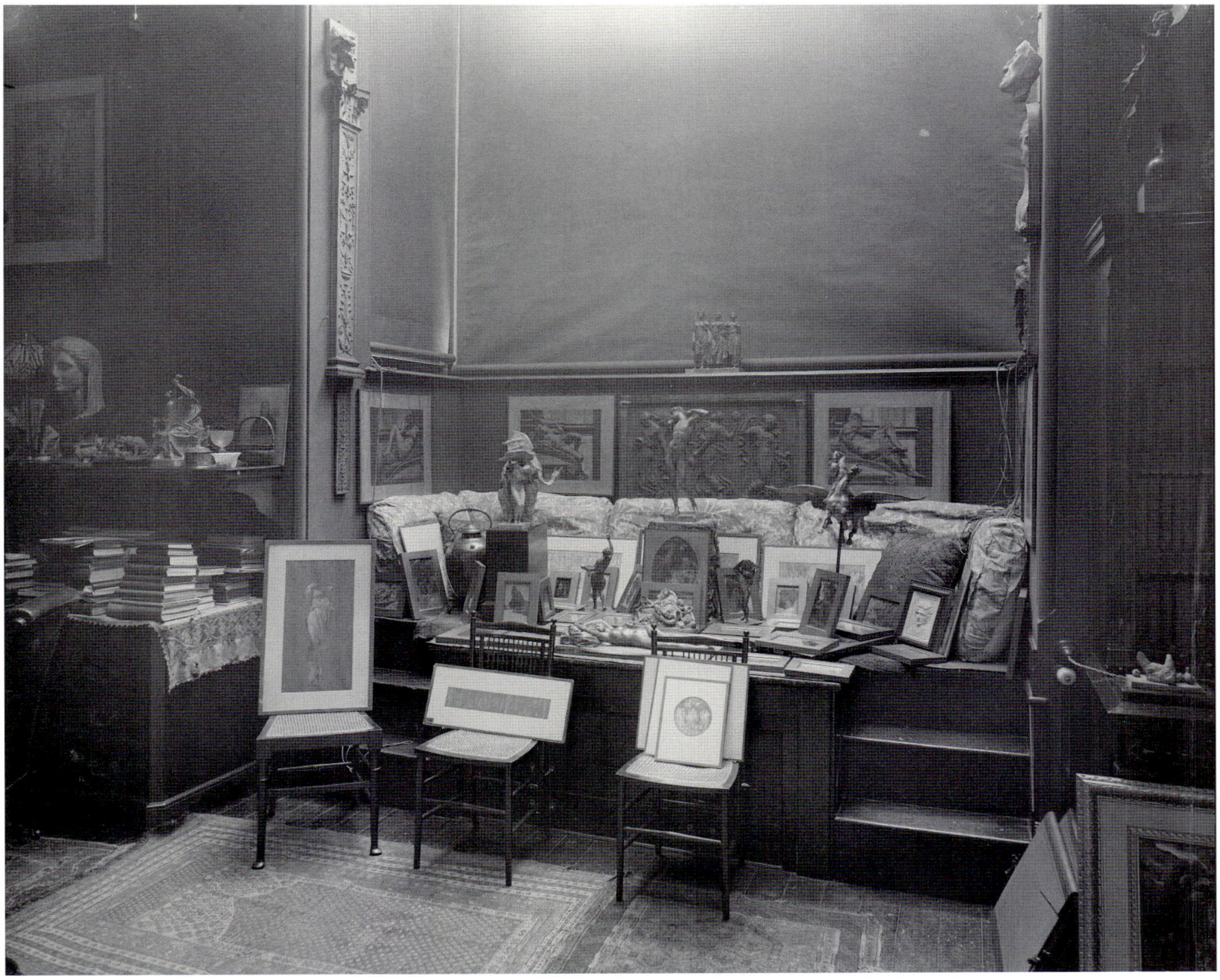

4.

fig. 4. Photograph of the display under the north window of the studio at 12 Holland Park Road, 1895, including framed drawings by Leighton. The drawing on the central chair may be the pencil study for the painting *Music* (*c.*1883–85, Leighton House Museum), purchased by Leighton House Museum in 2005 (see cat. no. 5.4).

but rather for the reason that studies from nature, for the artist himself, are of irreplaceable value... so far I have consistently refused to part with these documents, although I have often enough been asked to do so.'[30]

It is conceivable that, in preserving the collection, it was Leighton's intention that all the drawings would remain together as a public collection after his death. But as the painter William Blake Richmond noted, Leighton was 'far too modest of his attainments' to presume that his home and drawings would be considered worthy of 'general public interest', and he would have been anxious not to burden his sisters with the task.[31] However, by preserving his former home as a museum and establishing the largest collection of Leighton drawings in the world, his sisters, with assistance from Emilie Barrington, may have partially fulfilled one of the artist's own undisclosed ambitions. With today's technology allowing us to further amass the dispersed drawings – through the on-line database of drawings in public collections worldwide including the catalogue of the Leighton House Collection, launched in 2006 – we are able to come close to reassembling this carefully preserved collection, which offers a precious insight into the life and work of Frederic Leighton.

NOTES

1. Barrington 1896, vol. II, p. 313.
2. Last will and testament of Frederic, Lord Leighton. Leighton House Archives, ref. no. LH/1/6/7. This was not the only will Leighton had made. Just days after his death, under the heading 'Fine Art Gossip', the *Athenaeum* reported: 'It is true that the painter made a will some time since, the provisions of which concern no one now; for shortly before his death he made another, according to which his estate is to be divided between his sisters.' (1 February 1896, p. 156.)
3. **LONDON** 1896, p. 13. The drawing was probably a study of a female figure illustrated in *Studio*, vol. IX, 1897, opp. p. 206, with the caption 'The Last Study made by Lord Leighton'.
4. W.B. Richmond, 'Lord Leighton's House', *The Times*, 30 April 1896, p. 6.
5. **LONDON** 1900, p. 532.
6. **LONDON** 1896, p. 9.
7. In a minute paper of the Department of Science and Art of 19 November 1896, Victoria and Albert Museum, ref. no. MA/1/F540/1.
8. Anon. 1896b.
9. For further details, see: *Davenport Weekly Leader*, Friday 6 November 1896, p. 3; 'Lord Leighton's House', *The Times*, 28 January 1899, p. 13; Anon. 1900.
10. **LONDON** 1897, p. 7.
11. Walter Crane, letter of 3 May 1896, *The Times*, Wed 6 May 1896, p. 4.
12. Henry Moore Institute, Thornycroft Archive, ref. no. LL49.
13. Birmingham Museums and Art Gallery, ref. no. 1960P8. *Byzantine Well-Head* is now in a private collection.
14. At the same time drawings by Edward Linley Sambourne (1845–1910) were on exhibition at the Fine Art Society. Sambourne's former home in Kensington, and a large collection of his drawings, are also now owned by the Royal Borough of Kensington and Chelsea.
15. Barrington 1897.
16. Anon. 1897.
17. Leighton House Archives, ref. no. K71/107.
18. Anon. 1900.
19. Leighton was 'at home' each Sunday afternoon, offering his guests the opportunity to view his home, his varied collection of art works and the paintings he was at work on in his studio.
20. Anon. 1898.
21. W.B. Richmond, 'Appeal for an Endowment Fund'. Leighton House Archives, ref. no. K71/107.
22. Staley 1906, p. 223.
23. Barrington 1896, p. 92.
24. Anon. 1902.
25. 'Inventory of Pictures, furniture, etc. to be taken over by the Kensington Borough Council'. Leighton House Archives, ref. no. LH/4/1/4/89.
26. 'Exhibition of Paintings by Lord Leighton'. Leighton House Archives, ref. no. LH/3/11/6.
27. Handwritten document entitled 'Leighton House February 1933'. Leighton House Archives, ref. no. LH/4/3/3/14.
28. 'Report of the Leighton House Sub-Committee', 1936. Leighton House Archives, ref. no. LH/4/2/4/71.
29. Letter from Leighton to Harry Quilter, dated 6 March 1893. Leighton House archives, ref. no. LH/1/5/164i.
30. Letter from Leighton to an unknown recipient, dated 9 February 1895. Leighton House Archives, LH/1/5/335.
31. W.B. Richmond, *The Times*, 4 May 1896, p. 9.

'ART DISGUISING ART'
THE DRAWINGS OF FREDERIC LEIGHTON

Alison Smith

In the course of his distinguished career, Leighton's public persona was established primarily through the paintings and sculptures he exhibited at the Royal Academy and elsewhere. Given the prominence accorded these productions, some commentators nevertheless felt that many of his best and most characteristic works remained unknown to the general public during the time he was active as an artist.[1] After Leighton's death portfolios were found, crammed with drawings and studies from his early years to his maturity. Such a comprehensive collection had never been compiled by a British artist and, for the writer Edgcumbe Staley among others, this was positive proof 'not only of his skills as a draughtsman, but of his amazing diligence and devotion to his art'.[2] These drawings were first exhibited *en masse* at the Fine Art Society in 1896, and following their acquisition by the Leighton House Committee were subsequently displayed at Leighton House from 1897 to at least 1936.

It is not altogether surprising that Leighton's drawings were so little known during his lifetime, as the majority were produced as designs and studies for finished paintings rather than being conceived of as independent works in their own right. Although artists would often exchange drawings as gifts, there was no strong tradition of exhibiting preparatory drawings in public because such works were considered unfinished, stages in a generative process. Drawings that were shown at 'black and white' exhibitions held by the Royal Academy and London's Dudley Gallery from the 1870s were generally produced as collectors' pieces, such as the highly finished coloured chalk portrait drawings of Frederick Sandys. Leighton's drawings can be said to have functioned as a mechanism of the academic tradition he adhered to, by which a painting was constructed via a carefully calibrated process. Emilie Barrington defined this method in terms of three key stages: the 'sketch' or original idea for a picture, followed by the 'study' which determined the constituent parts of the work, and finally the 'design' which distributed these elements within the composition.[3] This system, which can be traced back to Giorgio Vasari and the Bolognese and Roman academies of the seventeenth century, viewed ideal art in terms of the gradual elimination of spontaneous and accidental elements – 'art disguising art'.[4]

Given the subservient role assigned to the study by this tradition, Leighton nevertheless ascribed a high value to his drawings, more so than did his fellow painter-sculptors Alfred Stevens and George Frederic Watts. Stevens was said to destroy his studies as they were absorbed into the finished statement, while Watts would work out a concept in his mind and then paint directly onto canvas, while also making as he progressed quick sketches in pencil and clay or wax maquettes.[5] By contrast, Leighton never found his drawings dispensable once they had played their particular function. Rather he would display selected examples with pride, as can be seen in the photograph of 1895 of the platform beneath his main studio window, where framed drawings and statuettes are arranged (fig. 4). According to Barrington, Leighton valued his sketchbooks more than any of his records. Describing an occasion when Leighton showed her and a friend a sketchbook containing studies of rocks, she recalled her companion exclaiming to Leighton: 'You had better take it [back], or I shall run off with it in my muff.' Barrington continues, '"You may take anything else in the place you like, but not that", Leighton answered, as he stretched out his hand and seized the little book eagerly.'[6] This testimony is amplified by a letter in which Leighton declined a request to sell a selection of his studies because of their irreplaceable value to himself as 'documents of relevance'.[7]

Given such territorial regard for his drawings, Leighton was however prepared to publish certain examples in the form of photographic reproductions. From 1884 these adorned the pages of specialist art magazines and drew attention to the aesthetic and intellectual side of his *métier*. In so doing Leighton may have deliberately been flaunting his sketches in defence of his practice as a painter. One of the presiding issues that dominated British art criticism of the 1880s and 1890s was the question of how far the academic system curtailed spontaneity. For advocates of Impressionism and the pursuant French avant-garde, 'academic' was a derogatory term connoting over-calculation at the expense of directness of application. Even a staunch acolyte like Barrington suspected that Leighton's relentless pursuit of perfection in his painting technique fettered unpremeditated expression, whereas in his drawings she perceived an antidote to the more academic aspects of his craft. For Barrington the crucial sense of 'vibration' that she admired in Watts was to be found in Leighton's sketches, not his paintings: 'A stray loose touch in charcoal will often possess a charm of quality which the most finished brushwork will fail in giving us'. Some of Leighton's drawings she perceived appeared so slight 'as to seem merely breathed upon the paper'.[8] From this perspective the drawings can be seen as a means of asserting his allegiance to the European academic tradition, but also, by virtue of their performative suggestive qualities, they demonstrate how he rose above any notion of the conventionally academic.

Leighton's Early Studies

The high esteem with which Leighton regarded his drawings owes much to his education which was, according to Stephen Jones, uniquely eclectic and international for a British artist of the time.[9] Following the peregrinations of his family Leighton received instruction at the academies of Florence and Berlin, and at the Städelsches Kunstinstitut in Frankfurt, where he studied assiduously from 1846–52. This cosmopolitan training liberated him from the constraints of the London Academy, where students were generally not permitted to draw from the nude until they had completed what would now seem an excessive three years in the Antique School, drawing from casts. By contrast, Leighton was proficient with anatomy by the age of fourteen (a discipline encouraged by his physician father) and had also benefited from an early exposure to the living model as well as Antique casts. However, seen in relation to his English contemporaries, the amount of time invested in Leighton's technical development seems inordinately long, for by the time he made his debut in Britain with *Cimabue's Celebrated Madonna is Carried in Procession through the Streets of Florence* in 1855, the younger Pre-Raphaelite artists John Everett Millais, Dante Gabriel Rossetti and William Holman Hunt had already established their reputations on the English exhibition scene.

Leighton's early drawings betray a seriousness of purpose and a deep reverence for early Italian art inculcated in him by his master at Frankfurt, Eduard von Steinle, and by the Nazarene school of Catholic German painters, and are marked by an extreme linearity coupled with an austerity of design. Leighton is said to have practised etching under Steinle, which may further account for the delicacy and precision of his line, which has led to several of his early studies having been mistaken as exercises in silverpoint (the highly refined means of making an inerasable line, practised in the Renaissance). The linear emphasis that went with the mistrust of effect instilled in him by Steinle can be clearly seen in a drawing the young artist made on the journey from Frankfurt to Rome during his *Wanderjahr* (year of travel) of 1852. The image shows a monk leading a youth away from his enemy and is rendered with what Alice Corkran termed 'a perfectly definite outline' and an 'almost remorseless severity'.[10]

If this drawing can be described as schematic, even mannered, Leighton was acutely aware of the danger of his art becoming flat and stereotypically academic – hence his embracement of the detailed observation of nature recommended in Ruskin's *Modern Painters* (1843–60). In a letter to his mother from Rome in December 1852, Leighton wrote, 'I long to find myself again face to face with Nature, to follow it, to watch it, and to copy it, closely, faithfully, ingenuously – as Ruskin suggests, "choosing nothing and selecting nothing"'.[11] The small fine studies Leighton executed around this time (with a hard pencil on white or tracing paper) of plants, vegetation and architectural detail bear witness to the extent of his commitment to Ruskinian principles.

Some of the most exquisite of these studies date from 1854–56, such as the drawing of a cyclamen viewed from different angles and inscribed with the colour notations 'stem onion col. / flow. pale pink / 2 streaks of lake' (fig. 5). In this and other botanical studies of crocuses, thistles and pumpkin heads, Leighton is focused primarily on the exploration of fact and structure, allowing nothing in his mind or art to obfuscate this abiding quest for accuracy apart from the elegant disposition of forms within the composition. Ruskin himself became particularly enamoured with two early drawings by Leighton: *Byzantine Well-Head* (1852, Private Collection) and *Study of a Lemon Tree* (cat. no. 2.8) and in 1883 asked the artist if he could borrow these as illustrations of exact draughtsmanship for his Slade lectures in Oxford. Leighton would have concurred with Ruskin's belief in delineation as the first skill of the painter, and is known to have preached the maxim, 'Learn to draw correctly, facility is sure to follow' to students at the Royal Academy.[12] Leighton exhibited *Study of a Lemon Tree* at the Pre-Raphaelite association, the Hogarth Club, in 1859, partly to prove that he could exceed the Pre-Raphaelites in their reverence for nature, but also to demonstrate his belief that selection and compositional arrangement should never be subordinate to a fixation with detail. Indeed with its judicious placement of the tree on the paper and the subtle adjustments in the strength of line and tone, this drawing exemplifies the cognitive process described by Barrington in which the eye transmits to the brain the structure of an object 'not only as it is outlined against other objects, but also as the different planes of which it is formed recede or advance, slant one way or another, curve or straighten'. The cult status accorded this drawing was largely due to its being the work on paper that Leighton exhibited most during his lifetime.[13]

Some of Leighton's early studies can be viewed as exercises in draughtsmanship for its own sake. Unlike his later sketches many are signed, indicating a precocious self-consciousness of his craft. Steinle was to warn Leighton against such pride in striving for excessive finesse, contending that art could only evolve through 'roughness' or a more impressionist use of medium.[14] It is worth noting that Leighton's drawings disclose little interest in the Antique at this stage of his career, and that his 'scientific' approach to nature was complemented by the scrupulous copies he made of fourteenth and fifteenth century masters studied in Italy. During his stay in Venice in September 1856, for example, Leighton spent time in the Accademia making precise copies of figures selected from Carpaccio's cycle from the *Scuola di Sant' Orsola* and *A Miracle of the Relic of the True Cross*. Extraordinary in these studies is the artist's power of concentration, his ability to isolate a figure from a densely crowded composition and to reproduce it with such exactitude. Particularly striking are the two men conversing, picked out from the sidewalk on the left in the latter painting (fig. 6), as well as the head study of a kneeling boy in the foreground. Copies like these would have caused a tremendous strain on the retina, and may have been at the root of eye problems experienced by Leighton in later years.

Drawing as Preparation

For the paintings produced in the early part of his career, Leighton adopted the practice of making many detailed studies of separate parts, such as the drawings of heads, feet and hands produced in relation to *Cimabue's Celebrated Madonna is Carried in Procession through the Streets of Florence* and *The Reconciliation of the Montagues and Capulets over the Dead Bodies of Romeo and Juliet* (1852–55, Private Collection). These 'fragments' were then traced and amalgamated into the composition, as worked out in a separate drawing. This process relates not only to his training but particularly to the influence of French painters like Elie Delaunay and Adolphe-William Bouguereau, whom he would have encountered in Rome. The French were as always a strong artistic presence in the city at that time, concentrated at the French Academy, and it was through this group that Leighton absorbed the rudiment that detail should be dependent upon form, a dictum that enabled him to move beyond the linear Germanic style of drawing towards placing a greater emphasis on modelling within a definite outline.

The three years that Leighton spent intermittently in Paris, from 1855 to 1858, were crucial in the development of a more systematic way of constructing a picture, by which the image would be realised through a painstaking attachment to a succession of preparatory steps as practised in the work of the French artists above. Once Leighton had finalised a design in his mind's eye he made a sketch. This was followed by nude studies, used to assemble the composition as a whole. Having made an oil sketch, and the drawing having been transferred to canvas with the aid of tracings, he worked on the painting in monochrome. The nude painted figures were then copied back into a drawing that served as a basis for detailed drapery studies. These were subsequently transferred to canvas for working up in monochrome and finally colour. Drawing thus acted as the foundation for painting, serving to discipline and control what Leighton considered to be the potentially distracting element of colour.

The emphasis Leighton placed in interviews on the undeviating nature of his system does risk exaggerating the consistency of his actual procedure, for a close examination of

fig. 5. ***Study of a Cyclamen***, dated 'Oct/56 Tivoli' (LHO/D/0978).

fig. 6. ***Study of three figures in Carpaccio's 'A Miracle of the Relic of the True Cross'*** (LHO/D/0930).

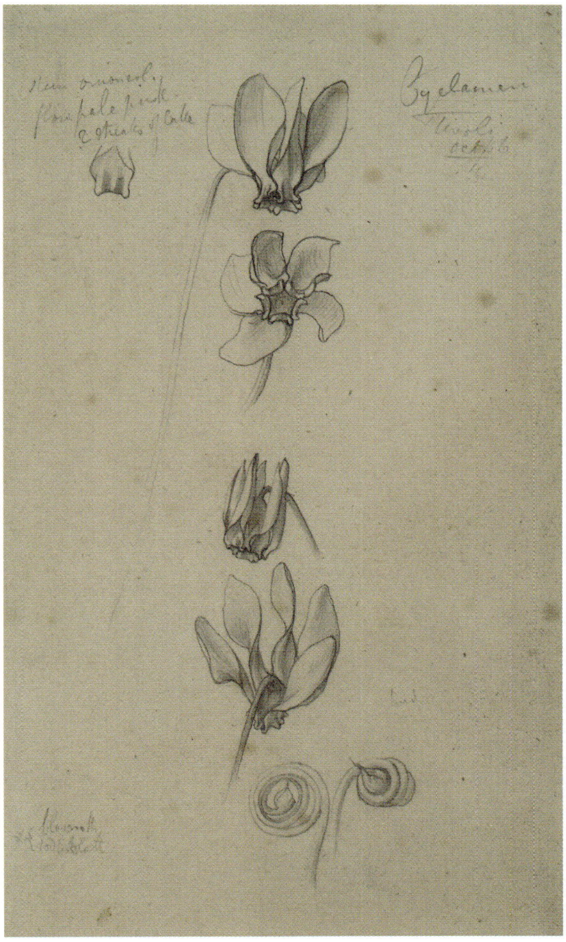

5.

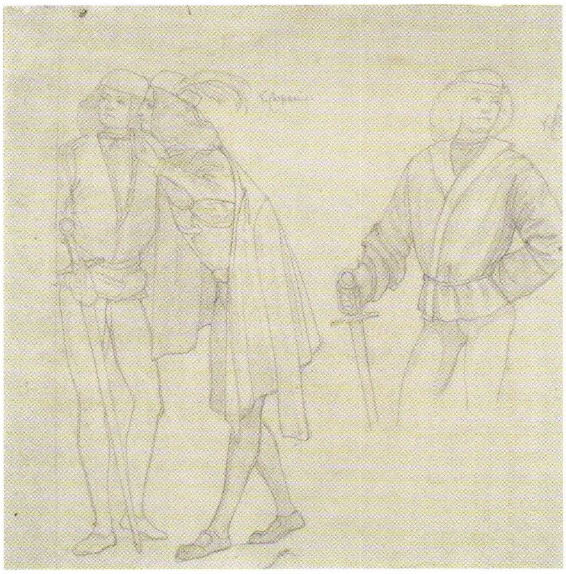

6.

his works on paper reveals that he did adjust figure postures and the arrangement of drapery folds in the course of a composition. Because there were so few witnesses to Leighton's system from inception to completion, it is impossible to ascertain precisely just how his method functioned. What is clear, however, is that from the time he settled permanently in London in 1859 his drawing assumed a mainly preparatory role. Few works were executed as independent studies. Not many drawings for portraits exist, which would indicate that he increasingly came to view draughtsmanship as a means of refining his ideas along ideal, abstract lines. Leighton's concern to distil through his drawings a sense of beauty developed in tandem with George Aitchison's building and extension of his studio house from 1865. As Elizabeth Prettejohn has demonstrated, this was organised through its structure and lighting scheme to allow Leighton maximum control over the conditions under which his pictures were executed.[15] The artist's avocation of an indoor working method further relates to his preoccupation with the figure as the basis for composition.

Leighton's contact with French academic painters had stimulated an interest in the nude, and it is significant that his acquisition of an Ingres pencil drawing, *Odalisque and Slave* (*c.*1835–41, Fogg Art Museum, Cambridge, MA) in 1867, coincided with his own foray into the realm of nude painting during the late 1860s. Leighton's promotion of the nude as the foundation of design can, in this sense, be seen as a renunciation of his former Ruskinian principles and his substituted allegiance to a group of artists who aspired beyond nature to an ideal corporeality associated with Classical, Renaissance and contemporary French academic art. Alongside this ambition developed a concern to reform the teaching of life-drawing in Britain along Continental lines, so that students would have access to the model much earlier in their training in order to comprehend the generalised forms that underpinned ideal art.

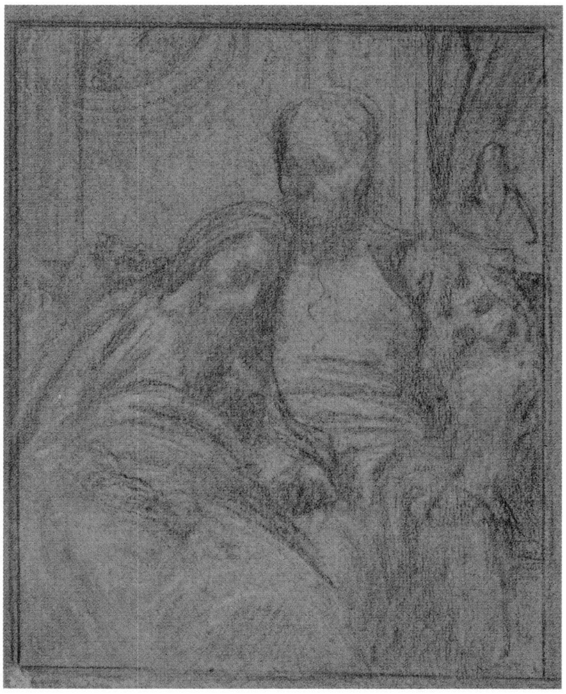

7.

Edward Poynter, who knew Leighton from his time in Rome, was the first to implement the French system of drawing from the model in conjunction with the Antique when he became professor at the Slade, on its opening in London in 1871.[16] Leighton's own practice was centred on drawing from life above the study of past masters. Few copies exist among his drawings, indicating that he had both assimilated key influences and could retain images in his mind, liberating him to focus almost exclusively on exploring idealism through the observation of living models.

The emergence of a softer, sensuous manner in Leighton's painting parallels changes in his drawing practice. Working from the model encouraged him to experiment with more 'responsive' materials like black and white chalk, which further allowed for rapid execution to capture fleeting movements and poses. Although Leighton had used *carta azzurra* (bright blue paper) from the late 1850s, he now used it more regularly in combination with black and white chalks to explore forms in the round as solid projections or two-dimensional bas-reliefs. This tendency can also be observed in the drawings of artists Leighton was associated with (including Watts, Albert Moore, Poynter, Whistler and Burne-Jones) who were all stylistically close in the 1860s although diverse in the way they treated the figure.

One of the key aims of the classically minded artists who emerged at this time was to reconcile the two traditional polarities of *disegno* (design) and *colore* (colour) by fusing sculptural and painterly elements and through a trans-historic association of different schools – for example, Venetian and fifth-century Greek. According to Barrington, Leighton continually struggled to prevent the sensuous or romantic qualities of his art from subsuming the preoccupation with line and form inculcated in him by Steinle.[17] Visually this dichotomy manifests itself as a tension between a desire to create rich colour harmonies and a self-imposed obsession with disciplined composition. The drawings often express a simultaneous impulse to both confine and release form by varying the medium and strength of line employed. Thus the studies produced in relation to *Michelangelo Nursing His Dying Servant* (1862, Private Collection) are drawn in a soft combination of black and white chalks on blue paper (fig. 7) as if establishing a counterpoint to the sombre heavy subject, and offer a visual equivalent to the theme of sleep and death. By contrast, the sensuous *Helios and Rhodos* of 1869 (Tate) was worked up from fine pencil drawings on white paper in which floating bodies are contained within clear binding contours.

Drawing as Expression

Leighton's drawing style can be said to have become more sculptural as he entered his Michelangelesque or Hellenistic phase around 1875. From around 1872 he began to experiment with using black and white chalks on two shades of brown paper, which became his favourite surfaces together with the coarse brown wrapping paper he employed for making rapid sketches. Working on a dark ground encouraged a bold and expressive treatment of the human figure in complex positions, and lent his drawing the quality of roughness that

Steinle had encouraged. This shift coincided with Leighton's venture into sculpture around the mid-1870s, which further stimulated a renewed interest in anatomy. (Following his election as PRA he became a regular attendee at the Academy's anatomy lectures.) The familiarity with the human figure that came from modelling in the round gave Leighton's figures a sense of organic life and freedom. As was the case with Stevens and Watts, drawing and sculpture were approached as complementary pursuits in the exploration of the dynamics of the human body. Working with speed and facility became vital at this time of high productivity. Samuel Pepys Cockerell writes of Leighton's devoted industry, estimating that he made 36 drawings and two clay maquettes of figures for *The Daphnephoria* (1876, Lady Lever Art Gallery, Port Sunlight), 56 drawings and three models for *Cymon and Iphigenia* (*c.*1884, Art Gallery of New South Wales) and 56 drawings for *Captive Andromache* (*c.*1888, Manchester Art Gallery).[18]

One striking feature of Leighton's mature draughtsmanship is the way drapery takes on a life of its own. Just as Hellenistic sculpture is distinguished by the agitated ridges and grooves of cloth, so Leighton's treatment of material became increasingly contorted, however tranquil the pose of the figure.[19] One could argue that his earlier passion for delineating the intricate folds of plants and bird plumage was re-channelled in his later years towards the expression of a complicated play of drapery. In studies such as the uppermost figure in *The Return of Persephone* (fig. 8) or the cascading tresses of *Clytie* (fig. 9) chalk is dextrously employed to capture rippling movement and tremulous contrasts of light and shade, a quality surely grounded in his earlier meticulous observations of the sinuous forms of plants and flowers.

It was these late drawings that came to public notice as illustrations in art periodicals, a development abetted by new reproductive technologies. The *Art Journal* led the way in 1884 when it published a selection of studies for *Cymon and Iphigenia*, followed by the *Magazine of Art* from 1888 when Leighton drawings were first used to adorn annual reviews of the Royal Academy summer exhibition. (The 1889 review provided the first detailed account of the artist's system.)[20] Leighton's relationship with influential editors such as Marion Spielmann of the *Magazine of Art* will have facilitated this flattering exposure, but it may also, as has already been suggested, have been encouraged by a growing willingness on the part of artists to promote their drawings in defence of their ideals, at a time when academic draughtsmanship was challenged by Impressionist techniques permeating British art from abroad. Watts, for instance, made red chalk drawings after the major subject paintings he intended to donate to the nation in defence of British art, twelve of which were exhibited and sold at Agnew's in May 1891. Poynter, who was closest to Leighton as an exponent of academic draughtsmanship, extolled the centrality of drawing to ideal art in his *Ten Lectures*, collectively published in 1897. Like Leighton, Poynter was himself a connoisseur and collector of drawings, and the eclectic nature of both artists' collections is testimony to the importance they ascribed to drawing as the key indicator of artistic personality.[21]

fig. 7. ***Study for 'Michelangelo Nursing his Dying Servant': Composition*** (LHO/D/0467).

fig. 8. ***Study for 'The Return of Persephone': Drapery*** (LHO/D/0698).

fig. 9. ***Study for 'Clytie':Hair*** (see cat. no. 6.9).

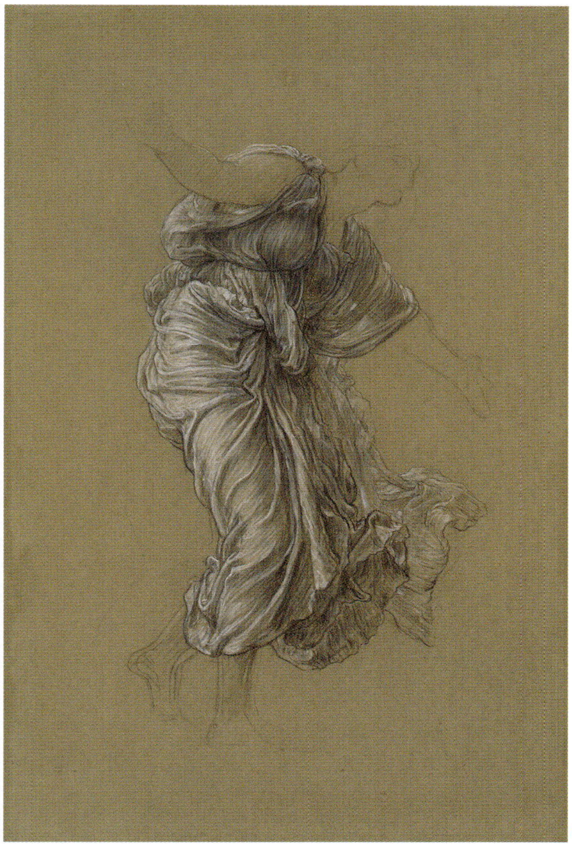

8.

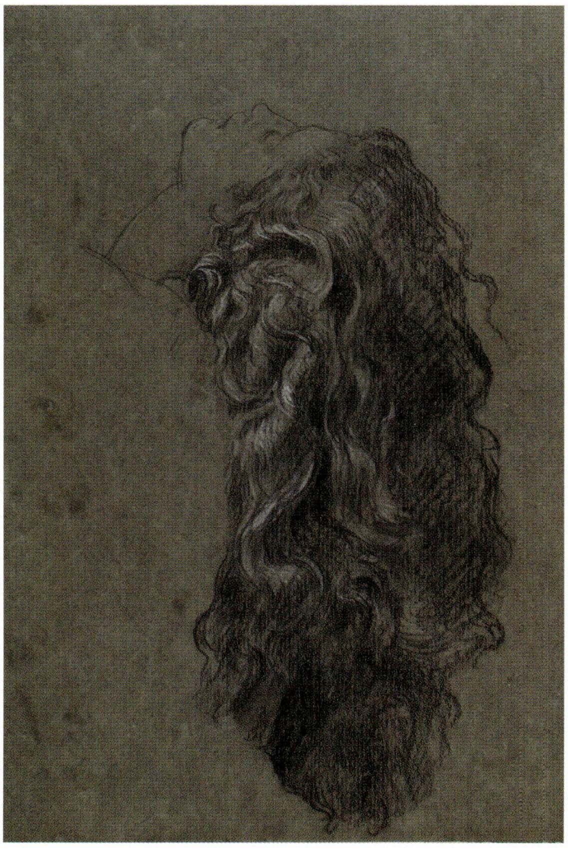

9.

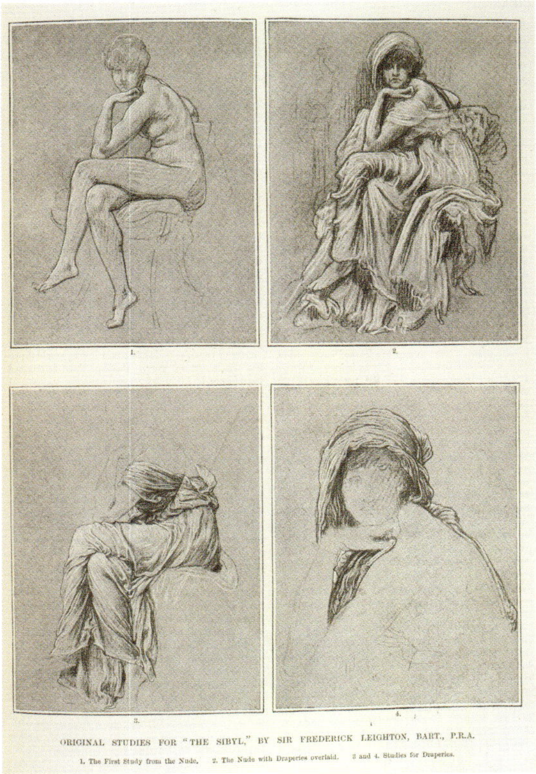

10.

fig. **10.** 'Original studies for *The Sibyl*, by Sir Frederic Leighton', from 'Current Art: The Royal Academy- 1', by Marion Harry Spielmann, *Magazine of Art*, 1889, p. 225.

It would seem that Leighton had commenced his career in London as a radical importer of foreign academic art, but rose in reputation to stand as a defender of the British school against a new wave of Continental influence. As President of the Royal Academy, Leighton inaugurated a series of pragmatic reforms, adjusting regulations and methods of instruction but never questioning the foundations of academic pedagogy. By the 1880s the teaching of the institution was perceived by outsiders to be moribund in contrast to the reformist agenda set by the Slade and Royal College of Art.[22] Thus Leighton's compositional system, which was itself a foreign importation, came with the new critical alignments of the 1880s to be identified with the institution of which he was president. It was seen as retrogressive in comparison to the latest Impressionist methods, which were set up in opposition to the 'progressive' art Leighton had championed earlier in his career.

Spielmann, a zealous spokesman of tradition in British art, recognised that Leighton's method was 'wholly out of tune with the realistic tendency of our rising Franco-English school'.[23] By replicating sequences of carefully composed preliminary drawings – such as a group of figure and drapery studies for Sibyl (1896, Private Collection; see fig. 10) – Spielmann set out to prove that idealism in art depended upon a time-consuming mode of procedure. This point was subsequently reiterated by William Blake Richmond, who thought that Leighton's drawings represented the culmination of a tradition threatened by the advance of 'slovenly' painting and drawing, and also by Samuel Pepys Cockerell, who called for reproductions of the artist's drawings to be hung in schools of art all over the country as a corrective to the fashionable disregard for sound draughtsmanship.[24] For Leighton's defenders the drawings thus epitomised an ideal yet to be embraced by the Royal Academy, as well as acting as a bulwark against new naturalistic trends in British art.

The idea that Leighton's art was dependent upon a carefully prescribed system does to an extent misrepresent the various ways he would use his preparatory studies. Indeed a survey of the works stored at Leighton House would suggest that he conceived of his vast collection of drawings as a sort of archive or database, from which he would select a pose or motif and re-work it in a different context (an important reason why he was loathe to part with his studies). An example of the ingenious way in which Leighton would mine his archive for images includes a small figure of a water-carrier on a sheet with other studies made on his 1857 trip to Algiers, which was later enlarged and reversed for the figure in the background of *Lieder Ohne Worte* (1860–61, Tate). Another example is the drawing of a tree made in Florence in 1854, which was re-used in the highly finished illustration for Heinrich Heine's *Buch der Lieder* of the following year, and then again, much later, was adapted for the background of *Lachrymae* (*c.*1895, Metropolitan Museum, New York).[25]

Assumptions concerning the inflexibility of Leighton's system, promoted by both his supporters and detractors, further overlook the accidental origins of his works in small doodles and unexpected sightings which connoisseurs prized as tokens of his genius. Cockerell quotes Leighton recalling that the design for *The Spirit of the Summit* (1894, Auckland Art Gallery) was 'suggested by certain blots on the drop-scene at one of the theatres as he sat staring at it between the acts in enforced idleness', while other accounts note that his most beautiful designs were prompted by the unconscious attitudes of his models.[26]

Although aleatory effects were a crucial springboard for Leighton's creativity, his preferred *modus operandi* was emphatically cerebral in working from chaos towards order. One commentator thus compared the claustrophobia and disorder of his studio 'cumbered with bric-a-brac' to the spacious tidiness of John Everett Millais, while noting that the fastidiousness of Leighton's procedure represented the antithesis of Millais' thoroughly modern spontaneity.[27] Leighton's art may have been grounded in fugitive impressions, but his system was ultimately aimed at exorcising all traces of the contingent in seeking to transmogrify the artist's visual sensations into art. Such a contradiction encompasses the drawings themselves. These had no economic value whatsoever, never having been tested on the marketplace. Generally filed away, their purpose hidden to all who confronted his beautifully fashioned canvases, they were all made to be filtered into compositions. Leighton's drawings represent both his craftsmanship and connoisseurship, confirming the evolution of his style through ritualised stages of development, and his self-consciousness about that achievement as probably the most dedicated exponent of the academic tradition in Britain, yet one whose art remained distinctive, defying easy classification. ■

NOTES

1. See, for example, Cockerell 1896, p. 809.
2. Staley 1906, p. 170.
3. Barrington 1896, p. 76.
4. *ibid.*
5. Towndrow 1939, pp 71–72.
6. Barrington 1896, p. 85.
7. Autograph letter in German, signed Frederic Leighton, London 9 February 1895. Leighton House Archives, ref. no. LH/1/5/335.
8. Barrington 1896, pp 78–79. For a detailed consideration of Leighton's academicism, see Prettejohn 2000b.
9. LONDON 1996, p. 55.
10. This drawing is reproduced opposite p. 18 in Corkran 1904. See also Barrington 1906, vol. II, p. 371.
11. Letter dated 22 December 1852, Barrington 1906, vol. I, p. 197: misquoting Ruskin 1843.
12. Corkran 1904, p. 123.
13. Barrington 1906, vol. I, pp 203–04. *Study for a Lemon Tree* was also exhibited at the black and white exhibition at the Dudley Gallery in 1874 and at the Grosvenor Gallery in 1880.
14. Barrington 1906, vol. I, p. 152.
15. Prettejohn 1996, pp 17–21. See also Robbins 2005.
16. Poynter 1897, p. 101.
17. Barrington 1906, vol. II, p. 12.
18. LONDON 1896, p. 812. See also Cockerell's preface in Cockerell 1898, p. xi.
19. For a fuller account of the Hellenistic quality of Leighton's later drapery style, see Barrow 1999.
20. Meynell 1884. During Leighton's lifetime illustrations were published in the *Art Journal*, 1890 and 1895; the *Magazine of Art*, 1888, 1889, 1890, 1893 and 1894; the *Studio*, 1893; the *Review of Reviews*, 1893. Spielmann's account of Leighton's working procedure first appeared in the *Magazine of Art* (Spielmann 1889).
21. Leighton's drawing collection comprised works by contemporary artists ranging from Charles Ricketts and Burne-Jones to Hubert von Herkomer, Kate Greenaway, John Phillip and John Leech, as well as British Old Masters such as Gainsborough and Wilkie. Further back, he also had examples by Michelangelo, Leonardo, Andrea de Sarto, Annabile Carracci, Claude and Rembrandt. For a full list see CHRISTIES'S 1896.
22. Denis 1999, pp 255–56.
23. Spielmann 1889, p. 226.
24. Richmond 1900, p. 127; LONDON 1896, p. 814.
25. The Algiers drawing is catalogued as ref. no. LHO/D/0972. The tree study is cat. no. 1.6 and the Heine drawing is reproduced in LONDON 1996, p. 73.
26. Cockerell 1898, p. ix; Richmond 1896, p. 469.
27. Anon. 1896a; see also Monkhouse 1882, p. 557.

A VICTORIAN MASTER
EXHIBITION CATALOGUE

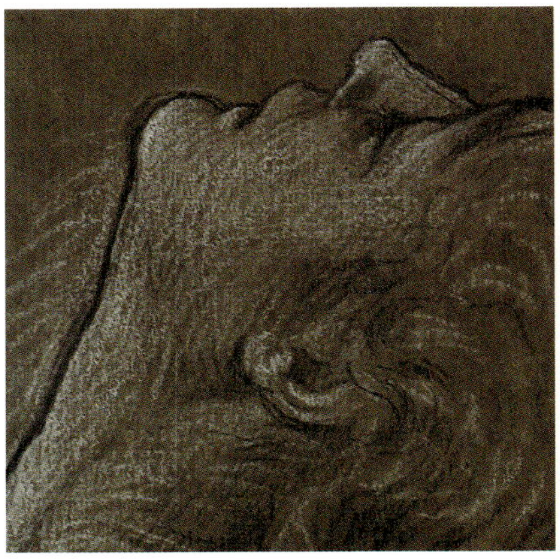
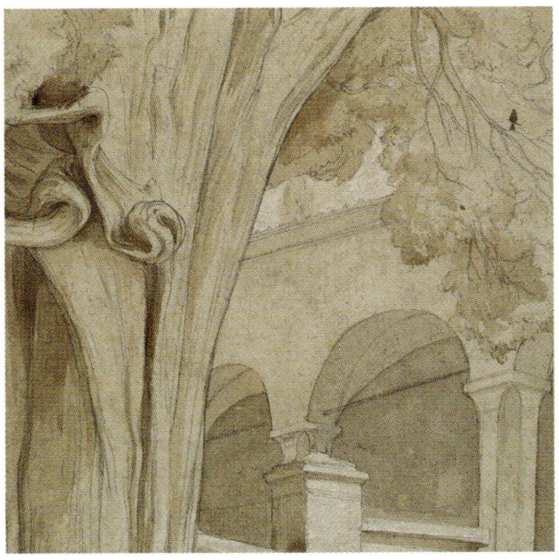
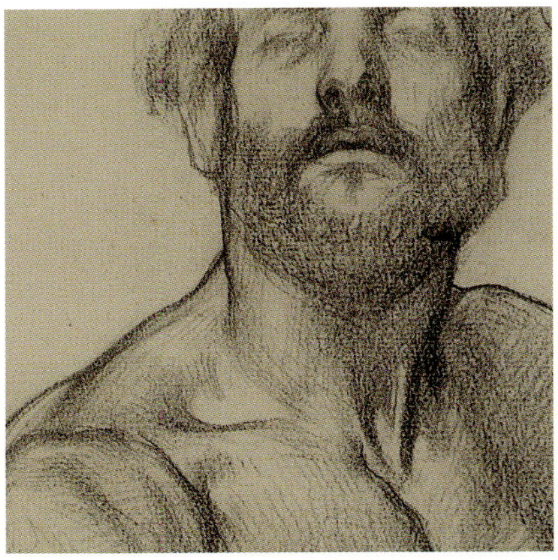
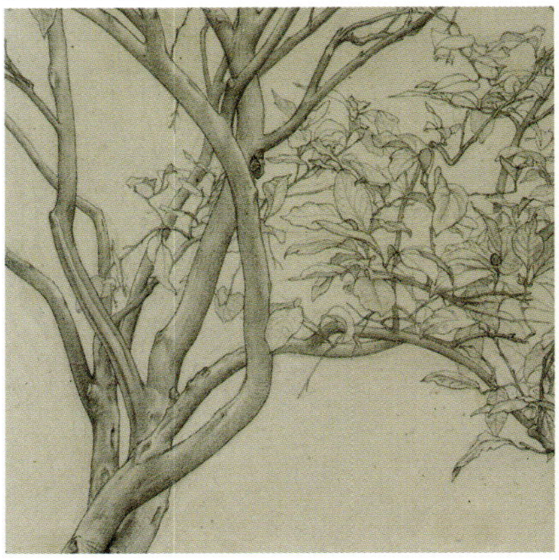
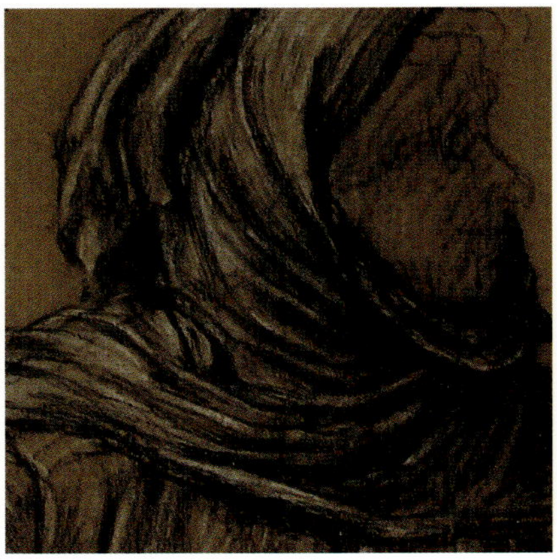
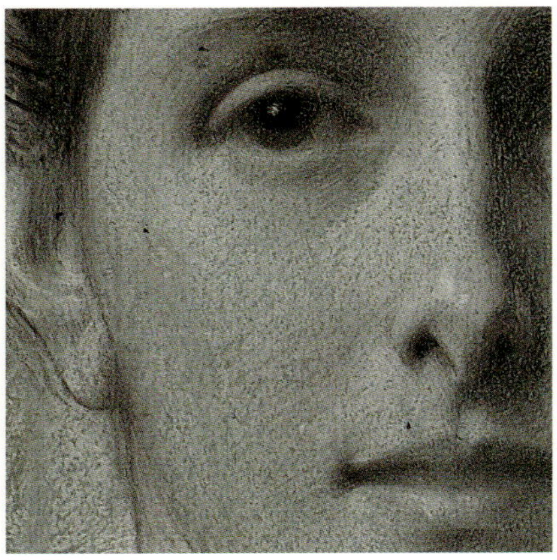

The 55 drawings in the exhibition are grouped into six sections. An overall chronological survey representing highlights from the collection is punctuated by three 'focus' years – 1859, 1877 and 1895 – when Leighton's drawing production is set into contrasting moments from his career. Each of the six sections is preceded by a short introduction to establish the details of Leighton's biography, and to outline how his use of drawing and technique evolved.

With the exception of Leighton's earliest drawings, that were signed and dated by the artist, the precise dating of his studies is problematic. The cycle of submissions to the Royal Academy in the spring of each year would suggest that the bulk of preparatory drawings for a composition would be made in the preceding year. However, in some instances the genesis of a painting started at a much earlier date and evolved over longer periods of time. Nevertheless, unless there is evidence to the contrary discussed in the relevant catalogue entry, the date given for the compositional studies is the year before the exhibition of the relevant work at the Royal Academy.

Discerning precisely when individual drawings entered the collection is also problematic. The earliest catalogues of the collection (1897 and 1900) are frustratingly imprecise in their descriptions of the drawings, and allow no easy way of distinguishing between multiple studies for a single work. Only when a drawing can be matched to a catalogue entry, or group of entries, with some certainty are these details provided.

All works illustrated in the catalogue are by Leighton. All drawings illustrated are part of the Leighton Drawings Collection, held at Leighton House Museum, unless otherwise stated. Bibliographical references are cited in abbreviated form in the catalogue entries and the chapter notes. The corresponding full citations are to be found in the bibliographical section that begins on page 128.

The following abbreviations have been used:

FAS: The Fine Art Society Ltd.
LHC: The Leighton House Committee
LLC: 'Lord Leighton's Collection'. This was stamped on the drawings purchased by the FAS after Leighton's death in 1896. All drawings stamped in this way were in his home at Holland Park Road at the time of his death.
RA: Royal Academy of Arts, London
RBK: Royal Borough of Kensington
RBKC: Royal Borough of Kensington and Chelsea

1

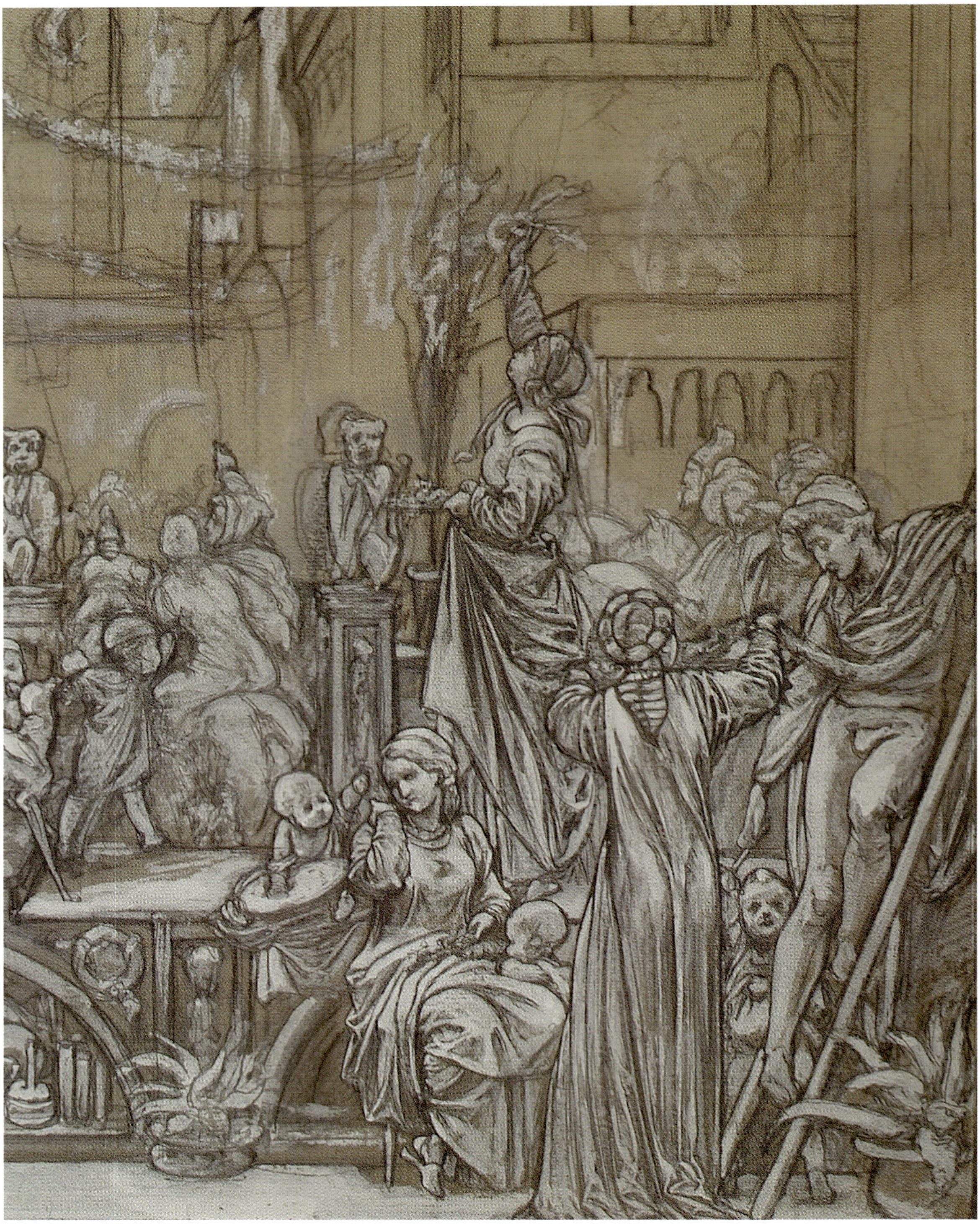

Detail of
cat. no. 1.2

A CONTINENTAL BEGINNING
1849–1858

Having lived much abroad during my youth, the years when one is wax, I have been in turn, thoroughly and sincerely, an Italian artist, a German artist, and a French artist.

[Letter by Leighton dated Thursday 27 November 1873, quoted in Comyns Carr 1908, p. 99.]

Frederic Leighton was born on 3 December 1830 at Scarborough, the second of the three children of Dr Frederic Septimus Leighton and his wife Augusta. The family moved to London in 1833, and Leighton subsequently attended University College School. In 1841, for the sake of Augusta's health, the family began spending extended periods on the Continent and it was as they travelled that Leighton's artistic training began. According to Emilie Barrington, 'from earliest days, drawing was Leighton's greatest amusement, and he had it always in his own mind that he would be an artist and nothing else'.[1] Having journeyed through Germany and Switzerland the family arrived in Italy, where Leighton received his first art lessons in Rome from a Francesco Meli. After a summer spent in England the family travelled to Berlin, and Leighton enrolled at the Academy before they then moved on to Munich and Frankfurt. Further tuition was received at the Accademia delle Belle Arti in Florence during the winter of 1845–46.

Anecdotal evidence suggests that it was the recognition of Leighton's precocious talent by established artists in Florence that persuaded his sceptical father to support him in his chosen career. When the family settled in Frankfurt in 1846, Leighton enrolled at the Städelsches Kunstinstitut and his formal training began in earnest. The school 'had acquired a strong Nazarene bias' under the directorship of the artist Philip Veit, and it was the particular influence of Eduard von Steinle, the school's professor of history painting and a Nazarene associate, that was to have a formative influence on Leighton's work.[2] Some of his earliest known drawings are contained in a sketchbook dated from *c.*1845 (ref. no. LHO/D/1135) and the first exhibition of his drawings held at Leighton House Museum in 1897 included two (untraced) studies of *Faust and Mephistopheles* signed and dated July and September 1847. Further undated drawings still in the Leighton House Collection, and almost certainly dating from these years, confirm this early enthusiasm for romantic, medievalised subjects – 'the atmosphere of Faust and the Nibelungen Lied', as Leighton recalled in 1879.[3] Rendered almost exclusively in pencil, they demonstrate the depth of his immersion in his German training.

Following an interval spent in Brussels and Paris from 1848 to 1849, Leighton continued his studies at the Städelsches Kunstinstitut until leaving for Rome in August 1852. Initially, he was accompanied by von Steinle, before the master symbolically left his pupil to complete the remainder of the journey alone. Rome remained Leighton's base for the next three years. The energy and drive allied to an engaging appearance and personality, that ultimately would take Leighton to the top of his profession, began to reveal themselves during this period. With the completion and exhibition of his first two major pictures, *Cimabue's Celebrated Madonna is Carried in Procession through the Streets of Florence* (exhibited RA, 1855) and *The Reconciliation of the Montagues and Capulets over the Dead Bodies of Romeo and Juliet* (exhibited Exposition Universelle, Paris, 1855) his professional career was launched. Exhibiting as a virtual unknown, the acquisition of his *Cimabue's Celebrated Madonna* by Queen Victoria on the first day of the Royal Academy exhibition, and the widespread critical acclaim that followed, marked a dramatic debut. However, Leighton was not yet ready to consolidate his reputation by settling in England. In the autumn of 1855 he moved to Paris, establishing himself in a studio at 21 rue Pigalle, where he would be based until 1858.

The move marked the first of what would be a series of definite and abrupt changes in Leighton's practice as a draughtsman. The detailed pencil preparatory studies made on white paper that had reached an apogee with the studies for *Cimabue's Celebrated Madonna* and *The Reconciliation of the Montagues and Capulets* were left behind. While he continued to make studies from nature in pencil, Leighton's preparatory studies for paintings were now typically produced in chalk on white paper.

The nine drawings that follow, span this Continental beginning. All were made abroad between the ages of 19 and 28, and besides expressing his uniquely cosmopolitan training as an artist (certainly amongst his British contemporaries) they reveal the extraordinary assurance and technical accomplishment that characterised Leighton's early drawing as he laid out the foundations for his career. *D.R.*

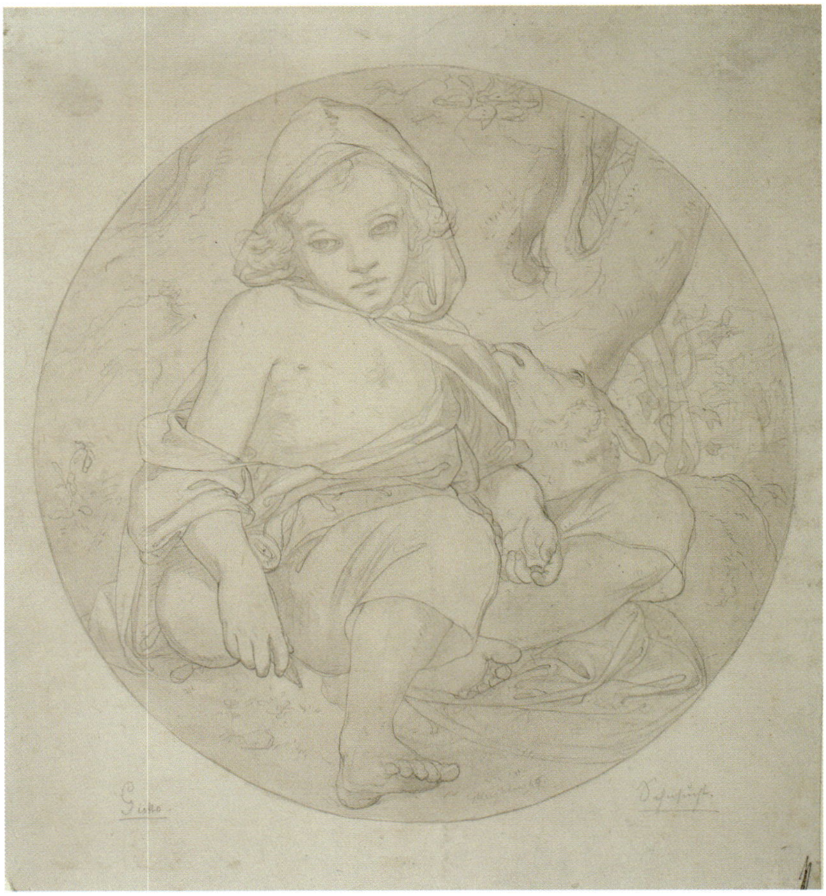

1.1

'Giotto as a Shepherd Boy', 1849

Graphite and watercolour on white paper
302 x 276 mm
LHO/D/0454

This drawing was produced during an enforced interlude in Leighton's studies at the Städelsches Kunstinstitut, Frankfurt. Political upheavals required his family to leave their adopted city in 1848, first moving to Brussels and then at some point in 1849 to Paris, before returning to Frankfurt in 1850.

In Brussels, Leighton produced the oil painting *Cimabue Finding Giotto in the Fields of Florence* (1848, Baroda Museum and Picture Gallery, India) turning to the same passage from Giorgio Vasari's *Lives of the Painters* for this composition. The youthful Giotto is shown prior to his discovery by the passing Cimabue, languidly guarding his father's sheep. In his right hand he holds a sharp stone with which he would scratch 'on the stones, the earth or the sand, some natural object that came before him or some fantasy that presented itself to his thoughts'.[4] Despite the best efforts of one of his charges, Giotto's attention is elsewhere. The 'longing' of the drawing's inscription is captured in his abstracted gaze as he day-dreams of a future as an artist. The appeal of this subject, with its implication that true artists are born to fulfil their destiny, and talent will inevitably be recognised, must have been irresistible to the young Leighton, himself longing fully to embrace an artist's life.

The study was preceded by a looser version in pencil and red chalk (ref. no. LHO/D/0455, Leighton House Museum) and despite Leighton's separation from his mentors in Frankfurt, this harmonious composition, with its controlled pencil outline and sense of dreamy otherworldliness, is a reaffirmation of the dominant influence of his German training at this time. *D.R.*

INSCRIPTIONS

Signed and dated, lower right, 'F Leighton 49' in graphite and 'Sehnsucht' (longing) in graphite, in the artist's hand. Inscribed, lower left, 'Giotto' in graphite, possibly in the artist's hand.

PROVENANCE

Emilie Barrington; by whom presented to the LHC by 1897; transferred to RBK in 1926 (now RBKC).

BIBLIOGRAPHICAL REFERENCES

Corkran 1904, ill. opp. p. 12; Staley 1906, p. 222; Ormond 1975b, pp 8–9.

EXHIBITION HISTORY

LONDON 1897, no. 54 ('Sketches for Early Designs'); **LONDON 1900**, no. 227.

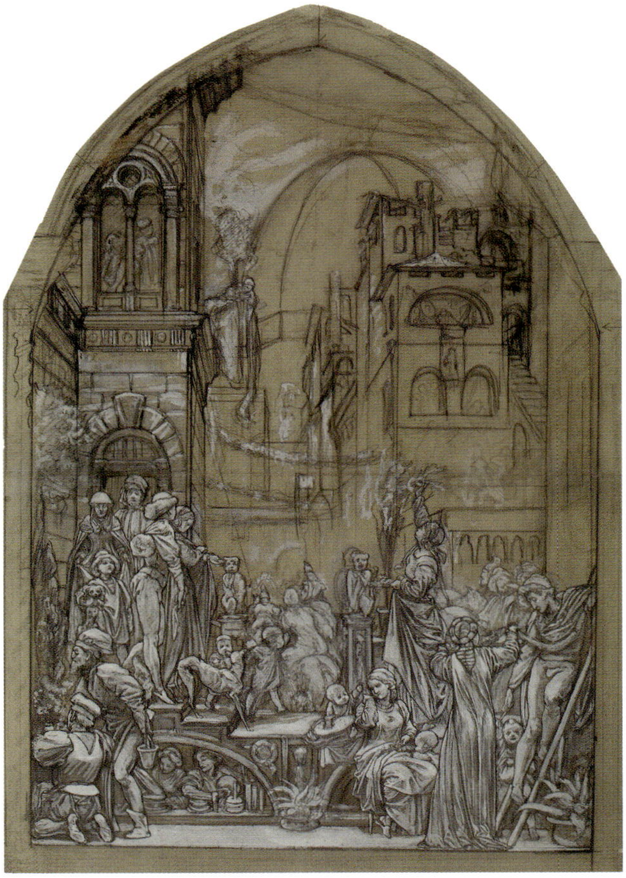

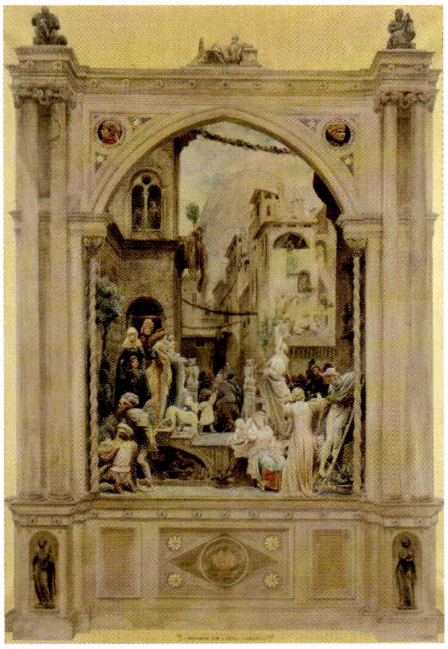

1.

cat. ill. 1. ***Preparing for a Festa***, 1851. Graphite and watercolour on white paper. 89 x 62 cm. Ashmolean Museum, Oxford.

1.2

Study for 'Preparing for a Festa': Composition, *c.*1851

Graphite, black chalk and bodycolour on buff paper
561 x 389 mm
LHO/D/0832

The second phase of Leighton's studies at the Städelsches Kunstinstitut continued from 1850 until his departure for Rome in August 1852. Dating from the middle of this period, this is a study for a highly finished watercolour in the collections of the Ashmolean Museum, Oxford (cat. ill. 1). However, contained within it are many of the elements that would characterise Leighton's first major paintings produced in the years immediately following.

The scene is an imagined Florence of the fifteenth century. The foreground, with its cross-section of citizens busily engaged in planting, hanging, cooking and arranging, has the same exuberant massing seen in the historical subject-paintings of Moritz von Schwind. Between 1844 and the spring of 1847, von Schwind had been 'in residence' at the Städelsches Kunstinstitut, working on a painting commissioned by the school. After subsequently moving to Munich, he returned to visit his friend Eduard von Steinle and was no doubt introduced to Leighton (if they had not already met).

Each figure is carefully rendered with a particular emphasis given to the modelling of draperies. Every fold was then transcribed, unchanged, into the final work, prefiguring the painstaking, methodical approach that would come to define Leighton's practice. According to Samuel Pepys Cockerell, Leighton followed the convention at the school and drew these draperies 'out of his head'.[5] This method did not last for long, and he would later go to great lengths to arrange fabrics carefully from which drapery studies were then made.

The background setting of Florence is more loosely sketched in. Dominated by the looming dome of the cathedral, the architecture of the city is fanciful, although the palazzo on the extreme left suggests a more definite architectural source. Numerous balconies populated by eager observers can be seen. Hanging banners add to the gaiety of the scene. A variation of this backdrop was used for Leighton's first major canvas, *The Death of Brunelleschi*, produced at the Städelsches Kunstinstitut the following year and now at Leighton House Museum. His next major work, *Cimabue's Celebrated Madonna is Carried in Procession through the Streets of Florence*, of 1855, is a further development of this formula, setting a densely populated pageant against a theatrical architectural backdrop. *D.R.*

PROVENANCE

John Hanson Walker; by whom presented to the LHC by 1897; transferred to RBK in 1926 (now RBKC).

BIBLIOGRAPHICAL REFERENCES

Ormond 1975b, p. 11.

EXHIBITION HISTORY

LONDON 1897, no. 29 ('Sketches for Early Designs'); **LONDON 1900**, no. 199; **LONDON 1969**, no. 46.

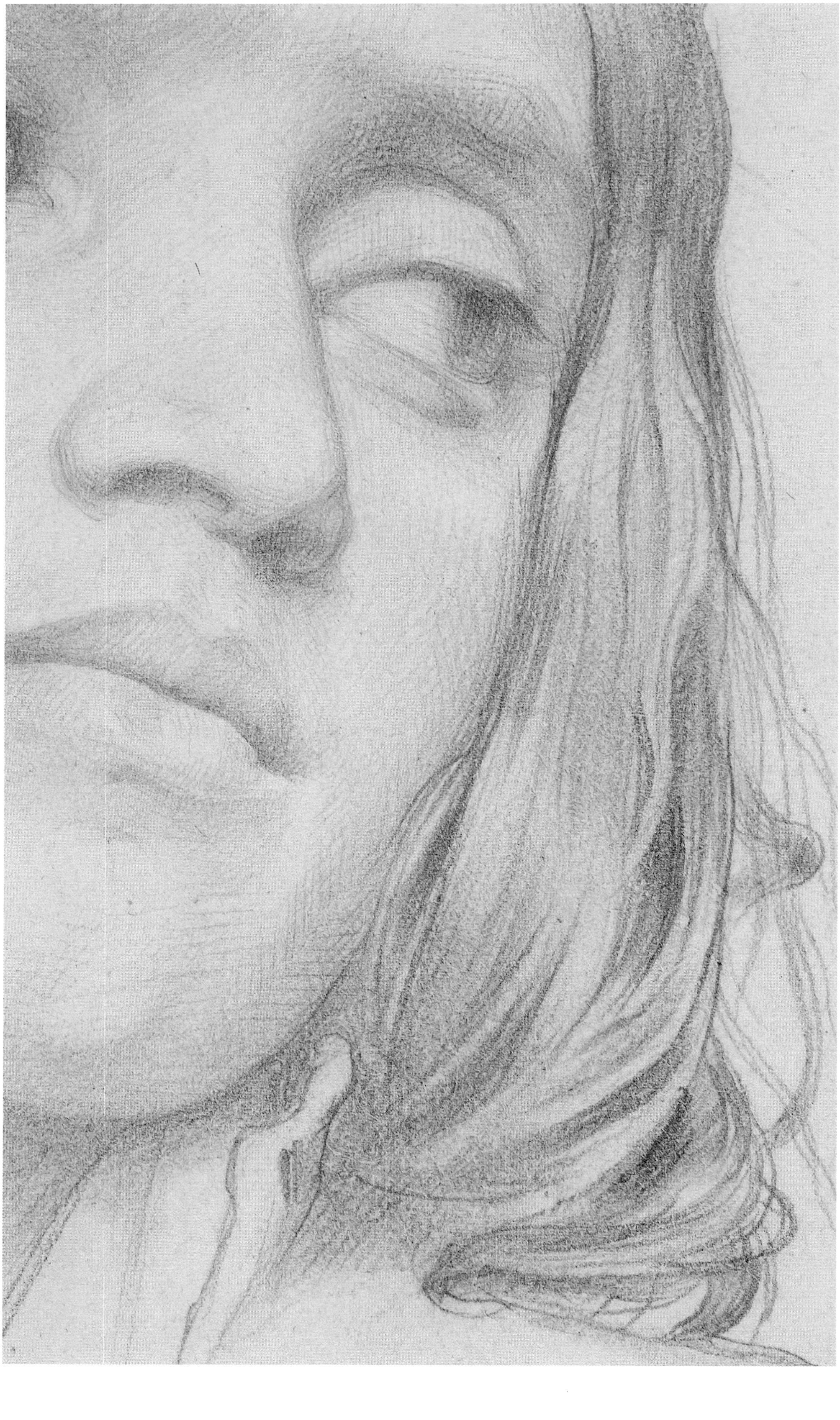

Detail of
cat. no. 1.4

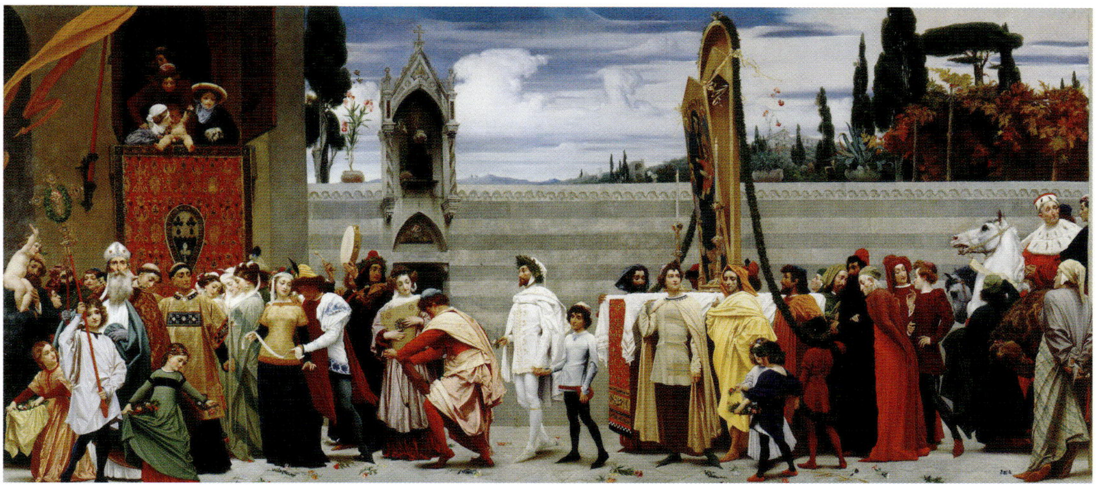

2.

cat. ill. 2. *Cimabue's Celebrated Madonna is Carried in Procession through the Streets of Florence*, RA 1855. Oil on canvas. 222.2 x 520.5 cm. The Royal Collection, London.

Three Studies for 'Cimabue's Celebrated Madonna', 1853–54
(Cat. nos 1.3, 1.4 and 1.5)

Leighton's intention in travelling to Rome in 1852 was to produce the paintings with which he would launch his career as an artist. After an uncertain start, early in 1853 he fastened on the subjects for two vast canvases that would preoccupy him for the subsequent two years: *Cimabue's Celebrated Madonna is Carried in Procession through the Streets of Florence* (1853–55; cat. ill. 2) and *The Reconciliation of the Montagues and Capulets over the Dead Bodies of Romeo and Juliet* (1853–55).

In both scale and complexity Leighton had set himself considerable challenges, and it is a mark of his confidence and ambition that, with so little experience behind him, he should have embarked on such undertakings. His approach was methodical and exacting. A total of over 50 preparatory drawings were made for *Cimabue's Celebrated Madonna*. Almost all were produced in a relatively short period, from December 1853 (when Leighton returned to Rome after travelling to Germany and Austria) to the middle of February 1854, when work began on the under-painting of the canvas.[6]

The two heads shown here (cat. nos 1.3, 1.4) demonstrate the assurance, precise observation, subtle modelling and sensuality of touch that characterise these studies. The models were drawn from amongst friends and the local population. Fra Giuseppe, a monk presumably attached to one of the Orders in Rome, posed for the head of the tall figure standing immediately behind the bier and possibly identified as Andrea Tafi (d. 1294).[7] The thick curls of hair emerging from beneath his skullcap and his clear-eyed expression clearly appealed to Leighton. He is also the subject of a second study, apparently unrelated to the painting, in the collections of Birmingham Museums and Art Gallery (ref. no. 1935 P527).

The study of the youth Alicante was used for the violin-playing musician who glances back at the following procession. This was the only head for which an oil study is known to have been made. Separate drawings were made for his hands, and a study for the left hand, holding the violin, is now in the collections of the Victoria and Albert Museum (ref. no. E.1844–1910). The exceptional number of hand studies made for the painting (see cat. no. 1.5) may have been prompted by nothing more than Leighton's need to get these most difficult anatomical challenges right, over the entirety of the composition. Certainly, as he became more experienced, detailed studies of individual hands were only occasionally made. At the same time, Leighton seems to have delighted in conceiving a great variety of gestures, almost drawing attention to his ability to render them accurately. The combination of these individual drawings resulted in pointedly harmonious, balanced and complete sheets of studies, produced to be seen and admired.

With the exception of *Helios and Rhodos* (1869), for no subsequent painting would such highly finished studies be produced, and after *c.*1860 almost no pencil drawings of this kind were made at all. Leighton's motivation in making them at this point seems partly to have stemmed from a youthful relish in his own abilities, now freed from years of training, and partly a determination that not only should the finished painting be somehow exceptional, but that all the stages leading up to its completion should reinforce the seriousness of his intent and extent of his abilities. He would later comment that he doubted any other artist enjoyed the act of making a painting as much as he did. In following such an exhaustive process for *Cimabue's Celebrated Madonna*, Leighton established a methodology that of itself set him and his work apart and which would be pursued, with some variation, for the rest of his career.

As the painting progressed, it is clear that the drawings were shown to many who visited the studio, and the response to them reinforced Leighton's confidence and assurance in carrying-off the painting itself. While he may have completed the studies to such a high degree of finish as an insurance against the complexity of the task in hand, they were developed beyond what was strictly 'necessary' to produce the painting. These studies became self-conscious, virtuoso demonstrations of Leighton's burgeoning talent. Completed at such an early stage in his career, before indeed it had really started, the studies made for *Cimabue's Celebrated Madonna* nevertheless represent one of the pinnacles in his entire output as a draughtsman. *D.R.*

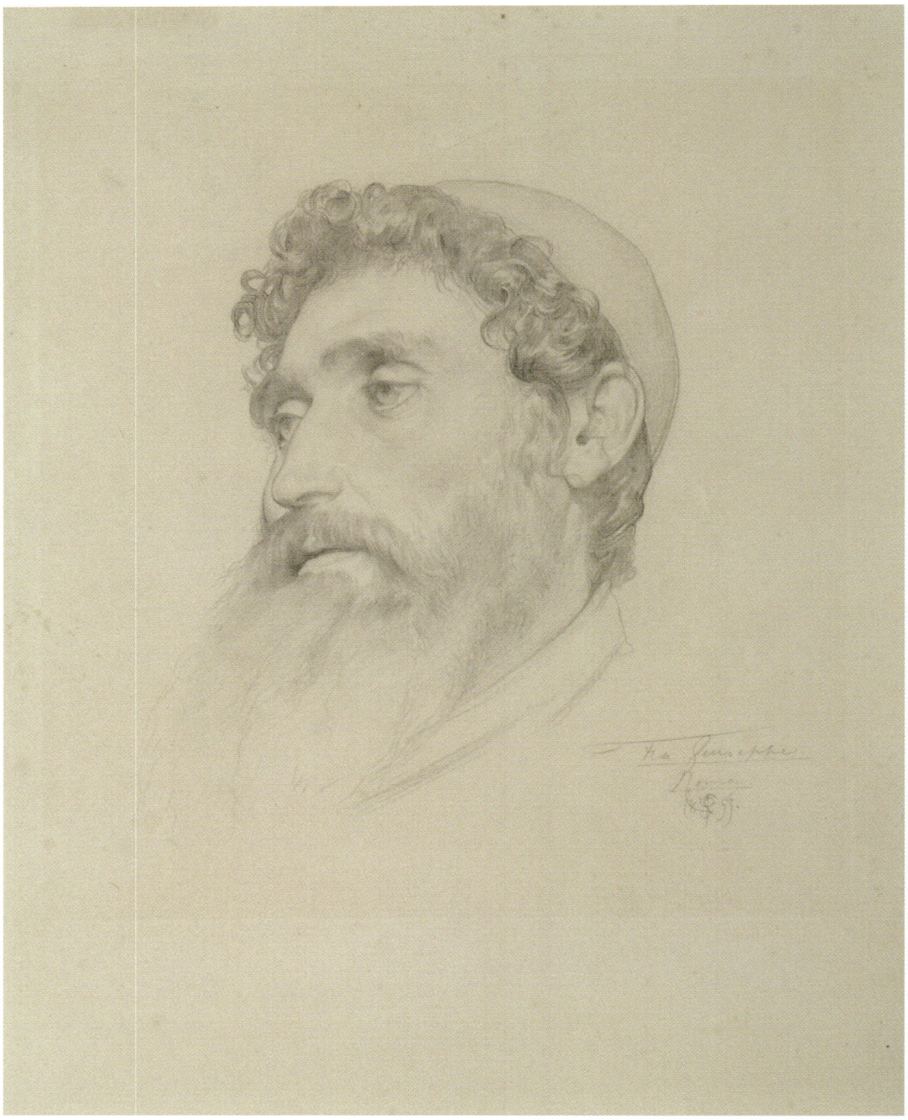

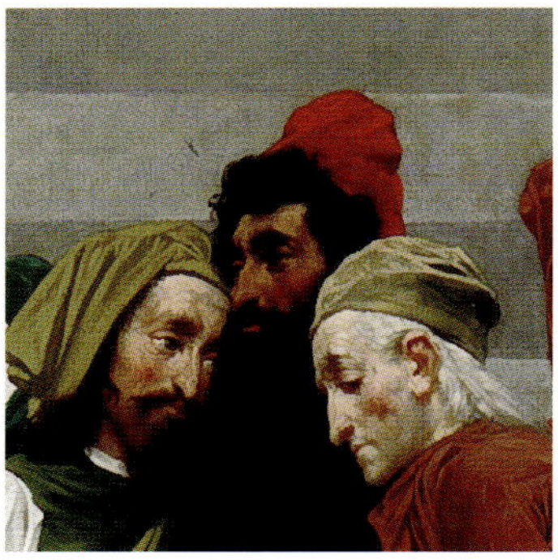

2a.

1.3

Study for 'Cimabue's Celebrated Madonna': Male Head, 1853

Graphite on white paper

275 x 224 mm

LHO/D/2177. Bequest of Stevan Beck Baloga

INSCRIPTIONS

Signed and dated, lower right, 'Fra Giuseppe. / Roma. / 18 FL 53' in graphite.

PROVENANCE

Purchased through the Robert Isaacson Gallery, New York, by David Daniels; Stevan Baloga; by whom bequeathed to RBKC in 2003.

BIBLIOGRAPHICAL REFERENCES

Ormond 1975b, p. 150 (listed under cat. no. 23).

EXHIBITION HISTORY

CAMBRIDGE, MINNEAPOLIS, CHICAGO, KANSAS CITY 1968, no. 37; MANCHESTER (UK), MINNEAPOLIS, NEW YORK 1978–79, no. 37; LONDON 2003.

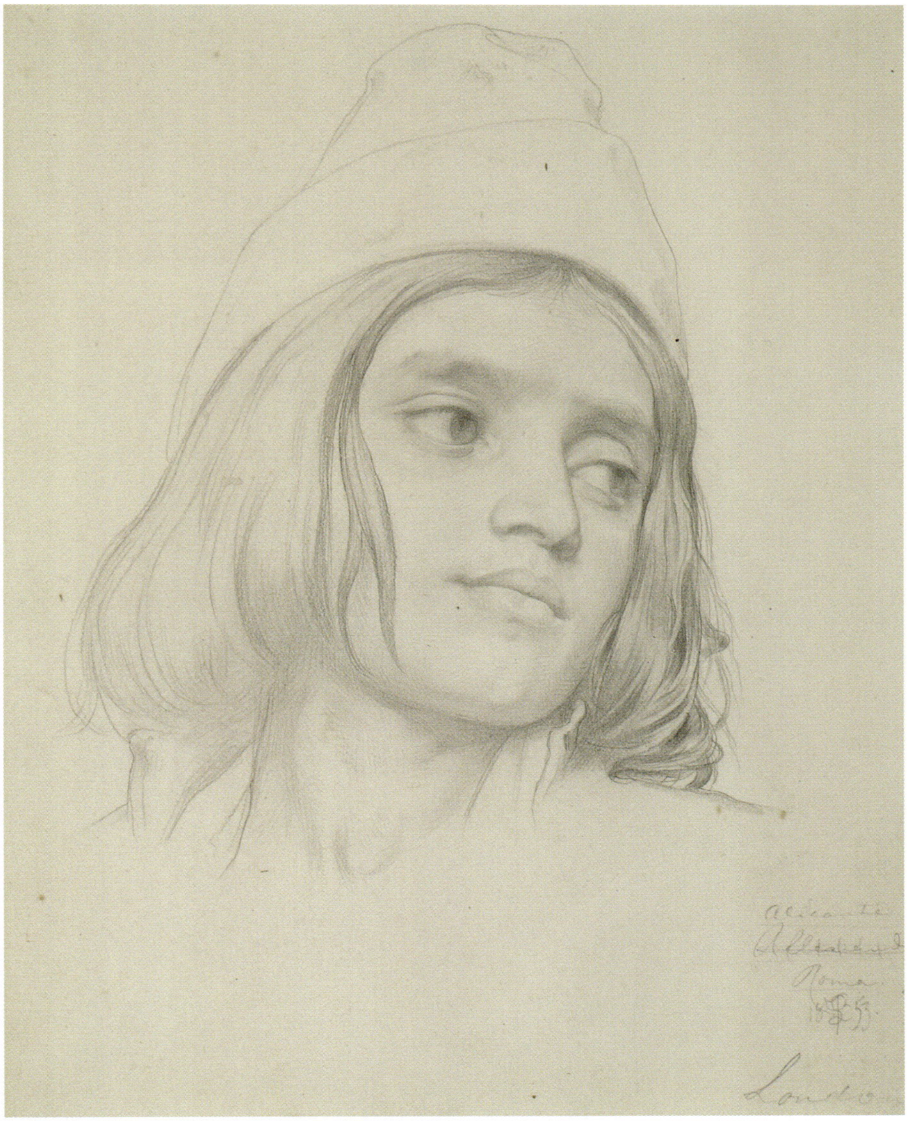

cat. ills **2a.** and **2b.** Details of *Cimabue's Celebrated Madonna*.

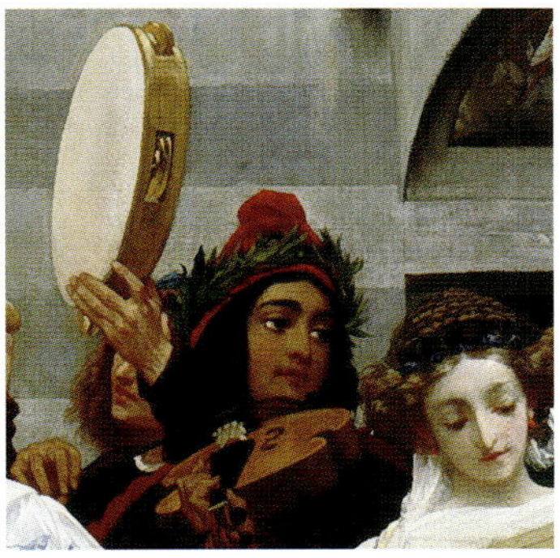

2b.

1.4

Study for 'Cimabue's Celebrated Madonna': Male Head, 1853

Graphite on white paper
226 x 182 mm
LHO/D/2178. Bequest of Stevan Beck Baloga

INSCRIPTIONS

Signed and dated, lower right, 'Alicante / Allessandro. [crossed out] / Roma. / 18 FL 53. / London' in graphite.

PROVENANCE

Purchased from the art dealers Durlacher Bros., New York by David Daniels in 1965; Stevan Beck Baloga; by whom bequeathed to RBKC in 2003.

BIBLIOGRAPHICAL REFERENCES

Ormond 1975b, p. 150 (listed under cat. no. 23).

EXHIBITION HISTORY

CAMBRIDGE, MINNEAPOLIS, CHICAGO, KANSAS CITY 1968, no. 37; **MANCHESTER (UK), MINNEAPOLIS, NEW YORK 1978–79**, no. 36; **LONDON 2003**.

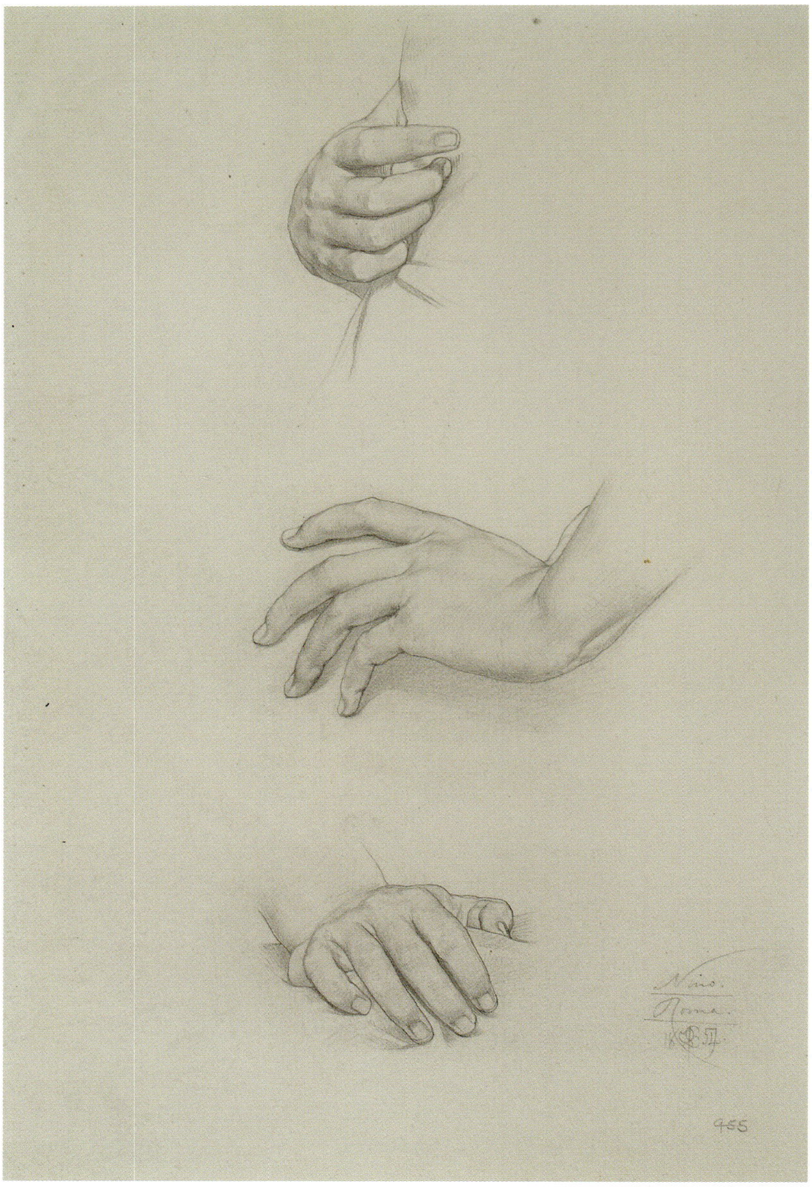

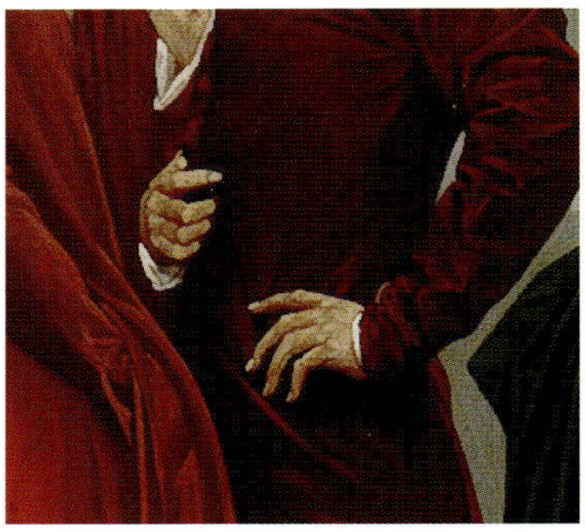

2c.

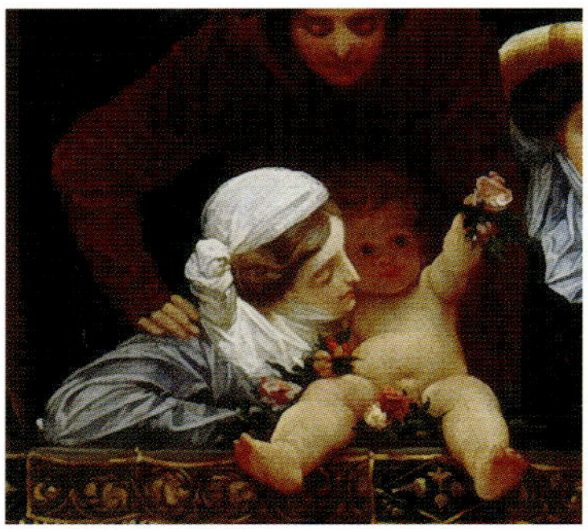

2d.

cat. ills **2c.** and **2d.** Details of ***Cimabue's Celebrated Madonna***.

1.5

Study for 'Cimabue's Celebrated Madonna': Hands, 1854

Graphite on white paper
290 x 230 mm
LHO/D/0965

INSCRIPTIONS

Signed and dated, lower right, 'Nino / Roma. / 18 FL 54' in graphite.

PROVENANCE

Bequeathed by the artist to his sisters, Mrs Augusta Matthews and Mrs Alexandra Orr; from whom purchased by the FAS in 1896; presented anonymously to the LHC by 1897; transferred to RBK in 1926 (now RBKC).

BIBLIOGRAPHICAL REFERENCES

Staley 1906, p. 214.

EXHIBITION HISTORY

LONDON 1897, no. 47 ('Sketches for Early Designs'); **LONDON 1900**, no. 49; **LONDON 1969**, no. 43.

1.6

Study of a Cypress Tree, Florence, 1854

Graphite and watercolour on white paper
408 x 266 mm
LHO/D/1028

At the end of August 1854, Leighton travelled from Bagni di Lucca (where he had spent the summer in the company of his great friend Adelaide Sartoris and her circle) to Florence, 'to work for a week or two'.[8] He had been in the city at the beginning of the year, but this study almost certainly dates from this second visit. The precise location is unknown, but Leighton was clearly captivated by the extravagant, sinuous trunk and branches of the old cypress tree set against the angled counterpoint of the loggia beyond. Rather than being produced for any specific purpose, it was probably made as an exercise in the close observation and recording of complex natural forms, something that would become prominent in Leighton's drawing as the decade ended. A second study in pencil of a similar tree, probably made in the same location, is also at Leighton House Museum (ref. no. LHO/D/1029). This is the only example of a finished watercolour in grisaille in the

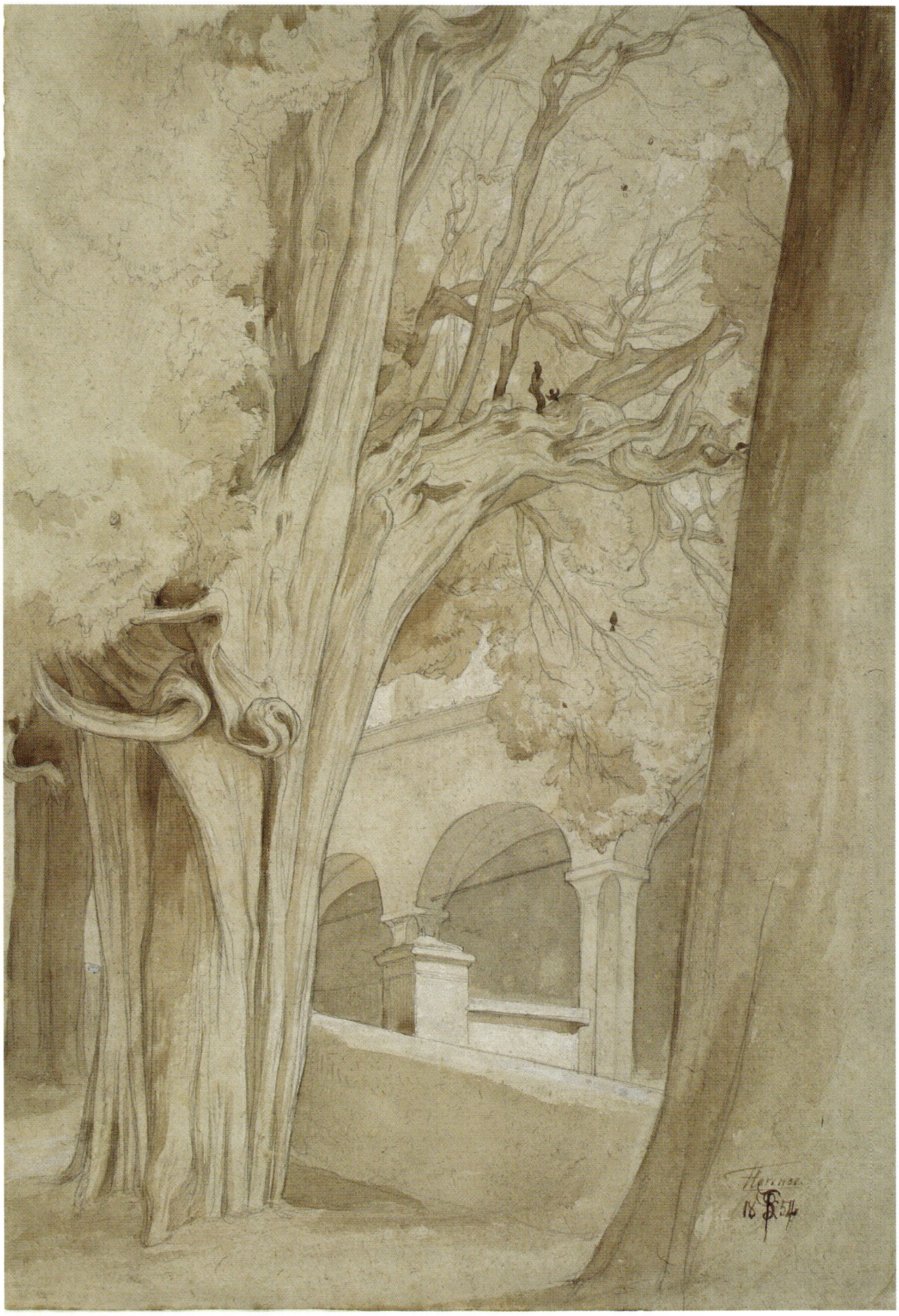

collection, again suggesting that Leighton had set himself a deliberate challenge in rendering the motif.

A simplified version of the same tree was used in Leighton's illustration made the following year of part of the poem 'Die Heimkehr', from Heinrich Heine's *Buch der Lieder*. A study for this composition is at Leighton House Museum (ref. no. LHO/D/0862). Remarkably, the trunk re-appeared on a further occasion. After an interval of 40 years it was used in the background of the painting *Lachrymae* (*c.*1895), part of Leighton's final submission to the Royal Academy in 1895. This retention of drawn studies of all kinds and from all phases of his career allowed Leighton to use and re-use them in this way, although the time span in this instance was exceptional. *D.R.*

INSCRIPTIONS

Signed and dated, lower right, 'Florence / 18 FL 54' in brown watercolour.

PROVENANCE

Bequeathed by the artist to his sisters, Mrs Augusta Matthews and Mrs Alexandra Orr; from whom purchased by the FAS in 1896; purchased by the LHC by 1897; transferred to RBK in 1926 (now RBKC).

BIBLIOGRAPHICAL REFERENCES

Ash 1995, opp. pl. 39.

EXHIBITION HISTORY

LONDON 1897, no. 24 ('First Section'); **LONDON 1900**, no. 91.

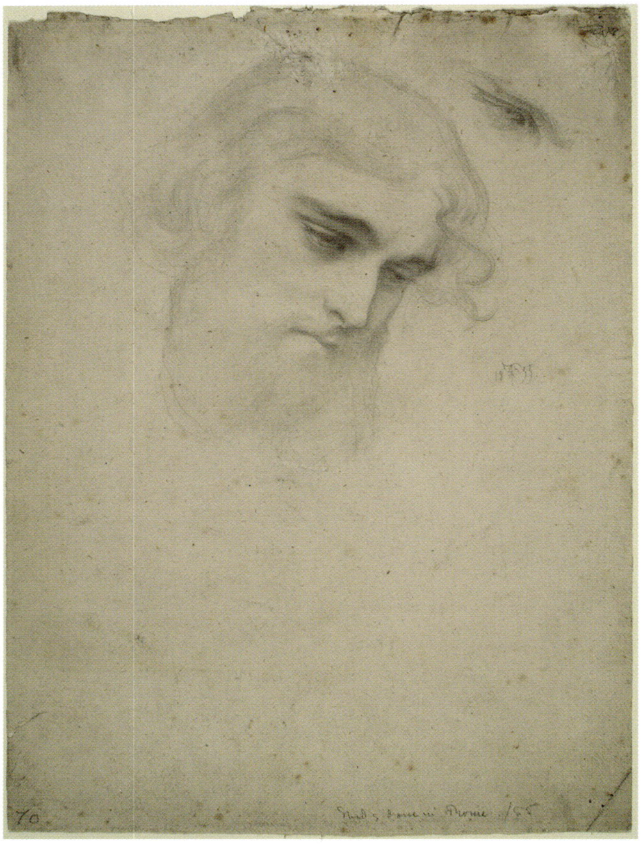

1.7

Study of a Male Head, probably Walter Pennington Creyke, 1855

Graphite on white paper
296 x 222 mm
LHO/D/0880

Writing to his father from Rome in early 1855, Leighton reported the widespread appreciation of 'a portfolio of heads which I have drawn at different times, and which are much admired by everybody'.[9] Whether this particular study was amongst them is not known, but it conforms to the finely drawn and highly finished group of head studies made at this time.

The subject so closely resembles Walter Pennington Creyke, whose portrait Leighton drew in the same year (now in the collections of the British Museum, ref. no. 1897, 0412.7), that it is almost certainly the same sitter. Creyke was an occasional painter, represented Ireland at cricket and was the Private Secretary and Chaplain to the 7th Earl of Carlisle when Lord Lieutenant of Ireland. He was also 'remarkable for his good looks. When in Rome he often sat to his artist friends as a model for "our Saviour"'.[10]

This comment gives some weight to the assertion that it was Creyke who modelled for the figure of Christ in Leighton's fresco *The Wise and Foolish Virgins* at St Michael's Church, Lyndhurst (1862–63). Certainly in this study, Creyke's flowing hair, full beard and intense, downcast gaze lend him a Christ-like appearance, and this drawing is clearly not a conventional portrait. The detailed study of the left eye in the top right corner of the sheet suggests this was a working study made with some other purpose in mind. The exceptional softness of the rendering of the face and delicacy with which hair and beard are suggested give the subject a heightened spiritual, insubstantial quality. The result is a remarkably sensitive, poignant study. However, it seems improbable that this drawing is linked directly to the Lyndhurst fresco, which was not to be painted for another seven years and in which the figure of Christ is turned in the opposite direction. More probable is that Creyke posed again for Leighton in the early 1860s. The head of the male figure in both *The Painter's Honeymoon* of *c.*1864 (untraced) and *Golden Hours* of *c.*1864 (Private Collection) bear striking similarities to the two studies of Creyke. *D.R.*

INSCRIPTIONS

Signed and dated, centre right, '18 FL 55' in graphite. Stamped, lower left, 'LLC' encircled. Inscribed, lower right, 'Studs done in Rome/55' in graphite, by the FAS.

PROVENANCE

Bequeathed by the artist to his sisters, Mrs Augusta Matthews and Mrs Alexandra Orr; from whom purchased by the FAS in 1896; presented to the LHC by Lady Bloomfield by 1897; transferred to RBK in 1926 (now RBKC).

EXHIBITION HISTORY

LONDON 1897, no. 20 ('Studies of Heads').

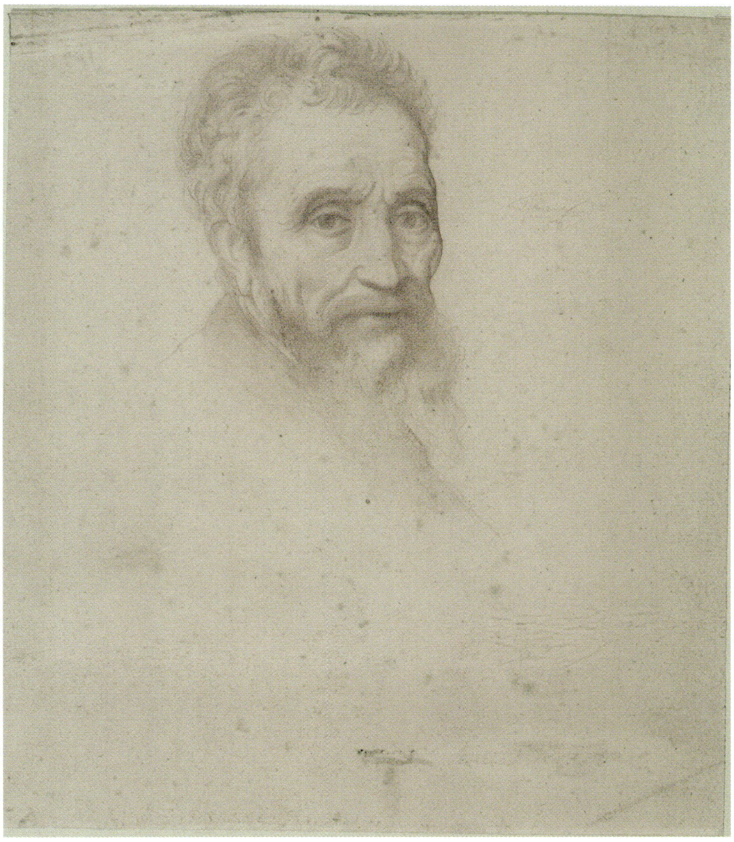

1.8
Study after Jacopino del Conte (1515–98), 1856
Graphite on white paper
226 x 199 mm
LHO/D/0465

Leighton's copying from Old Masters was given a particular purpose and momentum in the early 1850s as he collected material for the development of his *Cimabue's Celebrated Madonna*. This study had very different motivations, and is an early manifestation of what was to become one of the enduring preoccupations of Leighton's artistic life – his close personal identification with Michelangelo. The Renaissance master presented Leighton with a 'personal as well as an artistic ideal'[11] that was fundamental in shaping his sense of what it was to be a great artist, as well as fuelling his obsession with the representation of the nude.

The drawing was made in Florence in September or early October 1856 as Leighton travelled from Venice to Rome. Jacopino del Conte's unfinished portrait of Michelangelo painted in *c.*1540 and mentioned by Vasari[12] had left Florence by this date, and this study was made from one of its numerous derivatives – probably the version presented to the Uffizi Gallery by the Strozzi family in 1771. However, the Michelangelo depicted here is a more vulnerable, sorrowful personality than is portrayed in the original. Intriguingly, Leighton appears to have exaggerated his frayed beard, thinning hair and deeply lined face, reducing the pensive middle-aged Michelangelo of the Strozzi portrait into a frail and elderly man. In some of Leighton's other studies after Old Master paintings and sculpture, he appears to have similarly altered and re-worked the original. While remaining true to facial features, he would add facial hair, animate expressions and occasionally completely change the pose in order to make his subject 'real'.[13] His motivation here, as Østermark-Johansen noted, may derive from the 'unusual degree of identification between the young artist and the old master'.[14] Through this drawing, with its heightened sense of intimacy and empathy between artist and subject, Leighton was perhaps trying to go beyond the archetype and forge an image of Michelangelo that was both intensely human and very much his own.

In 1862, Leighton may have referred to this study in working on his painting *Michelangelo Nursing his Dying Servant*. Taken from an account in Vasari, it is a more robust Michelangelo who places his arm around his servant Urbino. As has been noted, rather than quoting from this study it is tempting to see Leighton's own features fused into the head of the Master. *D.R.*

INSCRIPTIONS
Inscribed, upper right, 'Florence / 56' in graphite, in the artist's hand. Inscribed, lower right, 'Michael Angelo' in graphite, by the FAS, partially erased.

PROVENANCE
Bequeathed by the artist to his sisters, Mrs Augusta Matthews and Mrs Alexandra Orr; from whom purchased by the FAS in 1896; presented to the LHC by Hamo Thornycroft by 1897; transferred to RBK in 1926 (now RBKC).

BIBLIOGRAPHICAL REFERENCES
Ormond 1975b, p. 154 (listed under cat. no. 80); Simon 1996, p. 35; Barringer & Prettejohn 1999, p. 114, pl. 38.

EXHIBITION HISTORY
LONDON 1897, no. 6 (Studies of Heads); **LONDON 1900**, no. 32.

cat. ill. 3. ***Study for 'Samson and Delilah'***, *c.*1858. Pencil on tracing paper. 10.9 x 10.6 cm. Royal Academy of Arts, London.

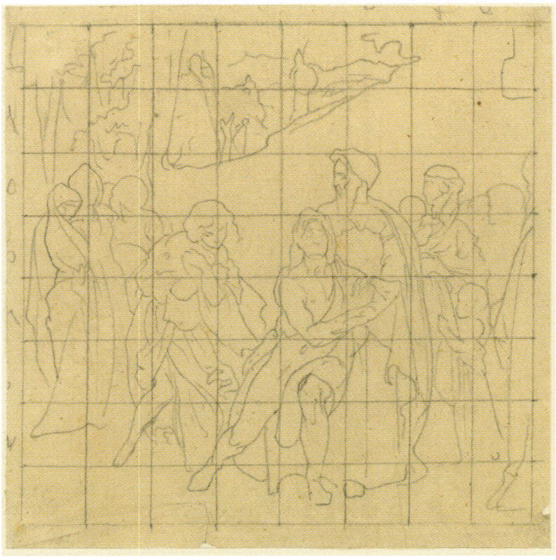

3.

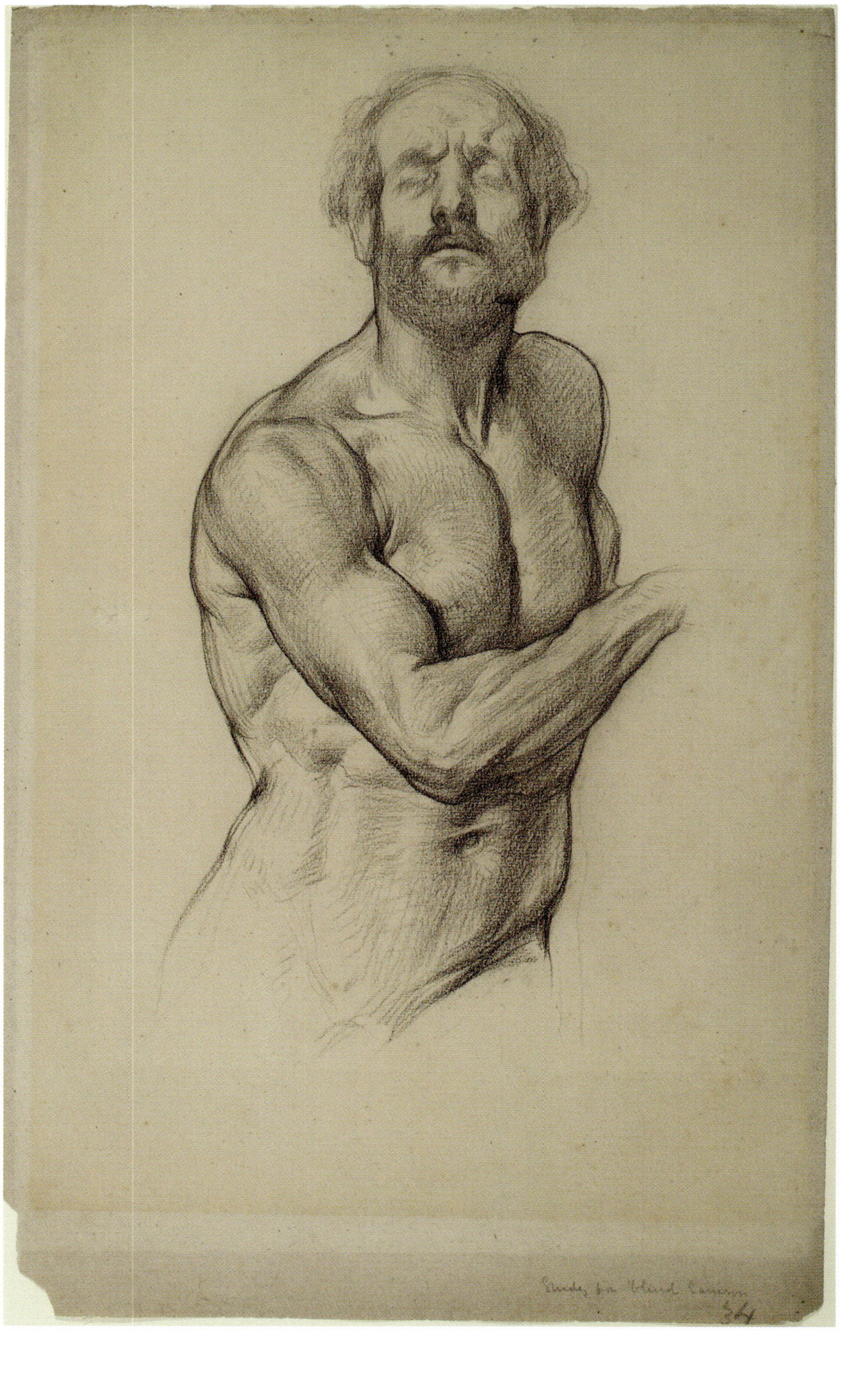

1.9

Study for 'Samson and Delilah': Samson, *c.*1858

Black chalk on white paper
467 x 293mm
LHO/D/0460

Samson and Delilah, an untraced work of 1858, was the source of considerable disappointment to Leighton. Writing to his mother from Rome in the spring of 1859, he made light of a recent setback: 'you will be rather amused to hear that my "Samson" has been *refused* at the British Institution, which this year is particularly weak and insignificant. Neither I nor anyone else has the least idea what is the cause of this strongish measure.'[15] A true sense of the impact this rejection had on him is given by his great friend, Giovanni Costa, who wrote that during this period in Rome, Leighton 'was far from contented with himself. I think that the cause of this discouragement was the refusal of his "Samson" by the British Institution'.[16]

This recent setback compounded the hostile reception his work had enjoyed at the Royal Academy since the triumphant success of *Cimabue's Celebrated Madonna* in 1855. In 1857 Leighton had submitted nothing, and remained some distance from the acceptance that would come with election as an Associate of the Academy in 1864.

Described as 'one of Leighton's darkest pictures',[17] the only visual evidence of the composition is a small squared-up outline drawing on tracing paper in the collections of the Royal Academy (ref. no. 04/1184; cat. ill. 3). This, together with three drawings at Leighton House Museum, give some sense of the overall arrangement and the pose of the central figure of Samson. Fanny Kemble, sister of Adelaide Sartoris, saw the work on exhibition in Boston in 1861 and, while being 'charmed' by it, wrote to Leighton that 'you have chosen a different moment for illustration than the one I had imagined'.[18] The RA tracing confirms that Leighton chose not to illustrate the cutting of Samson's hair nor the entry of the Philistines to seize him – both of which had been depicted by artists on numerous occasions. As can be seen from this study, Samson has already been blinded, and it appears that Leighton selected the moment just after this has taken place, when the incapacitated Samson is being pulled to his feet by one of the Philistines to be taken away to Gaza. The uncertainty over whether this is indeed the scene depicted stems from the grip of Samson and the figure behind him. They clasp each other's wrists (ref. no. LHO/D/0461 verso) in a gesture that suggests some empathy or concern for Samson's plight, at a moment when there should be none.

Samson's pose clearly owes a debt to the figure of Christ in Michelangelo's unfinished canvas *The Entombment*, which Leighton must have seen prior to its acquisition by the National Gallery in 1868. In addition to this study of the upper torso of the figure, Leighton also made a study of his left leg (ref. no. LHO/D/0461). Both are in chalk and on a larger scale than the figure drawings he had conventionally made up until this point and, with their vigorous but controlled cross-hatching, they point the way to his use of drawing over much of the rest of his career. *D.R. & P.M.*

INSCRIPTIONS

Inscribed, lower right, 'Study for blind Samson' in graphite, by the FAS.

PROVENANCE

Bequeathed by the artist to his sisters, Mrs Augusta Matthews and Mrs Alexandra Orr; from whom purchased by the FAS in 1896; purchased by the LHC by 1897; transferred to RBK in 1926 (now RBKC).

BIBLIOGRAPHICAL REFERENCES

Ormond 1975b, p. 151 (listed under cat. no. 40).

EXHIBITION HISTORY

LONDON 1900, no. 215a; **LONDON 1969**, cat. no. 138.

NOTES

1. Barrington 1906, vol. I, p. 37.
2. Ormond 1975b, p. 7.
3. Comyns Carr 1908, p. 98.
4. Vasari 2005, p. 2.
5. Cockerell 1896, p. 811.
6. Barrington 1906, vol. I, p. 177.
7. Murray-Fennell 2003, p. 54.
8. Ormond 1975b, p. 24.
9. Barrington 1906, vol. I, p. 177.
10. Francis A. Gerard (pseud.): *Picturesque Dublin Old and New*, Hutchison & Co., London, 1898, p. 226.
11. Barringer & Prettejohn 1999, p. 112.
12. Vasari 2005, p. 183. The original portrait by del Conte is in the Metropolitan Museum of Art, New York. Vasari also cites the portrait by Giuliano Bugiardini (1475–1554).
13. For example, the Leighton Drawings Collection includes a pencil study of the head of Savonarola (ref. no. LHO/D/0949), which is not a copy from any known source but appears to be based on Fra Bartolomeo's portrait of *c.*1498.
14. Barringer & Prettejohn 1999, p. 114.
15. Barrington 1906, vol. II, p. 39.
16. Costa 1897, p. 376.
17. Rhys 1900, p. 56.
18. Barrington 1906, vol. II, p. 74.

2

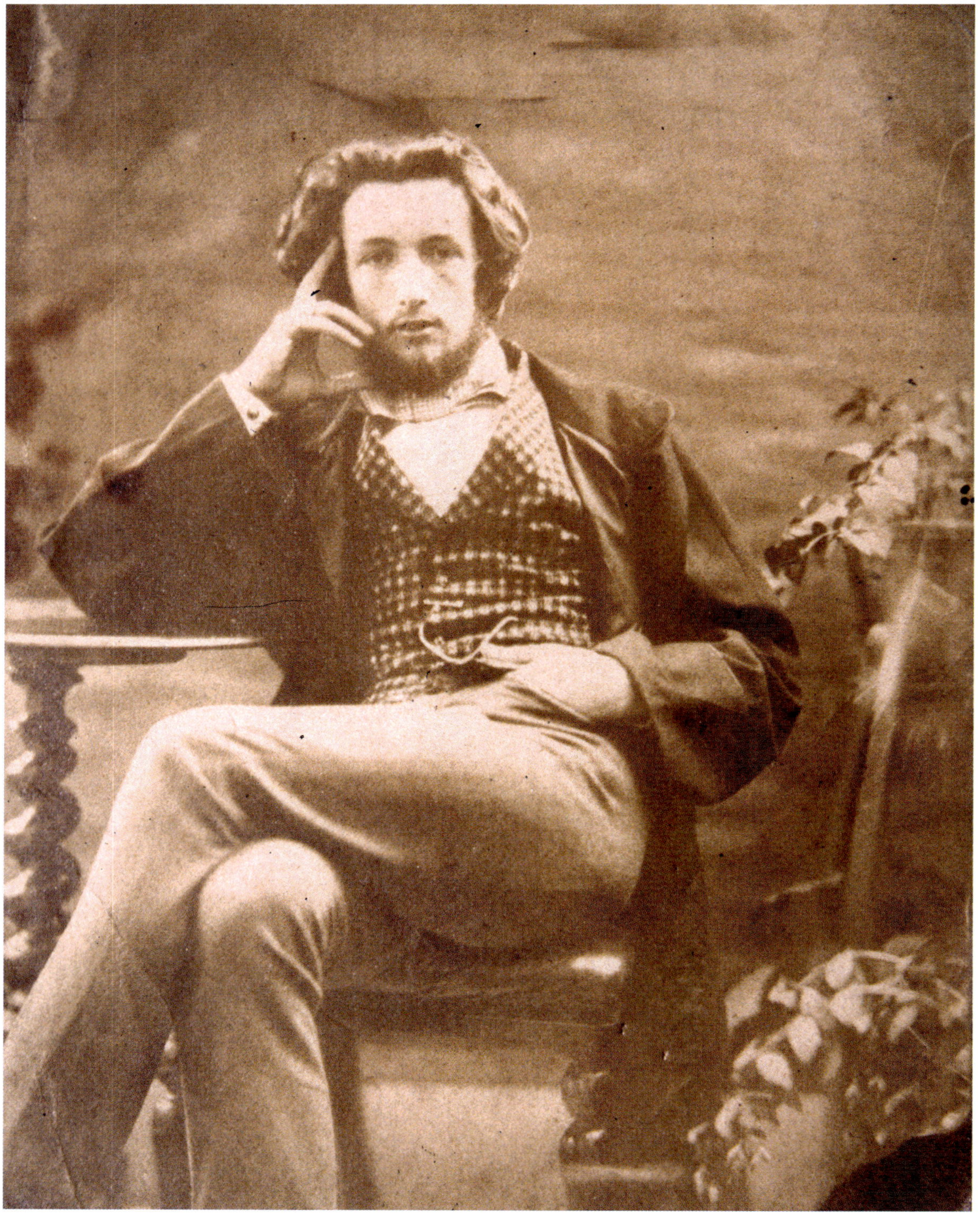

cat. ill. **4.** Photograph of Frederic Leighton, c.1859. Private Collection.

SIX WEEKS IN CAPRI
1859

In 1859, while at Capri, he drew the celebrated Lemon Tree, working from daylight to dusk for a week or two, and giving large details in the margin of the snails on the tree.

[Aitchison 1896, p.264.]

In about 1855, Leighton expressed the desire to make 'a trip to Naples, Capri, Ischia, Amalfi, and all the spots about which artists rave'.[1] In April 1859 he set out from Rome to travel southwards, via Naples, to the island of Capri where he was to spend the early summer.

Six weeks in Capri offered Leighton the opportunity to take stock of his position, prior to his move to London and his entry upon the English art world. The period since the exhibition of *Cimabue's Celebrated Madonna* four years earlier had been far from easy. In 1856 he had suffered a humiliating failure with *The Triumph of Music* (untraced), while early in 1859 *Samson and Delilah* (untraced) had been refused at the British Institution. Perhaps shaken by these setbacks, the artist used his time in Capri to regain confidence in his abilities by the exercise of drawing.

The English had long been interested in Capri, with eighteenth- and early nineteenth-century travellers describing the place in their published journals. English troops garrisoned the island during the Napoleonic wars. Henry Wreford, special correspondent for *The Times* in Rome and Naples and an untiring supporter of the cause of Italian liberty and unity, settled on the island in 1842 and lived there until his death in 1892. Among the English painters who visited or settled permanently on Capri, James Talmage White was there from the late 1850s. The American painter William Stanley Haseltine, who certainly knew Leighton in later years and who lived on Capri for long periods in the 1850s and 1860s, may have encouraged him to visit the island. Leighton stayed at Pagano's Hotel;[2] among other guests there in the summer of 1859 were Arthur Murch and Val Prinsep.

From the 1820s onwards Capri had also been much visited by travelling Germans. The neo-classical poets Stolberg, Stegmann, Rückert and Platin, and the painter Karl Blechen, stayed there. The illustrator von Führich and a group of painters who named themselves 'Die Odyseer' (to mark their admiration for Homeric legend) lived and worked on Capri. Leighton's enthusiasm for the island may have owed more to his contact with European writers and artists than with English-speaking painters.

Free from anxieties about works intended for exhibitions, Leighton occupied himself by drawing landscape, architectural and botanical subjects, and by making a series of ravishing *plein-air* oil sketches. The Capri drawings are both personal and introspective works, intended as meditations on the architectural and natural forms that make the island's physical appearance so distinctive. The drawing of buildings, landscape and nature was a personal therapy for Leighton, in which he might search for objective statements about the physical world by the simplest means of line and shade. Not made for display in public exhibitions or for sale, nor intended to serve as *aides-mémoire* of detail which might be incorporated in paintings with landscape settings, these drawings are works of art in their own right, done as intellectual and technical exercises in which Leighton learned to concentrate his mind absolutely, and focus his eye with the utmost clarity.

The oil sketches were likewise done without any object beyond that of training the eye to be observant of the qualities, intensities and direction of light. This was the first occasion that Leighton had made such a series of small studies, which in their variety of effect and differences according to time of day seem to have been intended to transmit the overall experience of the place. Two of the Capri oil-sketches – *Capri – Sunrise* and *Garden of an Inn, Capri* – were worked up as larger landscape compositions, each shown at the Royal Academy. He must have realised that the entrancing intensity and particularity of observation of the original sketches were lost in these scaled-up versions, and after 1861 he abandoned the practice.

Leighton's Capri drawings and oil sketches are perhaps the least academic and the most personal works he ever made. Indicating a mood of profound reflection of a kind which the painter was seldom to enjoy in the years to come (they may, however, be compared with the series of about 30 views that he made in 1868 during a six-week journey up the Nile – an artistic project Leighton described as 'a sort of discipline'[3]), they are complete in themselves and are unique to the circumstances of time and place. Their austere simplicity and the avoidance of all bravura effects of technique speak both of a sense of introspection during this period of self-exile, and of Leighton's determination to re-establish his creative confidence. C.S.N.

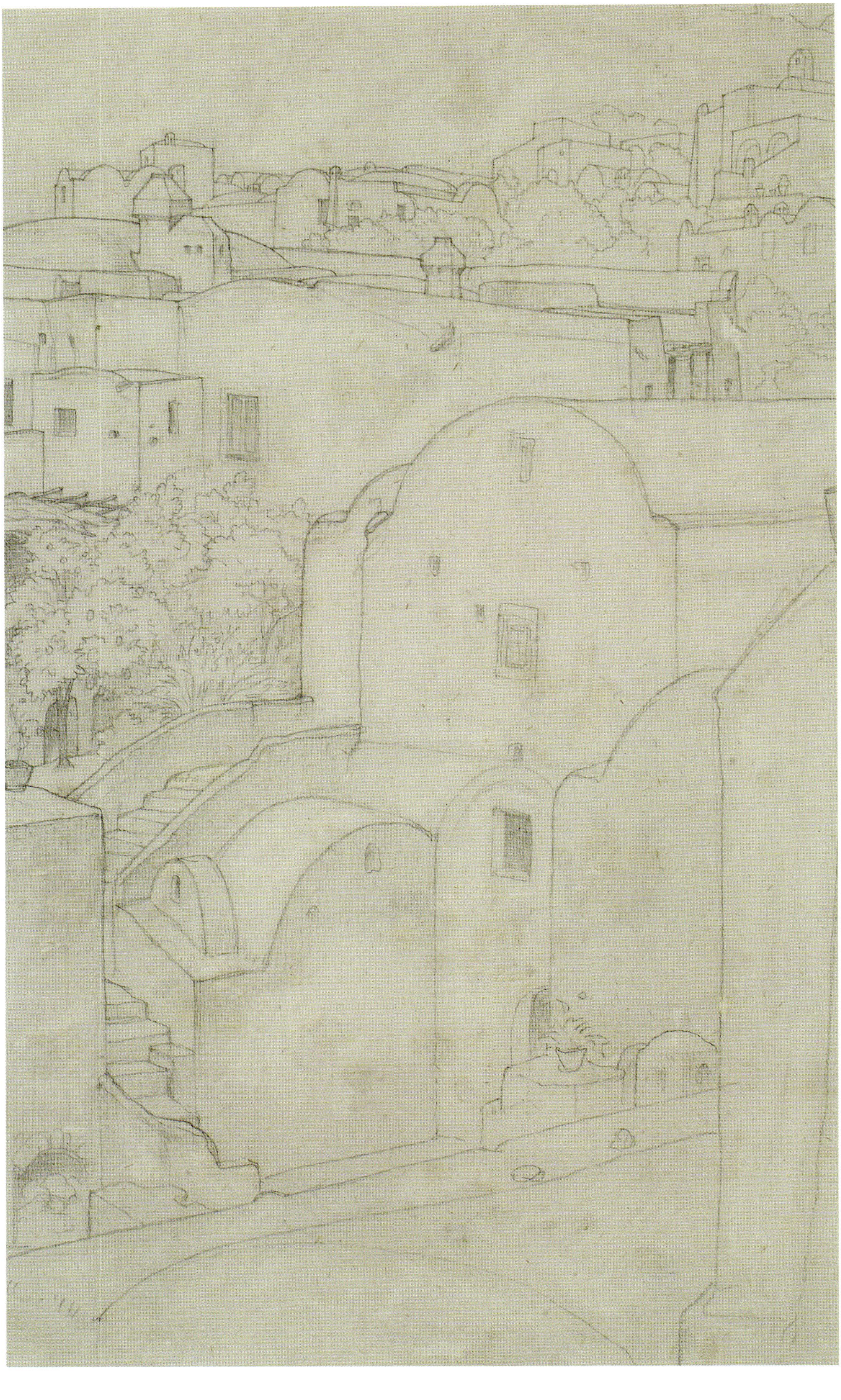

Detail of
cat. no. 2.2

cat. ill. 5. ***Capri – Sunrise***, 1859.
Oil on canvas. 27 x 41 cm. Private Collection.

cat. ill. 6. ***The Staircase of a House at Capri***, 1859.
Oil on canvas. 27.6 x 29.8 cm. From the Loyd Collection.

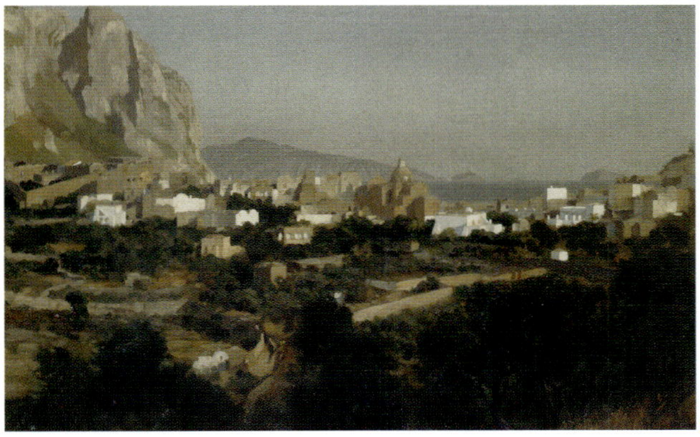
5.

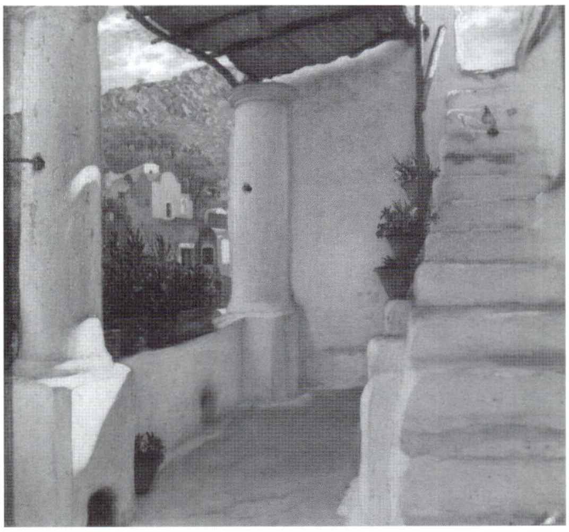
6.

Four Views of Capri, 1859

(Cat. nos 2.1, 2.2, 2.3 and 2.4)

Pagano's Hotel, where Leighton stayed for the six weeks that he spent on the island in April and May 1859, stood on the narrow street that runs around the east end of the cathedral of S. Stefano (the reconstructed hotel is now called La Palma, and the street is named Via Vittorio Emanuele).

Of the two elaborate views of distinctive low cubic buildings and their gardens, both may be assumed to be views of the town from close to Pagano's. In drawings of this type, Leighton seems to have taken particular pleasure in the shapes of the piled-up and overlapping forms, which extend in complex patterns across the sheet. The architectural and landscape forms are treated, almost without exception, in lines of delicate but definite character, without volumetric toning either in graphite or wash. These drawings were made directly from the motif, and represent the characteristic topography with careful attention. Each was probably made in the course of a single session, and therefore may be regarded as having resulted from two or three hours of concentrated inspection.

One of the drawings (cat. no. 2.2) offers a glimpse of the sea, presumably that on the island's south coast close to the Marina Piccola. This is likely to be another view taken from Pagano's itself, from which there were southerly views over the hillside that led down to the shore, looking towards the southwest. The other drawing (cat. no. 2.4) looks up towards the centre of the town, and while again there are no particular buildings that can be recognised, the lie of the ground and the elevated vantage point suggests that the view was from the hotel, looking to the north. Photographs of the building as it existed in the nineteenth century show that there were terraces or balconies on each side. Leighton is known to have painted from a bedroom window or balcony of the hotel itself. His oil-sketch *Garden of an Inn, Capri* (Private Collection) is undoubtedly a view from the hotel looking westwards towards Monte Solaro and with the sanctuary of Santa Maria Cetrella at its crest (the scaled-up version of this composition, entitled *Capri – Pagano's*, is in Birmingham Museums and Art Gallery).

Only one of the 1859 Capri drawings can be identified topographically. *View of a Landscape with Buildings* (cat. no. 2.3) shows the church of S. Michele della Croce, which stands on a small hill on the north-eastern fringe of the town, and is recognised by its distinctive belfry. The building on the right side in the same drawing, with three prominent archways cut into its wall, was a farm building converted in the nineteenth century for use as an annexe to Pagano's (and therefore where Leighton may have slept). Another open landscape subject to derive from the 1859 visit is the oil-sketch *Capri – Sunrise* (cat. ill. 5), which shows the town from the southeast, with its buildings resting in the saddle between the Tuoro and Solaro hills and with the islands of Ischia and Prócida on the horizon.

The distinctive character of the town of Capri, the limestone and whitewashed buildings of which are crowded together on the sloping ground, is given in the drawing *Study of a House in Capri* (cat. no. 2.1). Leighton was clearly fascinated by the complex patterns of stairways leading up to terraces and roofs, as well as the narrow alleyways across which the buildings face, some hardly wider than corridors and sections of which are closed over. The severe architectural pattern is softened by the leaves of an oleander, while various figures are glimpsed as they pass up and down the stairways and rest on the balconies. This sense of the labyrinthine complexities of the architecture, even despite the tiny scale of the town, and the seclusion of its hidden and private spaces, was explored by Leighton both in this drawing and in the oil sketch *The Staircase of a House at Capri* (cat. ill. 6). C.S.N.

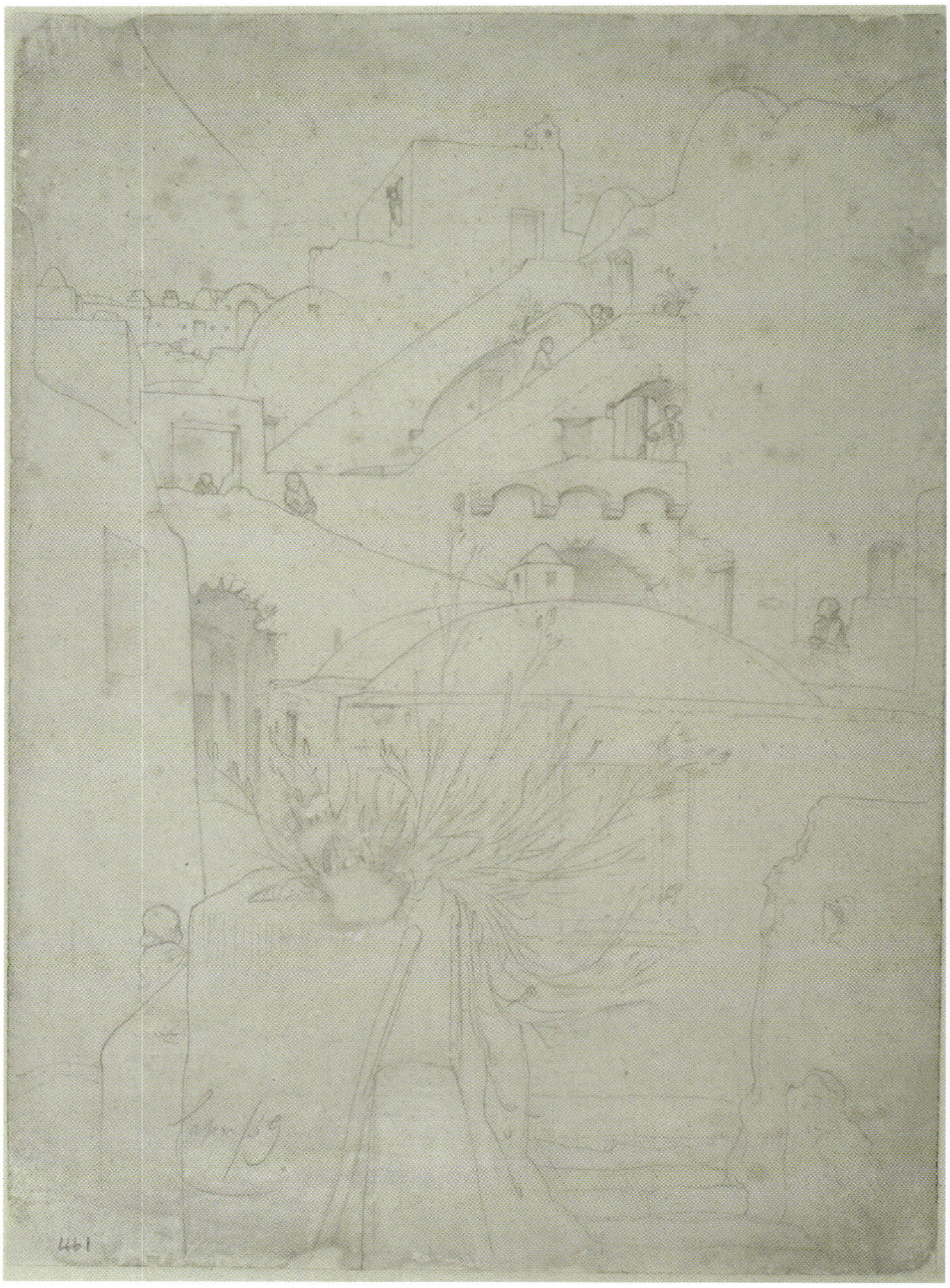

2.1

View of Houses in Capri, 1859

Graphite on white paper
271 x 200 mm
LHO/D/0914

INSCRIPTIONS

Inscribed and dated, lower left, 'Capri/59' in graphite, in the artist's hand.

PROVENANCE

Bequeathed by the artist to his sisters, Mrs Augusta Matthews and Mrs Alexandra Orr; from whom purchased by the FAS; acquired by the LHC by 1897; transferred to RBK in 1926 (now RBKC).

EXHIBITION HISTORY

LONDON 1897, nos 4–8 ('Landscapes'); **LONDON 1900**, possibly no. 99 or 104.

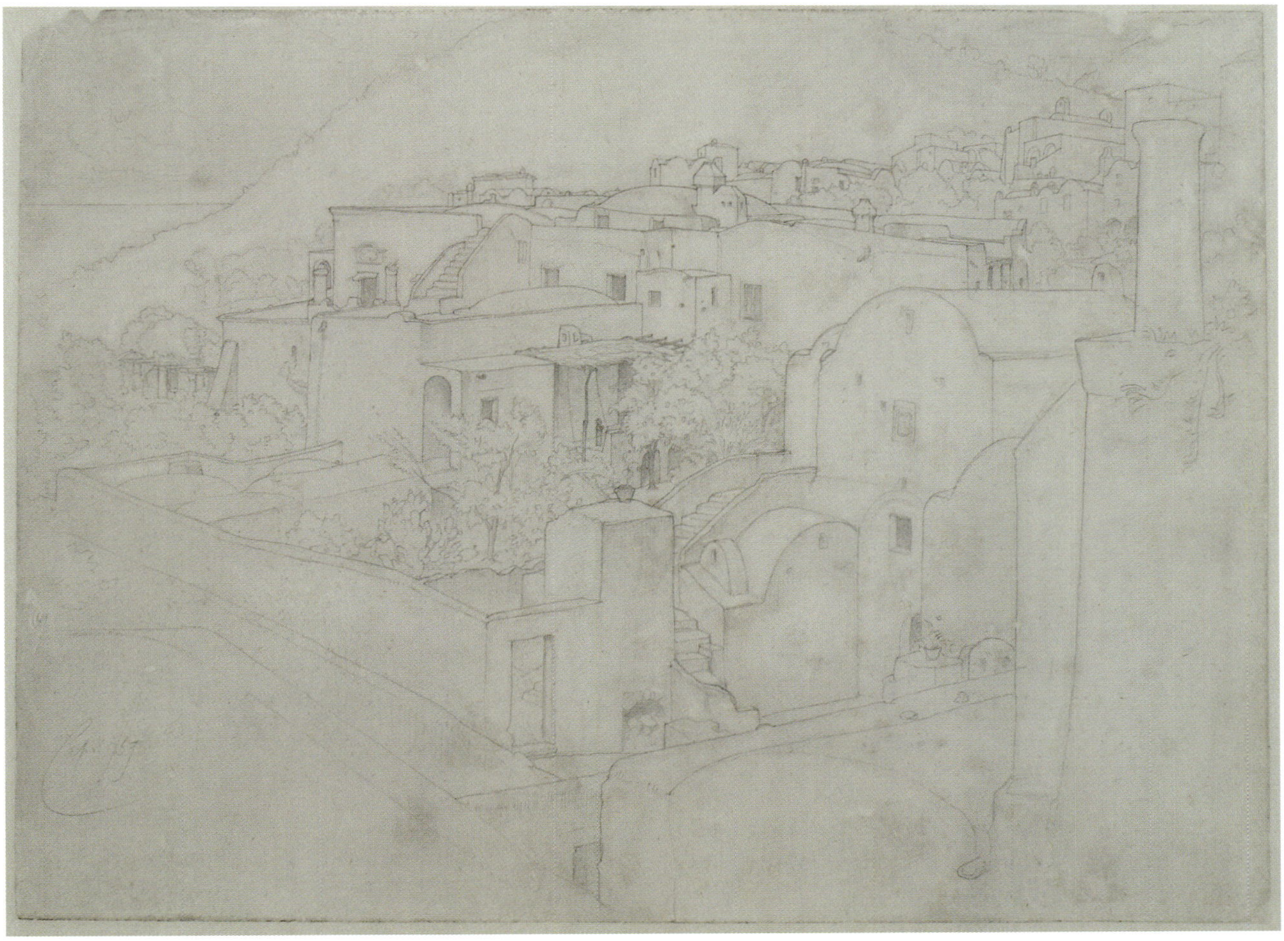

2.2

View of Capri, 1859

Graphite on white paper

201 x 273 mm

LHO/D/0916

INSCRIPTIONS

Inscribed and dated, lower left, 'Capri/59' in graphite, in the artist's hand.

PROVENANCE

Bequeathed by the artist to his sisters, Mrs Augusta Matthews and Mrs Alexandra Orr; from whom purchased by the FAS; acquired by the LHC by 1897; transferred to RBK in 1926 (now RBKC).

EXHIBITION HISTORY

LONDON 1897, nos 4–7 or 8; **LONDON 1900**, possibly no. 99 or 104.

2.3

View of a Landscape with Buildings, Capri, 1859

Graphite on white paper
201 x 273 mm
LHO/D/0917

INSCRIPTIONS

Inscribed and dated, centre left, 'Capri/59' in graphite, in the artist's hand. Stamped, lower left, 'LLC' encircled. Inscribed, lower right, 'Casa Scale' in graphite, by the FAS, partially erased.

PROVENANCE

Bequeathed by the artist to his sisters, Mrs Augusta Matthews and Mrs Alexandra Orr; from whom purchased by the FAS in 1896; acquired by the LHC by 1897; transferred to RBK in 1926 (now RBKC).

EXHIBITION HISTORY

LONDON 1897, nos 4–7 or 8; **LONDON 1900**, possibly no. 99 or 104.

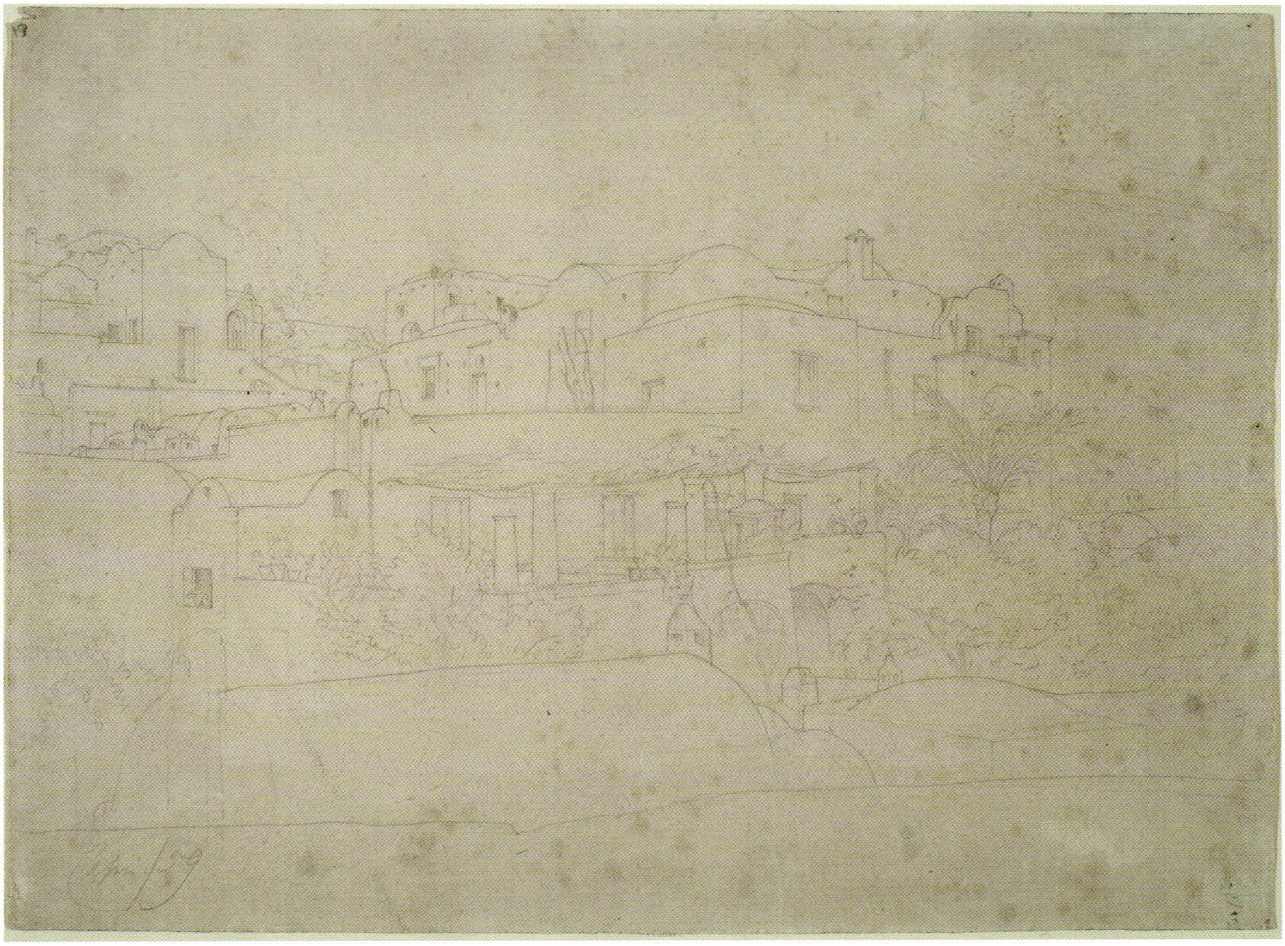

2.4

View of Capri, 1859

Graphite on white paper
200 x 274 mm
LHO/D/0915

INSCRIPTIONS

Inscribed and dated, lower left, 'Capri/59' in graphite, in the artist's hand. Stamped, lower left, 'LLC' encircled.

PROVENANCE

Bequeathed by the artist to his sisters, Mrs Augusta Matthews and Mrs Alexandra Orr; from whom purchased by the FAS in 1896; purchased by the LHC by 1897; transferred to RBK in 1926 (now RBKC).

EXHIBITION HISTORY

LONDON 1897, nos 4–7 or 8; **LONDON 1900**, possibly no. 99 or 104.

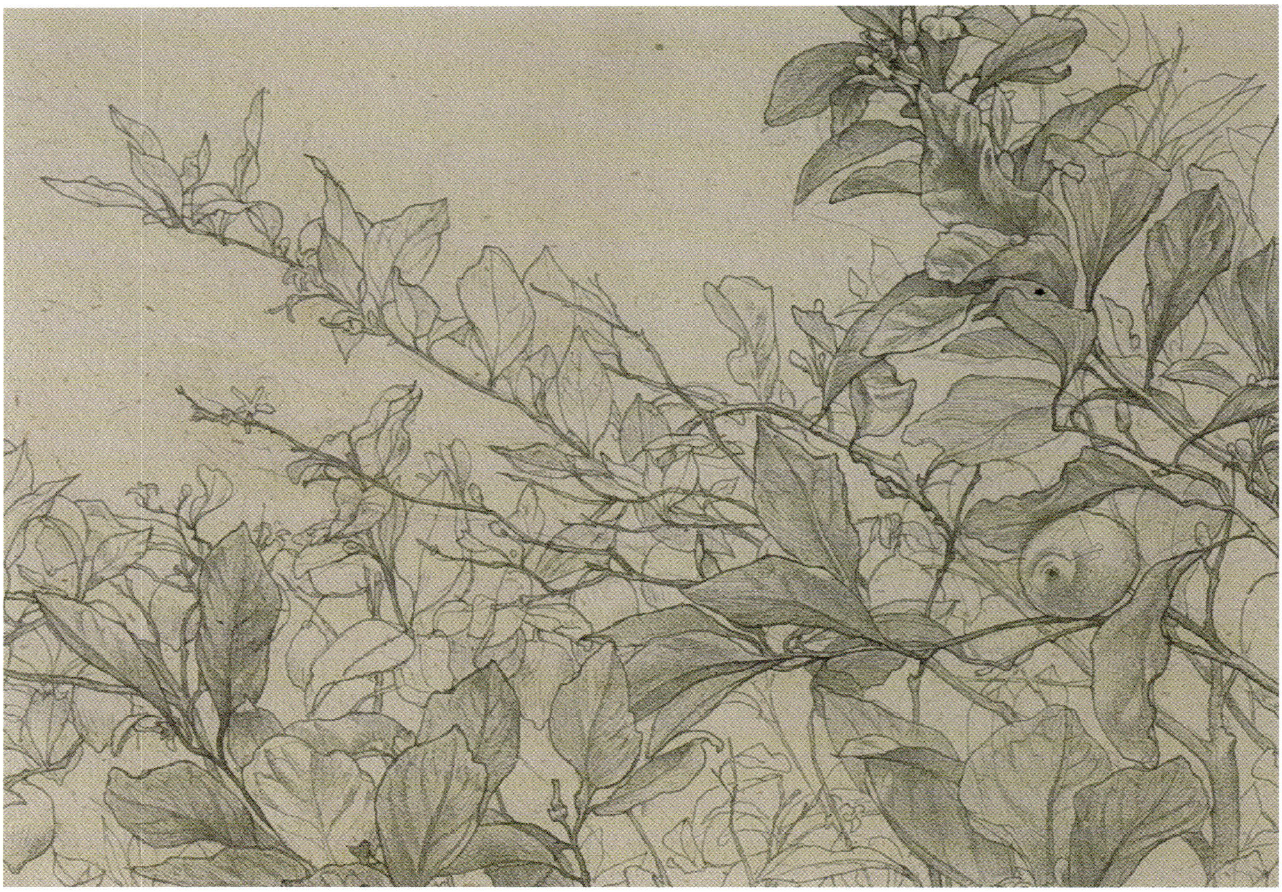

Detail of cat. no. 2.8

Three Botanical Studies, Capri, 1859

(Cat. nos 2.5, 2.6 and 2.7)

The gardens and fields of Capri are effulgent in their growth because of the mild climate and fertile soil. Leighton was there in the spring and early summer, and seems to have taken particular pleasure in observing a variety of plants and flowers. The most famous of these nature studies is *Study of a Lemon Tree*, but in addition he made drawings of vines, fig trees, and maize leaves and flowers. A further example of Leighton's meticulous observation of flowers and foliage, probably from the 1859 Capri trip, is the ravishing *Study of Jasmin*, also in the Leighton House collection (ref. no. LHO/D/0997). The great palm tree that grew in the garden of Pagano's Hotel was the principal motif of the oil sketch *Garden of an Inn, Capri*.

The beautiful study of a lemon flower (cat. no. 2.7) makes a perfect complement to the more famous *Study of a Lemon Tree*. It is not known where he made either drawing, but of course lemon trees grow freely on all parts of the island. In his book *The Masque of Capri* (1957) Edwin Cerio described the hotel as it existed in the nineteenth century as 'the charming house of the Paganos, situated on a property of theirs where even today *die Zitronen blühn*', so it seems the artist did not need to travel far to find his subject.

The drawing of the lemon flower shows two main studies, the upper one treated in graphite tone so as to give a sense of the volume of the leaves, buds and petals. This study is closely observant of the botanical specimen, with weird protuberant swellings that are the unburst buds, and a spray of fresh petals and stamens in another part. The other drawing is purely linear. In both, Leighton manifests an interest in the plant's different parts, and in the irregular patterns that they describe.

In these botanical drawings Leighton may have been responding, whether deliberately or not, to the programme of recommended subjects that John Ruskin laid out in his book *The Elements of Drawing*, published in the late spring of 1857. Intended in the first place as a course of instruction for amateurs and students, and owing much to the teaching that Ruskin had given at the Working Men's College in London, this was nonetheless read and followed by many young artists and was widely influential. Couched in terms of utter simplicity and directness, its essential purpose was to encourage readers to find beauty in familiar and easily overlooked aspects of nature and the countryside.

Ruskin was himself entranced by nature, as he was also by the geological structure of man's environment, and brought the faculties of a scientist to the processes of inspection in his own drawings as in his prose. Likewise, he demanded that artists who adopted his principles should observe with understanding, and should respect scientific principles of type and differentiation as they drew. The draughtsman's duty was to see the essential characteristics of his chosen subjects, as a botanist might analyse and identify a specimen. *C.S.N.*

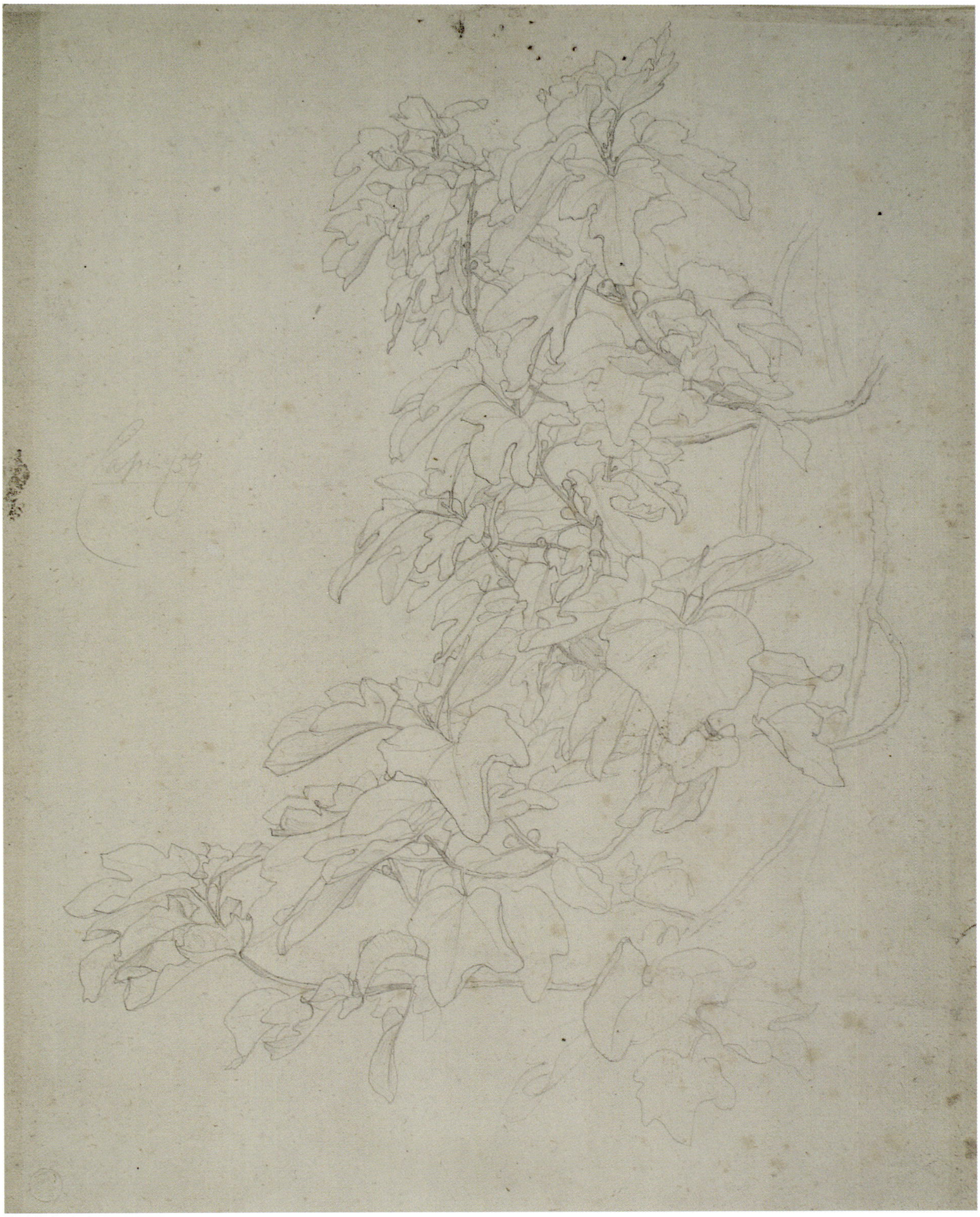

2.5

Study of the Branch of a Fig Tree, Capri, 1859

Graphite on white paper
270 x 200 mm
LHO/D/1019

INSCRIPTIONS

Inscribed and dated, centre left, 'Capri/59' in graphite, in the artist's hand. Stamped, lower left, 'LLC' encircled. Inscribed, lower right, 'A fig tree' in graphite, by the FAS.

PROVENANCE

Bequeathed by the artist to his sisters, Mrs Augusta Matthews and Mrs Alexandra Orr; from whom purchased by the FAS in 1896; from whom probably purchased by Matthews and Orr and presented to the LHC by 1900; transferred to RBK in 1926 (now RBKC).

BIBLIOGRAPHICAL REFERENCES

Staley 1906, p. 220.

EXHIBITION HISTORY

LONDON 1900, no. 243.

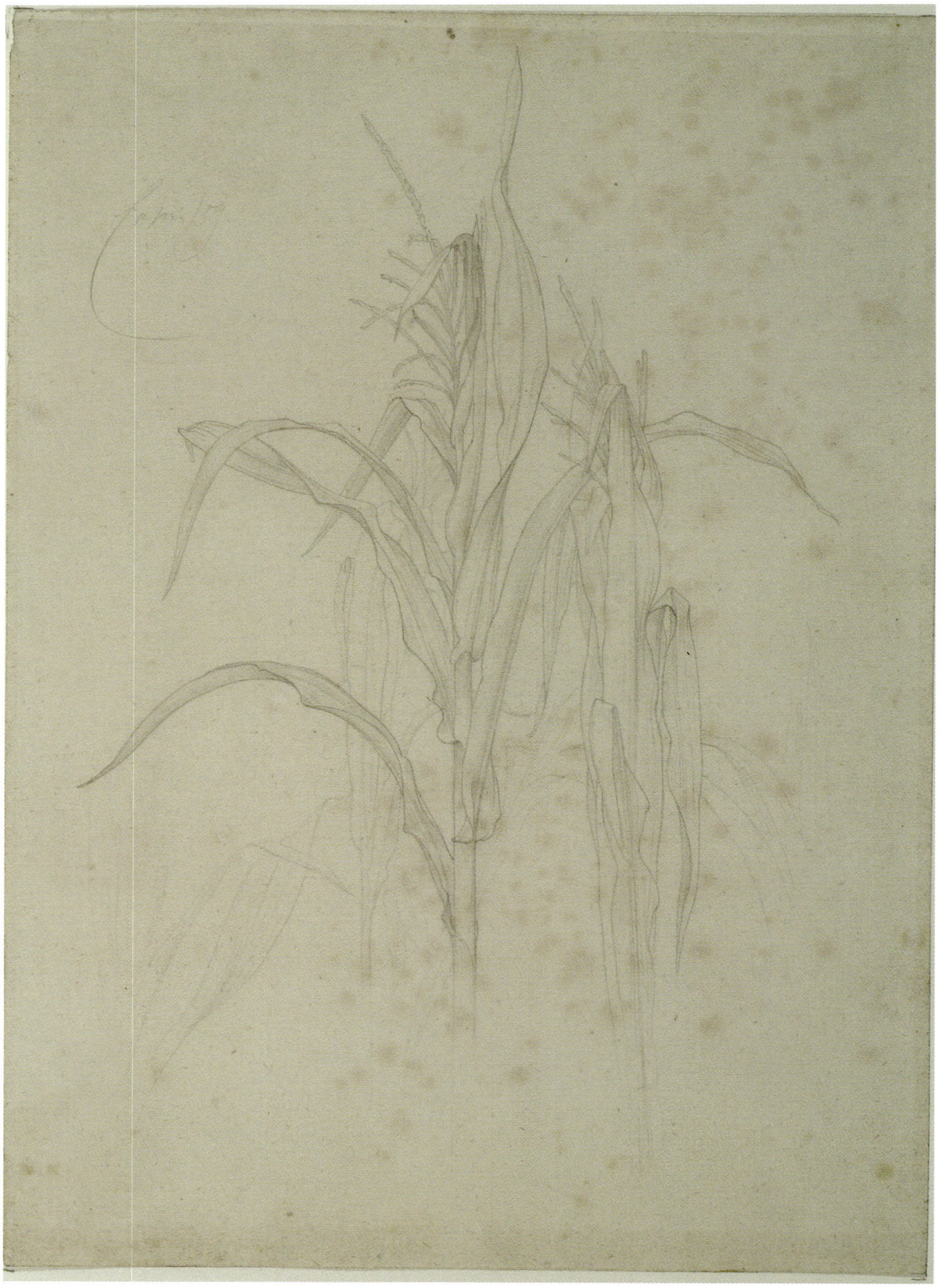

2.6

Study of Maize, Capri, 1859

Graphite on white paper
276 x 202 mm
LHO/D/1005

INSCRIPTIONS

Inscribed and dated, upper left, 'Capri/59' in graphite in the artist's hand.

PROVENANCE

Bequeathed by the artist to his sisters, Mrs Augusta Matthews and Mrs Alexandra Orr; from whom purchased by the FAS in 1896; purchased by the LHC by 1897; transferred to RBK in 1926 (now RBKC).

EXHIBITION HISTORY

LONDON 1897, no. 17 (First Section); **LONDON 1900**, no. 40.

2.7

Studies of a Lemon Blossom, Capri, 1859

Graphite on white paper
268 x 192 mm
Victoria and Albert Museum, London (E.3803–1910)

INSCRIPTIONS

Inscribed, upper right, 'Lemon blossom / Capri/59 / buds pink violet' in graphite, in the artist's hand.

PROVENANCE

Inherited by the artist's sisters Mrs Augusta Matthews and Mrs Alexandra Orr; from whom purchased by the FAS, 1896; purchased by the Victoria and Albert Museum, 1897.

BIBLIOGRAPHICAL REFERENCES

Caldwell Hutchinson 1893, ill. in two parts: p. 125 fig. 82, p. 127 fig. 83; Staley 1906, p. 226.

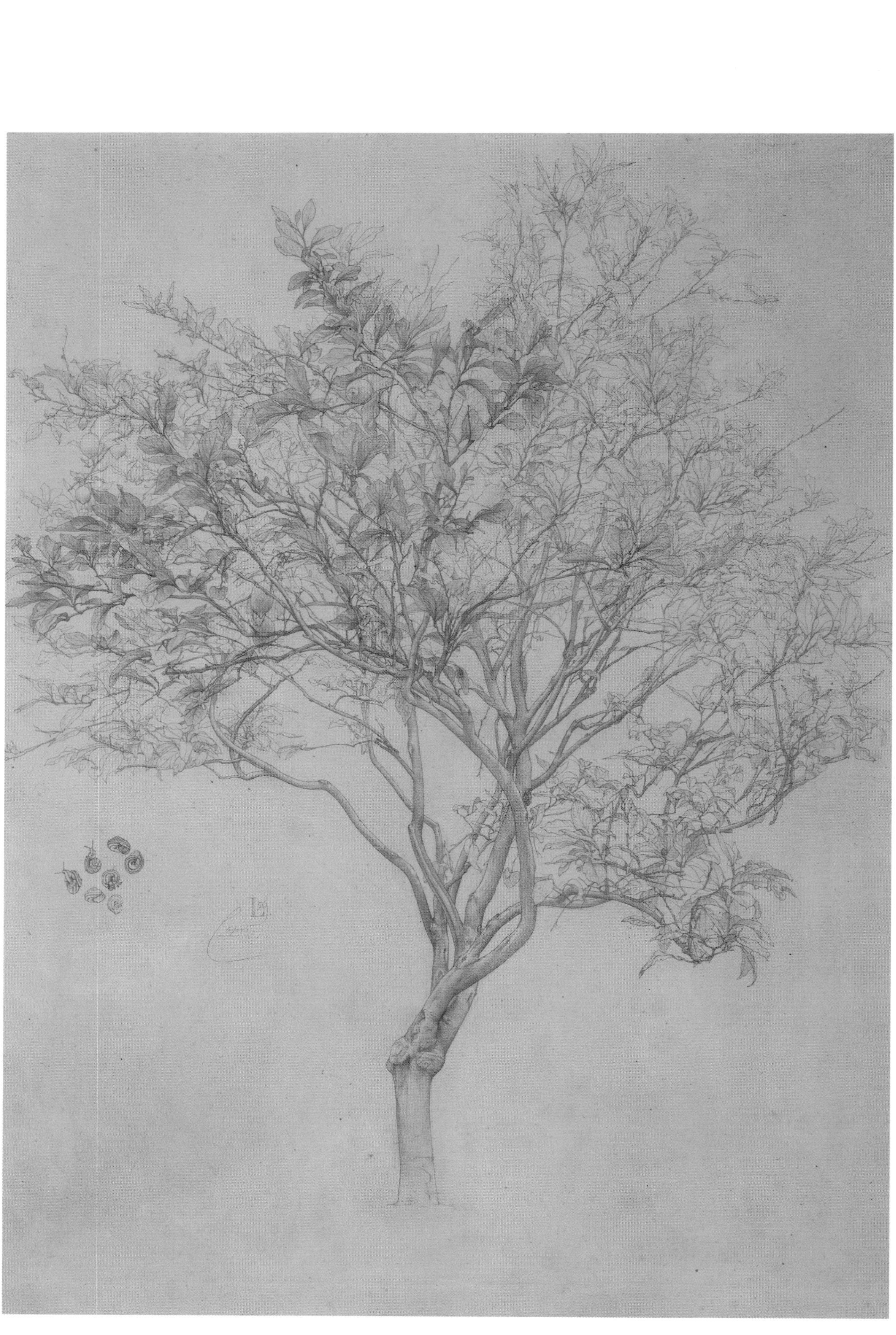

2.8

Study of a Lemon Tree, Capri, 1859

Graphite on white paper
534 x 394 mm
Private Collection

Leighton's *Study of a Lemon Tree* is the most famous and most elaborate drawing that he ever made. It has an intensity of observation that serves the exact replication of the forms of stem, branches, foliage and fruit. In making the drawing, Leighton resisted all abbreviations or mannerisms of line in favour of searching and objective observation, finding in the very austerity of its pure draughtsmanship a degree of creative anonymity. At the same time, the work exerts a fascination upon the viewer by the deliberate manipulation of degrees of finish in its different areas – some parts of the composition appear almost schematic while others are exhaustively and minutely represented, thus simulating the very function of seeing. This was a work of enormous industry and inventiveness, which was undertaken both as a personal manifesto and as a means of self-investigation.

Whereas the majority of Leighton's 1859 drawings took a couple of hours or so to do, and each of his oil-sketches perhaps half a day, *Study of a Lemon Tree* occupied him for many sessions and over an extended period. Manifestly demonstrated by the sheer complexity of the drawing, the length of time he spent on it is corroborated by the account given by George Aitchison, who described how Leighton worked 'from daylight to dusk for a week or two'.[4] In an article in the *Studio* in 1894, it was said that Leighton still reminisced about 'the many days spent upon the production of this study' thirty-five years before, and how he especially recalled 'the difficulty he experienced in finding again and again each separate leaf in the perspective of the confused branches, as morning after morning he returned at sunrise to continue his work'.[5] In embarking on this particular project, Leighton was declaring himself an earnest and devoted student of nature, and one who was prepared to endure discomfort as well as physical and mental exhaustion in pursuit of his objective. The seriousness and determination of this approach – the consequence of which was a slight sense of self-consciousness in a drawing that in all other respects is utterly self-denying – certainly owed much to the training that Leighton had received among German artists. When drawing from nature in the 1850s, Leighton is likely to have had in mind the botanical studies of Nazarene artists such as Friedrich Olivier and Julius Schnorr von Carolsfeld, as well as those of his own master Eduard von Steinle.

Study of a Lemon Tree has also been seen as a bid on Leighton's part to show that he could match the Pre-Raphaelites in terms of detailed replication of the forms of nature. Emilie Barrington described her 'first introduction' to the drawing:

> [it was] on an occasion when Leighton and I had an argument respecting the principles of the Pre-Raphaelite school. He fetched the drawing from a corner in his studio and... said words to the effect that it was not only the Pre-Raphaelites who reverenced the detail in Nature, and who thought it worth the time and labour it took to record the beauty in the wonderful minutiæ of her structure.[6]

The drawing was first exhibited at the Hogarth Club, in the winter of 1859–60. The Hogarth was a meeting place for the quondam Pre-Raphaelites (all the original Pre-Raphaelites, with the exception of John Everett Millais and James Collinson, were members there, as briefly was John Ruskin; Leighton had become a founder member of the club during his visit to London in the summer of 1858). Showing the drawing at the Hogarth may have been a bid for recognition among that progressive circle.

Notwithstanding the microscopic attention to detail demonstrated in *Study of a Lemon Tree*, the subject remains fresh and animated with rippling life. The leaves appear to rustle before our eyes, and the sappy stems of the tree's branches seem to flex in the soft wind. The drawing represents a living nature in which the artist finds pleasure and delight. In the *Studio* article devoted to the drawing, it was described as:

> broad and simple, and [a work that] scarcely suggests the enormous patience which must have been needed to carry out the self-imposed toil. Nothing is shirked, nothing scamped, from the stem to the uttermost leaf; every part in succession reveals equal interest, and yet the whole is not devoid of a large quality which brings it together in a harmonious whole, so that it is as much the study of a tree as the study of each separate item that composes it.[7]

Study of a Lemon Tree emerged as a transcendent and complex work of art, and one that is both earnest and ecstatic. In the context of Leighton's entire career it has been uniquely famous and intensely admired since the time it was made. *C.S.N.*

INSCRIPTIONS

Signed, dated and inscribed, lower left, 'L59/Capri' in graphite, in the artist's hand.

PROVENANCE

Loaned by the artist to John Ruskin, December 1882; collection of Samuel Pepys Cockerell; by descent to Frederica Huddart, 1921; by descent to E.W. (Bill) Huddart, 1957; purchased by a private collector, 2005.

BIBLIOGRAPHICAL REFERENCES

Anon. 1874a, p. 867; Anon. 1874b, p. 232; Anon. 1880, p. 24; Anon. 1894; Rhys 1895, pp xviii, 10, 11, ill. opp. p. xviii; Aitchison 1896, p. 264; Cockerell 1896, p. 812; Spielmann 1896, p. 210; Cook 1903–12, vol. XXXIII, pp 318–19, ill. opp. p. 319, vol. XXXVI, p. 334, vol. XXXVII, p. 424; Corkran 1904, pp 37–38, 186, 209; Barrington 1906, vol. I, pp 201–02, ill. opp. p. 202, vol. II, pp 41–42, 55–56, 373; Staley 1906, pp 57, 96, 212, 238; Ironside 1948, pl. 94, p. 49; Staley 1973, p. 177, pl. 100b; Ormond 1975b, pl. 66, pp 43, 52; Newall 1990, p. 31, ill. on half title page; Prettejohn 2000a, pl. 138, pp 173–74.

EXHIBITION HISTORY

LONDON 1859, not numbered; **LONDON 1874**, no. 171; **LONDON 1880**, no. 408; **OXFORD 1894**, not numbered; **DUBLIN 1907**, no. 568; **MANCHESTER (UK), MINNEAPOLIS, NEW YORK 1978–79**, no. 40; **LONDON 1996**, no. 3; **LONDON 2004**, no. 16.

NOTES

1. Barrington 1906, vol. I, p. 172.
2. Leighton's entry in the Visitors' Book at Pagano's Hotel, Capri reads: 'Fred Leighton, painter, in England / spent six weeks at this inn and never found in Italy greater liberality / or more obliging civility'.
3. Barrington 1906, vol. II, p. 158.
4. Aitchison 1896, pp 264–65.
5. *Studio* 1894, vol. III, pp 25–26.
6. Barrington 1906, vol. I, p. 202.
7. *Studio* 1894, vol. III, pp 25–26.

3

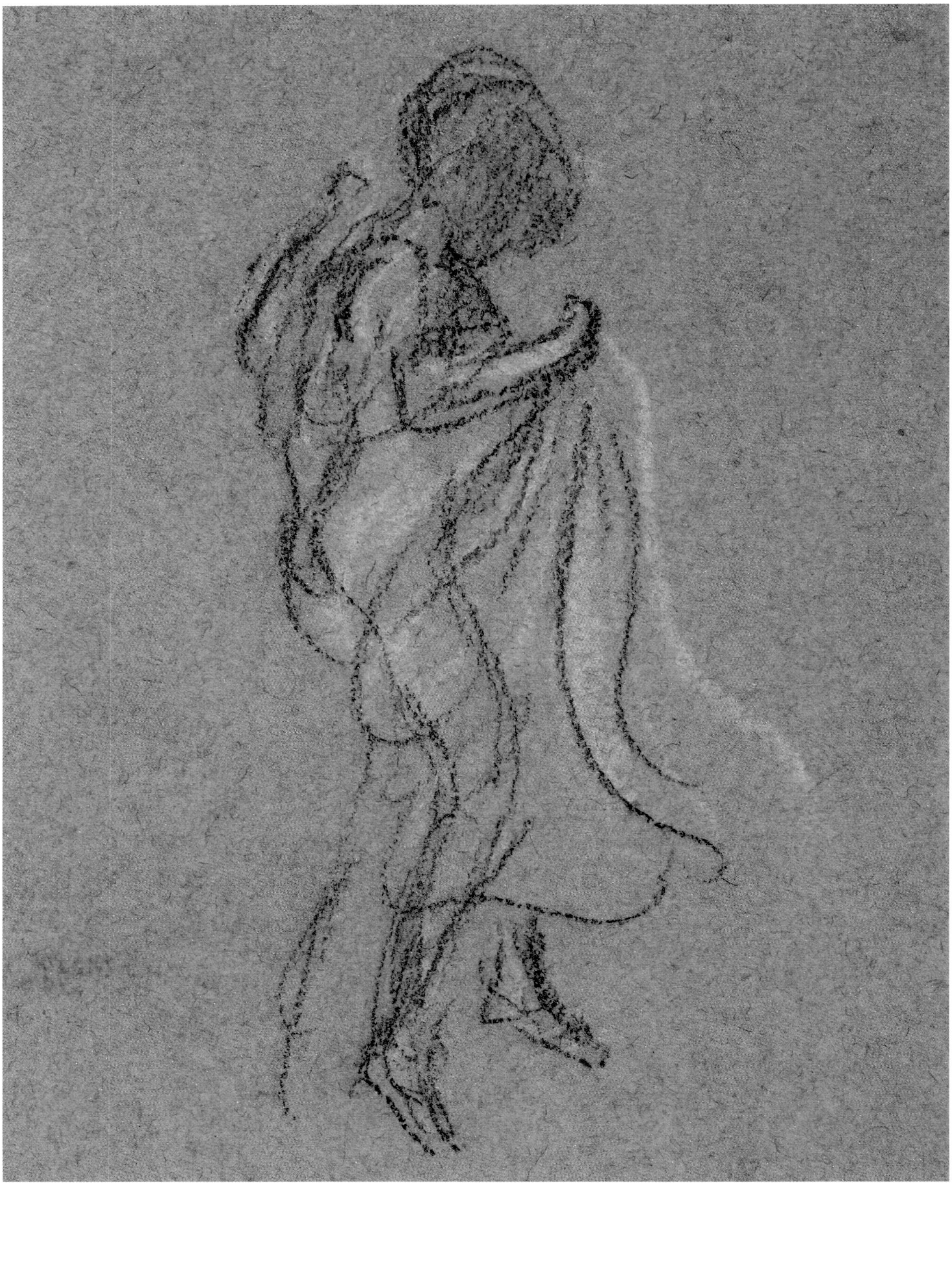

Detail of cat. no. 3.8.

CONSOLIDATION AND ADVANCE
1859–1876

If the Public receives my pictures as favourably as the Private has done, I shall have no cause to complain; as far, at least, as the maintenance and increase of my reputation is concerned.

[Leighton writing to his father from London in 1861, quoted in Barrington 1906, vol. II, p. 58.]

In the autumn of 1859 Leighton settled in London, taking a studio at 2 Orme Square, Bayswater. While he seamlessly entered London society and gained the admiration of his contemporaries, Leighton's professional standing was at a low ebb. Stylistic uncertainties and significant disappointments continued to surround his work, as he encountered further difficulties in his relationship with the Royal Academy. However, a turning point came in 1864 with his election as an Associate. By the end of the decade he had been elected a full Academician, and his reputation and standing would continue to grow through the 1870s.

This period of transition started unpromisingly. Leighton's Academy submission of 1861 – composed of six important canvasses (including *Lieder Ohne Worte*, cat. ill. 7) – resulted in gallery placings that were so unsympathetic as to elicit protests on his behalf from figures such as John Everett Millais and Dante Gabriel Rossetti. Further disappointments were to follow, perhaps encouraging Leighton to turn towards the other dissenters of the Pre-Raphaelite Brotherhood through his membership of the Hogarth Club. Leighton felt keenly the antipathy he perceived to have been directed against him, but was similarly convinced of the value of his own position and that his abilities would eventually prevail.

In the early 1860s, work for the Dalziel Brothers' compendium of Bible stories required Leighton to produce sharp and compressed images suitable for reproduction. Leighton's interest in biblical subjects continued with the major canvas, *Jezebel and Ahab* (*c.*1863, Scarborough Art Gallery). At this time he also received the commission to decorate St Michael's Church, Lyndhurst, painting the fresco *The Wise and Foolish Virgins* (1862–64).

Illustrations were also completed in 1862 to accompany the serialisation of George Eliot's *Romola* in the *Cornhill Magazine*. This commission re-ignited Leighton's interest in Renaissance subject matter, and led to the production of a number of canvases that began slowly to cement his reputation as an artist. The most important of these, *Dante in Exile* (Private Collection), was exhibited in 1864 and sold for £1,050 – considerably more than had been realised for any of his works prior to this date. The studies for this work are in black and white chalk on blue paper. From the late 1850s Leighton had begun to produce his preparatory studies in this medium, and continued to do so almost without exception until about 1877.

The status of Academy membership also confirmed Leighton's financial independence. For some time he had been considering the construction of a studio-house, and in September 1864 he purchased a plot of land in Holland Park. Leighton engaged his old friend, the architect George Aitchison, to design and construct a building that would serve equally well as a space for working and for entertaining. He was in residence by 1866 and would remain at 2 Holland Park Road for the rest of his life, gradually enlarging both his house and his collections of fine and decorative art.

Leighton continued to travel extensively, and in the late 1860s undertook several important trips. Enthused by a brief sojourn in Algeria in 1857, Leighton journeyed to Turkey and Greece in 1867. A year later he sailed along the Nile. Taking advantage of favourable contacts made on his behalf by the Prince of Wales, Leighton spent several weeks aboard a steamship, living in some luxury and stopping wherever he pleased. In 1873 this spate of travels to the Middle East ended in a trip to Damascus. These journeys provided the opportunity for Leighton to increase his collections of tiles, pottery, vases and other Eastern wares significantly, and to experience at first hand the Arabic world that had fascinated him since his first interest in the Moorish influences within Spanish art. However, of the greatest practical value was the opportunity to produce numerous sketches. These were mostly landscapes in oil, but he also made a number of fine pencil studies of heads.

As Leighton approached the zenith of his career, his style became more assured and his technique consistent. The era of his great canvasses was approaching, signalled by *The Daphnephoria* of 1876, a masterpiece of decorative style. The ambitious *The Arts of Industry as Applied to War* (1878–80, Victoria and Albert Museum) for the South Kensington Museum brought his art into a major public space, and prepared the ground for Leighton's emergence as one of the pre-eminent artists of his day. R.S.

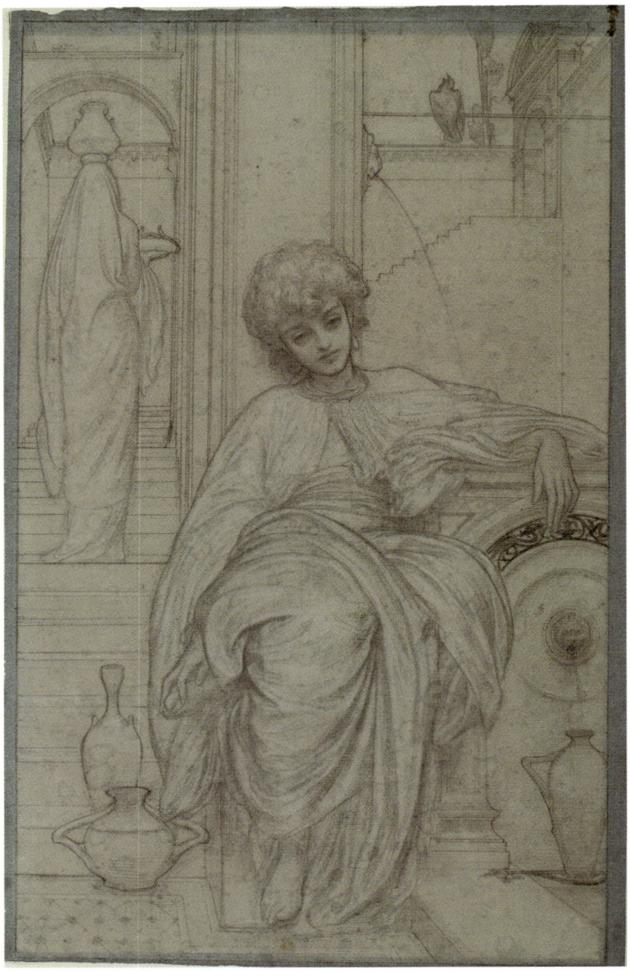

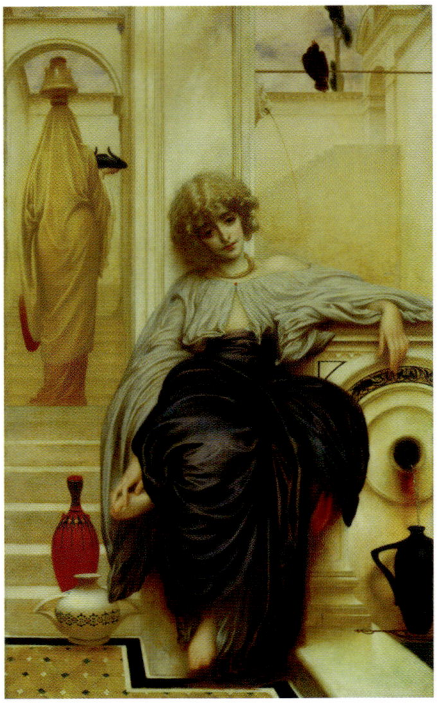

7.

3.1

Study for 'Lieder Ohne Worte': Composition, *c.*1860

Black and white chalk on blue paper
595 x 385 mm
LHO/D/0834

Leighton's working title for this composition was *The Listener*, and this study amply conveys the subject lost in thought whilst contemplating the sounds of running water and of birdsong. This study appears to be one of the last occasions when Leighton concluded the process of studying individual elements of the composition by the production of a worked-up and highly finished drawing of the whole design. His later practice was to make only small outline drawings of the composition on tracing paper in readiness for the design to be squared-up on the canvas. The subsequent adoption of the title *Lieder Ohne Worte* (cat. ill. 7) after the piano pieces by Felix Mendelssohn, was suggested by a visitor to his studio, Mrs Ralph Benson (sister of his friend Frederick Pepys Cockerell) and is entirely consistent with the evolution of the painting in the artist's mind.[1]

Some debate exists as to the identity of the female model, who was assumed by Emilie Barrington to be, in fact, a boy – John Hanson Walker.[2] Leighton's desire to introduce a more abstract quality to the work led to a stylised depiction of the face, making the identity of the sitter less relevant. In doing so Leighton set about feminising the face, introducing features taken from studies of female models. The hands of the figure may also have their origin in a female sitter. Although the most striking, *Lieder Ohne Worte* was not the only example of Leighton combining studies of models of different ages or sexes to create a single figure in one of his paintings.

To further distance the picture from any sense of naturalism, Leighton treats the architectural framework with a considerable degree of eclecticism, mixing eastern styles observed and documented on his trip to Algiers with a classical Roman influence reflecting his travels around Italy. The Algerian journey of 1857 which Leighton undertook, 'partly to make some landscape studies, but also to make acquaintance with that very interesting race',[3] had a more specific impact upon the painting. Leighton adapted the tall figure on the left from sketches made of a woman in Algiers (ref. no. LHO/D/0972), introducing an 'authentic' eastern element into an exotic display of buildings and artefacts.[4] *R.S.*

PROVENANCE

Bequeathed by the artist to his sisters, Mrs Augusta Matthews and Mrs Alexandra Orr; from whom purchased by the FAS in 1896; acquired by the LHC by 1900, transferred to RBK in 1926 (now RBKC).

BIBLIOGRAPHICAL REFERENCES

Staley 1906, p. 214; Ormond 1975b, p. 60, pl. 82, p. 153 (listed under cat. no. 64).

EXHIBITION HISTORY

LONDON 1900, no. 36a.

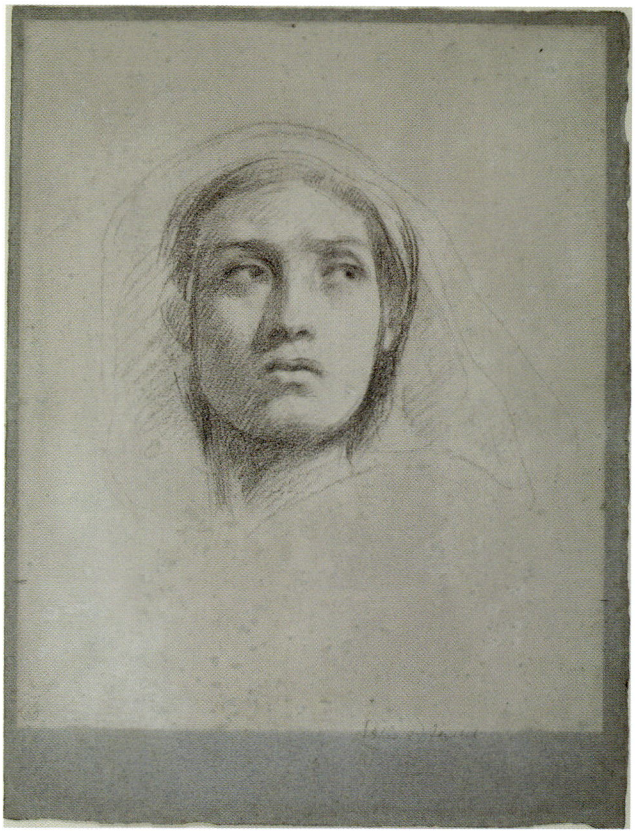

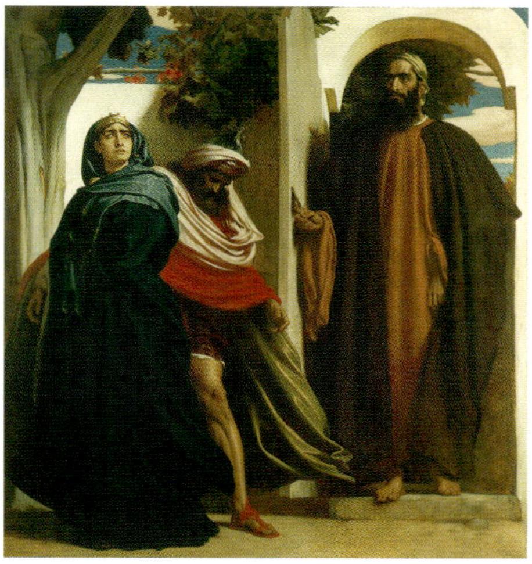

8.

cat. ill. 7. ***Lieder Ohne Worte***, RA 1861.
Oil on canvas. 101.6 x 62.9 cm. Tate, London.

cat. ill. 8. ***Jezebel and Ahab***, RA 1863.
Oil on canvas. 238.8 x 231.1 cm. Scarborough Art Gallery.

3.2

Study for 'Jezebel and Ahab': Head of Jezebel, *c*.1862

Black chalk on blue paper
320 x 242 mm
LHO/D/0475

Leighton had considered the subject of Jezebel as one of his illustrations for the Dalziel Brothers' *Bible Gallery*. When this suggestion was not taken up, he decided to devote a full canvas to his interpretation of the subject of Jezebel and Ahab (cat. ill. 8). Contemporary critics were largely positive in reviewing the painting, which helped to re-establish Leighton's reputation following the setbacks of recent years. He must have taken some comfort from a review describing him as 'an artist whose genius of late years has fallen into chaos, but who now rises once again into the spheres of well ordered creation'.[5]

The face of Jezebel in this study does not have the villainous features of the face in the painting. This may indicate that it is an early study, made before Leighton achieved the desired effect. The story of how Leighton was 'despairing of finding a model to assume a sufficiently dramatic expression of wickedness', is recalled by the model herself, Fanny Kemble, an actress and the sister of Adelaide Sartoris. Henry Greville (a prominent figure in society and part of Sartoris' social group) was sympathetic to Leighton's plight and pointed out Kemble, suggesting, 'Why don't you ask her?' Kemble recalled how she used her experience on the stage 'to assume as thoroughly as possible the character which I was representing'. However, she found the pose a strain, and almost fainted as a result.[6] Although Kemble is drawn in the haughty and contemptuous pose required by the character of Jezebel, these features are deliberately distorted in the painting into an almost melodramatic mask of disdain. Interestingly, Leighton used the same model in a different attitude for the study of the head of Elijah. The effect of melodrama is further reinforced by the composition and scale of the finished work in which all three characters – Jezebel, Ahab and Elijah – are depicted life size.[7] *R.S.*

INSCRIPTIONS

Stamped, lower left, 'LLC' encircled. Inscribed, lower right, '(Ahab &) Jezebel' in graphite, by the FAS.

PROVENANCE

Bequeathed by the artist to his sisters, Mrs Augusta Matthews and Mrs Alexandra Orr; from whom purchased by the FAS in 1896; possibly acquired by the LHC by 1897, transferred to RBK in 1926 (now RBKC).

BIBLIOGRAPHICAL REFERENCES

Staley 1906, p. 218; Ormond 1975b, p. 154 (listed under cat.no. 86).

EXHIBITION HISTORY

Possibly **LONDON 1897**, no. 10, 10A or 10B ('Studies for Designs'); **LONDON 1900**, no. 166.

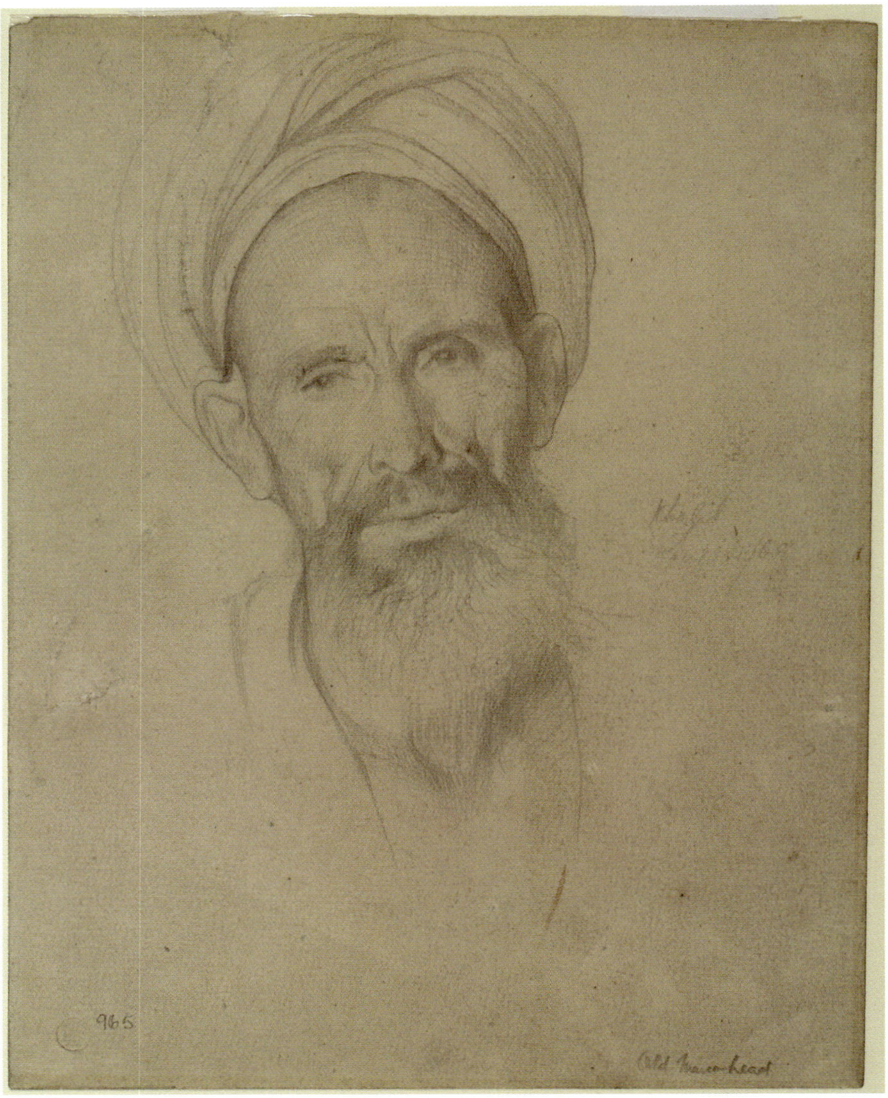

3.3

Study of a Male Head, 1868

Graphite on white paper
213 x 172 mm
LHO/D/0975

Leighton made a number of trips to the Middle East and North Africa, including a journey by boat along the Nile during October and November 1868. His friendship with the Prince of Wales secured him the patronage of the Pasha (Viceroy of Egypt), whose support extended to the loan of a steam tug. The benefits of this more speedy and reliable vessel allowed Leighton to make stops as he wished, and to spend more time ashore than would have been possible with a conventional sailing boat.[8] Leighton took full advantage, and a considerable number of sketches were made during the trip. In spite of his favourable travelling arrangements, his correspondence of the time expressed a sense of irritation at the urgency with which he was occasionally required to sketch. 'Hate sketching heads rapidly, it is unavoidably and odiously free and easy, and nearly all that is worth escapes'.[9] In fact, this excursion appears to be the last occasion that Leighton produced time-consuming, detailed studies of heads in pencil.

This sketch would appear then to be one of the more successful portraits from this trip. Drawn during a stop in Luxor, the sitter is identified as 'Khalid'. The sketch is strongly and sympathetically rendered; indeed in his late years, Leighton attested to the empathy he felt with the native Arab peoples. His affection for the subject seems evident within the sketch. The contemporary writer Ernest Rhys may be referring to this particular drawing when he observed: 'Of the studies made during the journey one is... the head of an old man, simple minded and philosophical.'[10] *R.S.*

INSCRIPTIONS

Inscribed and dated, lower left, 'Khalid / Lugsor / 68' in graphite, in the artist's hand. Stamped, lower left, 'LLC' encircled. Inscribed, lower right, 'Old mans head' in graphite, by the FAS.

PROVENANCE

Bequeathed by the artist to his sisters, Mrs Augusta Matthews and Mrs Alexandra Orr; from whom purchased by the FAS in 1896; acquired by the LHC by 1897, transferred to RBK in 1926 (now RBKC).

BIBLIOGRAPHICAL REFERENCES

Simon 1996, p. 70.

EXHIBITION HISTORY

LONDON 1897, no. 8 (Studies of Heads).

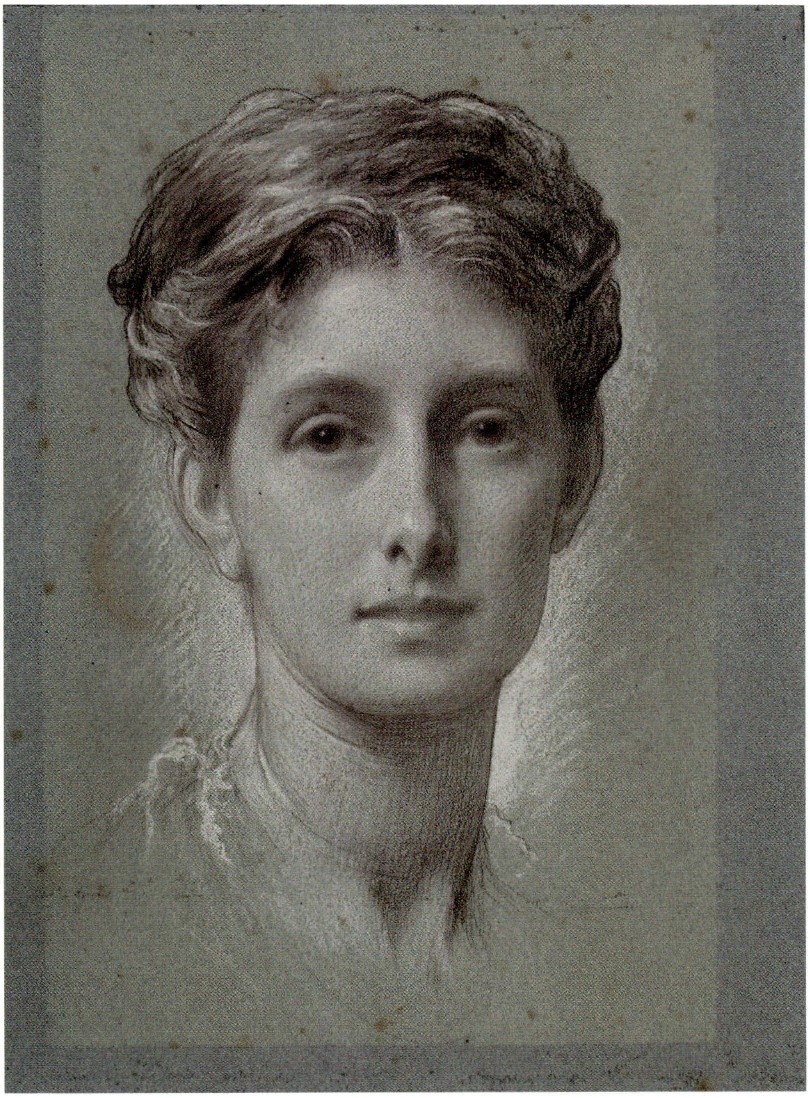

3.4

Study of a Female Head, *c.*1870

Black and white chalk on blue paper
317 x 233 mm
LHO/D/0895

The sitter for this affectionate study is unknown, but the treatment implies that it is a friend or close acquaintance rather than a professional model. A possible identity for the sitter is May Sartoris (b.1845), the daughter of Leighton's old friend Adelaide. When she was 15 years old May had been the subject of one of Leighton's most successful portraits, set against the background of a dramatic English landscape (*May Sartoris*, *c.*1860, Kimbell Art Museum, Fort Worth, Texas).[11] He painted her again, less successfully, as a married woman (*Mrs Henry Evans Gordon*, *c.*1875, Leighton House Museum) some 15 years later.

If this image is indeed May Sartoris, it most probably dates from a time before her marriage in 1871, when it was suggested that Leighton's regard for her mother might have been transferred, to some extent, to the girl herself.[12] It is an unusually highly worked chalk study, perhaps demonstrating Leighton's regard for his subject, and it may have been presented to the sitter on completion. *R.S.*

PROVENANCE

Possibly acquired by the LHC by 1897, transferred to RBK in 1926 (now RBKC).

EXHIBITION HISTORY

Numerous studies of women's heads were included in **LONDON 1897**, although it is not possible to determine which of them, if any, this was.

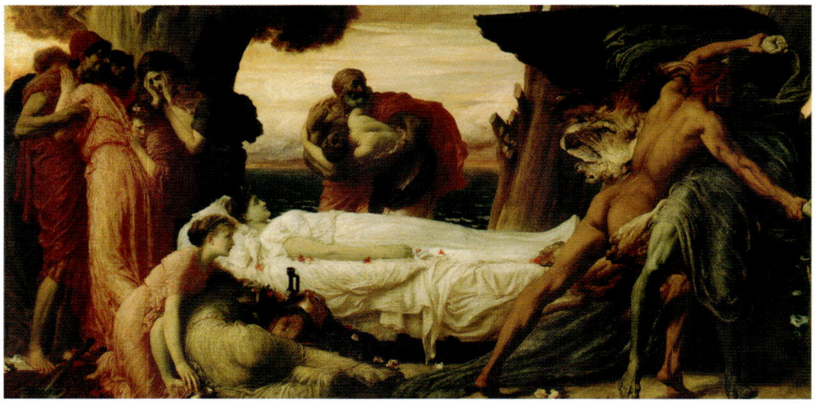

9.

cat. ill. **9.** ***Hercules Wrestling with Death for the Body of Alcestis***, RA 1871. Oil on canvas. 153 x 269 cm. Wadsworth Atheneum, Hartford, Connecticut.

3.5

Study for 'Hercules Wrestling with Death for the Body of Alcestis': Drapery for Death, *c.*1870

Black and white chalk on blue paper
405 x 284 mm
LHO/D/0824

The subject of this composition was probably inspired by interest in the Herculean legends amongst Leighton's close inner circle of artistic friends. Gluck's opera *Alceste* premiered in the spring of 1871, in a performance attended by Leighton and a number of his friends, while Robert Browning published his *Balaustion's Adventure* in the autumn of that year.[13]

The intensity of the struggle of Hercules with Thanatos, the winged emissary of death, seems also to have had something of a personal aspect for Leighton, occasioned perhaps by his concern for the health of his confidante, Adelaide Sartoris. The physicality of the work also foreshadowed what is considered to be Leighton's sculptural masterpiece, *Athlete Struggling with a Python* of 1877 (Tate Britain).

However, it is the sketch itself that is arguably of the greatest significance, as an early example of Leighton's large-scale study of drapery. This aspect of his work was to become of supreme importance. Contemporary accounts of his working method identify Leighton, 'arranging material on the studio floor over cunningly placed cotton-wool whereby not only forms, but depths, of folds and the effects of light [were] obtained'.[14] In later life, describing his compositional technique, Leighton would reveal how the scale and the position of draperies were almost fixed within the picture prior to the introduction of the human elements upon which the clothing was to be applied.[15] The abstract quality of the study, and the manner in which the drapery seems almost to overwhelm the figure of Thanatos in the finished painting (cat. ill. 9) amply demonstrate the role of drapery in Leighton's oeuvre. *R.S.*

INSCRIPTIONS

Stamped, lower left, 'LLC' encircled. Inscribed, lower left, 'Drapery for Hercules wrestling / with death' in black chalk.

PROVENANCE

Bequeathed by the artist to his sisters, Mrs Augusta Matthews and Mrs Alexandra Orr; from whom purchased by the FAS in 1896; from whom probably purchased by Matthews and Orr and presented to the LHC by 1900; transferred to RBK in 1926 (now RBKC).

BIBLIOGRAPHICAL REFERENCES

Staley 1906, p. 213.

EXHIBITION HISTORY

Possibly **LONDON 1897**, no. 3 (Drawings from Heracles struggling with Death for the body of Alcestis); **LONDON 1900**, no. 56b.

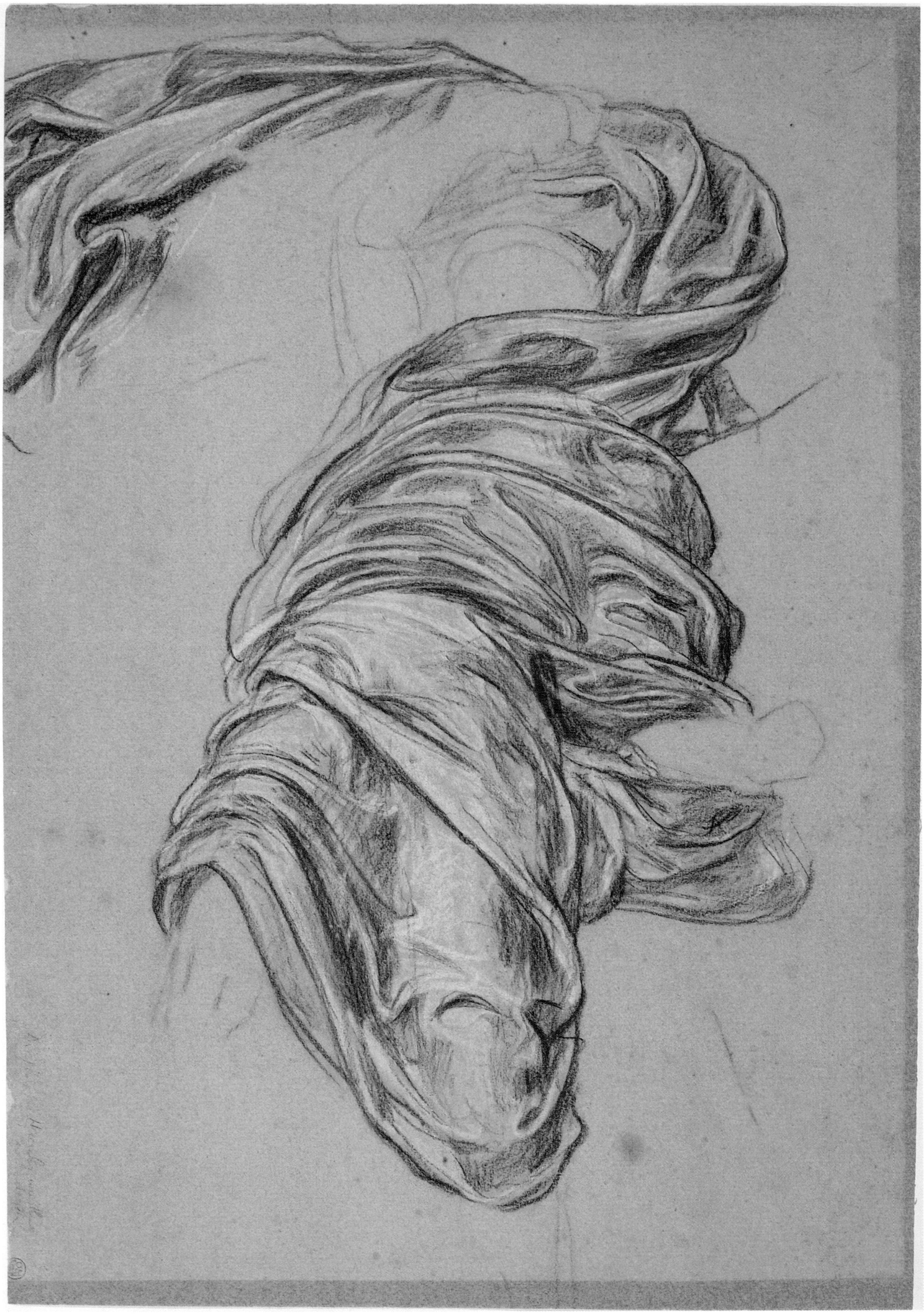

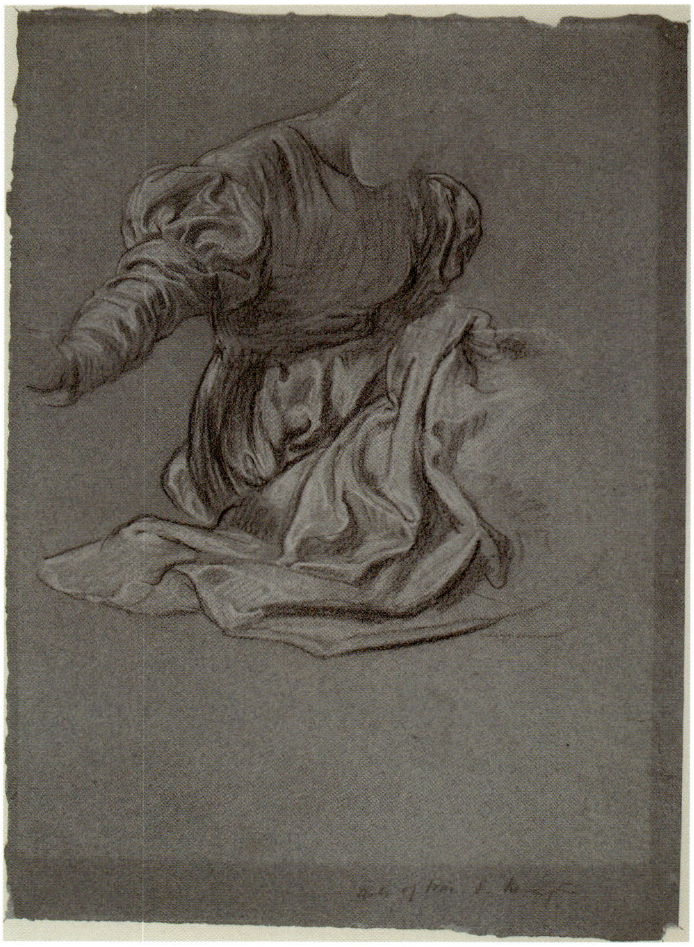

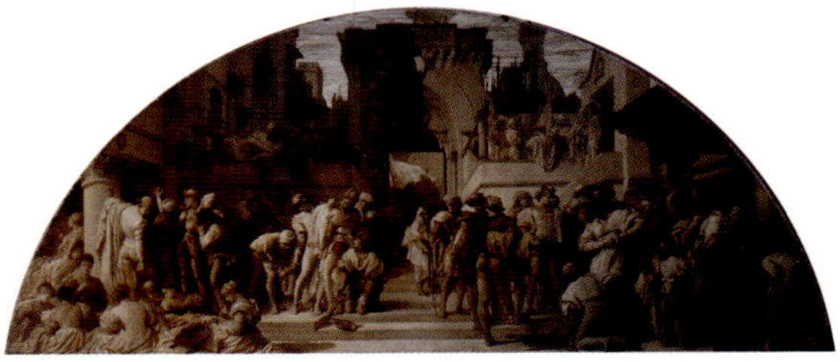

10.

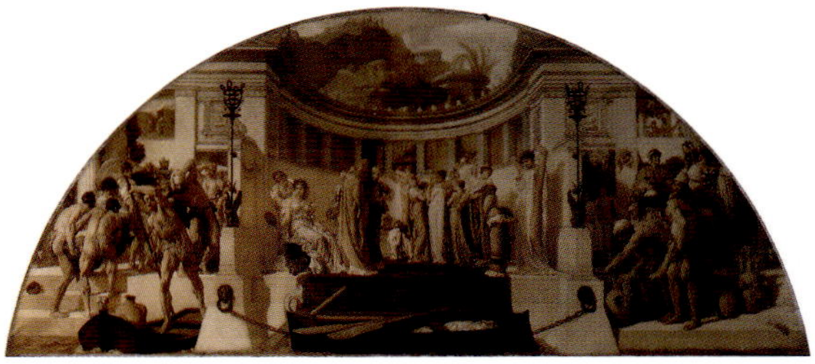

11.

cat. ill. **10.** ***Monochrome oil cartoon for 'The Arts of Industry as Applied to War'***, London 1872. Oil on canvas. 197 x 451 cm. Victoria and Albert Museum, London.

cat. ill. **11.** ***Monochrome oil cartoon for 'The Arts of Industry as Applied to Peace'***, RA 1873. Oil on canvas. 197 x 451 cm. Victoria and Albert Museum, London.

Studies for 'The Arts of Industry as Applied to War' and 'The Arts of Industry as Applied to Peace'

(Cat. nos 3.6 and 3.7)

For several years, the South Kensington Museum (now the Victoria and Albert Museum), and in particular its General Superintendent of Art, Henry Cole, had been looking to provide wall decorations to the museum's South Court. In 1868 Leighton was approached to provide a design for one of the lunettes. Modifications to the interior of the building, and the Court's subsequent extension by two further bays, created a second lunette at its opposite end. Henry Cole commissioned Leighton to design for this one also, enabling the artist to devise two grand compositions that referred to each other and yet were, in accordance with their position within the Court, at polar opposites.[16]

The Arts of Industry as Applied to War was the first of the two paintings to be undertaken. Leighton's design allowed him to return, by way of its theme, to the Renaissance Florence so beloved of his imagination. The scene in which a group of noblemen prepare for battle is, as has been noted by Richard Ormond, less a piece of martial organisation than an excuse for a display of masculine decoration.[17]

The principal female group, for which this study was executed, occupy a subordinate position at the bottom left-hand corner of the composition. A number of women are assembled to sew a banner, and the plainness of the costume contrasts with the militaristic decoration of the soldiers. However, true to his extraordinary talent for rendering drapery, Leighton has adorned what might best be described as contemporary Victorian dress with a richness of texture that belies the inferior status of the roles adopted by the female protagonists.

The process by which the sketches were transformed into a cartoon (cat. ill. 10) and ultimately into the completed fresco was elaborate, and was further complicated by delays in advancing the commission both on the part of the artist and his client. The 'War' fresco was thus not completed until 1880. Facing it, and not finished until six years later, was *The Arts of Industry as Applied to Peace*. Reflecting Leighton's concept for the two frescoes of relativity and opposition, *Peace* is set in the Hellenistic world and depicts an imaginary scene of commerce and trade. Again the composition serves as a vehicle for display, but in contrast to *War* the major grouping is female and occupies the centre of the canvas.[18]

In the study for the second fresco (cat. no. 3.7), groups of figures are roughly sketched over the architectural backdrop. Figures are drawn with rapid strokes from the artist's imagination. The study represents the painting as seen in the 'mind's eye' of the artist and is the initial stage in the process of creating a work. Its purpose is to give an overall impression of the design and to see the composition in its entirety, without focusing on individual elements. The alternative groupings of figures underneath the composition and to the upper right show Leighton exploring ideas for how the figures might be grouped and posed. These would be further developed through nude and draped studies from the model. *R.S.*

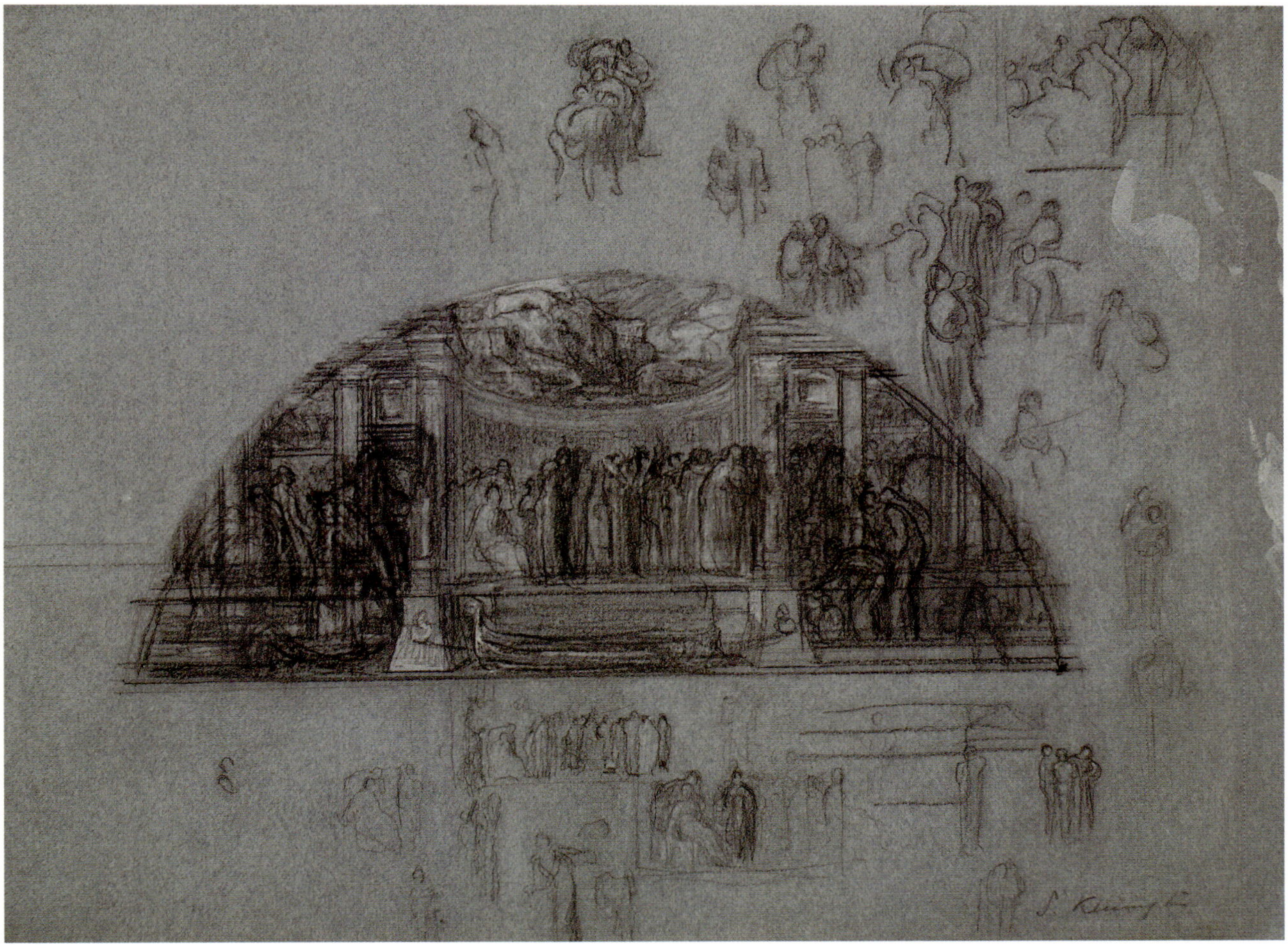

3.6

Study for 'The Arts of Industry as Applied to War': Drapery for Female Figure, *c.*1871

Black and white chalk on blue paper
329 x 240 mm
LHO/D/0545

INSCRIPTIONS

Inscribed, lower right, 'Arts of War S Kensington' in graphite, by the FAS.

PROVENANCE

Bequeathed by the artist to his sisters, Mrs Augusta Matthews and Mrs Alexandra Orr; from whom purchased by the FAS in 1896; purchased by the LHC by 1897; transferred to RBK in 1926 (now RBKC).

BIBLIOGRAPHICAL REFERENCES

Ormond 1975b, p. 160 (listed under cat. no. 194).

EXHIBITION HISTORY

LONDON 1897, no. 5 ('Arts of War').

3.7

Study for 'The Arts of Industry as Applied to Peace': Composition, Figures, *c.*1872

Black and white chalk on blue paper
231 x 315 mm
LHO/D/0554

INSCRIPTIONS

Stamped, lower left, 'LLC' encircled. Inscribed, lower right, 'S. Kensington' in graphite, by the FAS.

PROVENANCE

Bequeathed by the artist to his sisters, Mrs Augusta Matthews and Mrs Alexandra Orr; from whom purchased by FAS in 1896; from whom probably purchased by Matthews and Orr and presented to the LHC by 1900; transferred to RBK in 1926 (now RBKC).

BIBLIOGRAPHICAL REFERENCES

Ormond 1975b, p. 160 (listed under cat. no. 194); Newall 1990, pl. 52.

EXHIBITION HISTORY

Probably **LONDON 1897**, no. 1 ('Arts of Peace'); **LONDON 1900**, no. 196e.

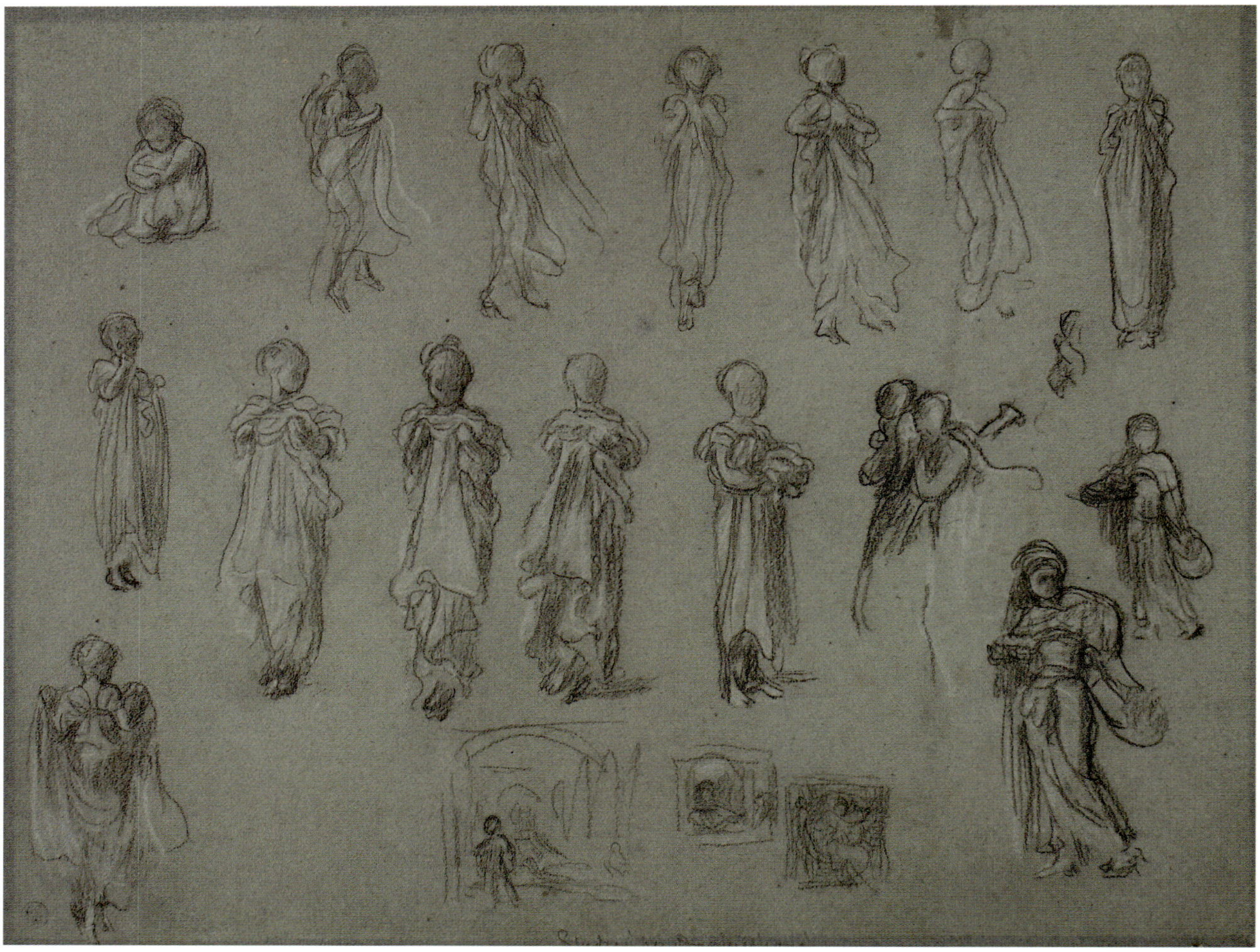

3.8

Study for 'The Daphnephoria' and 'Moorish Garden: A Dream of Granada': Girls, *c.*1873

Black and white chalk on blue paper
244 x 321 mm
LHO/D/0579

This sheet of studies illustrates Leighton's practice of simultaneously developing material for different compositions. The majority of sketches are studies for the processional painting, *The Daphnephoria* (*c.*1874–76; cat. ill. 12), commissioned by the wealthy banker James Stewart Hodgson. The subject matter relates to the Theban practice of honouring Apollo for victory in battle.[19] The two figures at the bottom right of the sheet and the thumbnail perspectives are for a separate painting, *Moorish Garden: A Dream of Granada* (*c.*1874, Private Collection; cat. ill. 13), developed from a number of *plein-air* studies made by Leighton at the *Generalife* (the walled garden of the Alhambra) at Granada.[20] However, all the sketches are of a single model – Connie Gilchrist – whom Leighton had employed regularly since her early childhood. The drawings demonstrate Leighton's practice of allowing the model to move rhythmically about his studio as he captured various poses with quick strokes of his chalk.[21] For the *Moorish Garden* studies Gilchrist was dressed in eastern garments,

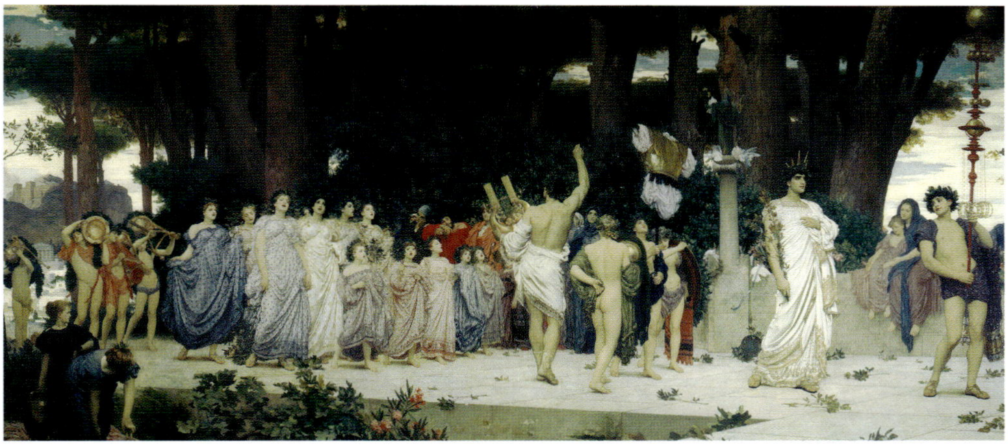

12.

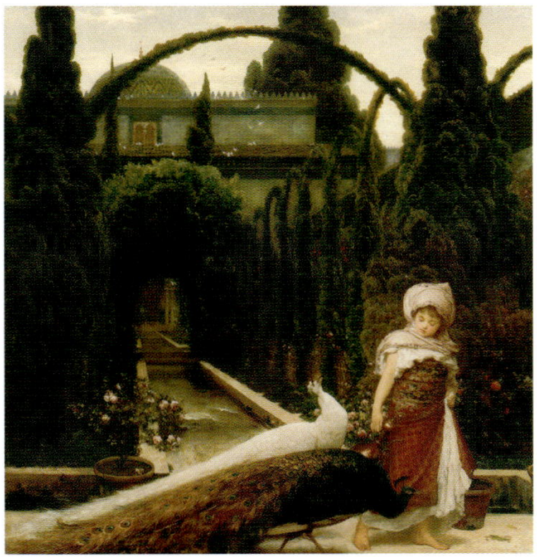

13.

cat. ill. 12. ***The Daphnephoria***, RA 1876. Oil on canvas. 226 x 518 cm. Lady Lever Art Gallery, Port Sunlight.

cat. ill. 13. ***Moorish Garden: A Dream of Granada***, RA 1874. Oil on canvas. 104 x 101.6 cm. Private Collection.

probably brought back by Leighton from his trip to Damascus in 1873, and is depicted bearing a copper water carrier and (in the completed picture) leading a pair of peacocks.

Leighton produced several similar sheets showing the young Gilchrist moving around the studio, all apparently related to *The Daphnephoria* (for example ref. no. 294-2 at the National Gallery of Victoria, Melbourne). In them, Leighton's skill at capturing a sense of spontaneity and movement through his chalk studies is demonstrated. However, these qualities were rarely apparent in the finished painting *R.S.*

INSCRIPTIONS

Stamped, lower left, 'LLC' encircled. Inscribed, lower centre, 'Studies for Daphnephoria' in graphite, by the FAS.

PROVENANCE

Bequeathed by the artist to his sisters, Mrs Augusta Matthews and Mrs Alexandra Orr; from whom purchased by the FAS in 1896; possibly purchased by the LHC by 1897; transferred to RBK in 1926 (now RBKC).

BIBLIOGRAPHICAL REFERENCES

Ormond 1975b, p. 163 (listed under cat. no. 237).

EXHIBITION HISTORY

Possibly LONDON 1897, no. 1 ('The Daphnephoria').

NOTES

1. Barrington 1906, vol. II, pp 57–63.
2. Morse 1987, pp 6–11.
3. Barrington 1906, vol. I, p. 296.
4. LONDON 1996, p. 123.
5. LONDON 1996, p. 133.
6. Anne Lyles and Robin Hamlyn: *British Watercolours from the Oppé Collection*, Tate Gallery Publishing, London, 1997, pp 234–35, no. 100.
7. LONDON 1996, pp 132.
8. Barrington 1906, vol. II, pp 131–87.
9. Barrington 1906, vol. II, p 169.
10. Rhys 1900, p. 28.
11. LONDON 1996, p. 121.
12. Ormond 1975b, p. 45.
13. Ormond 1975b, pp 64, 78, 89–90.
14. Spielmann 1892, p. 637.
15. Barrington 1906, vol. II, pp 12–13.
16. LONDON 1996, pp 37–39.
17. Ormond 1975b, pp 29–35.
18. LONDON 1996, p. 38.
19. *ibid.*, pp 17, 34–36.
20. Ormond 1975b, p. 98.
21. *ibid.*, p. 92.

4

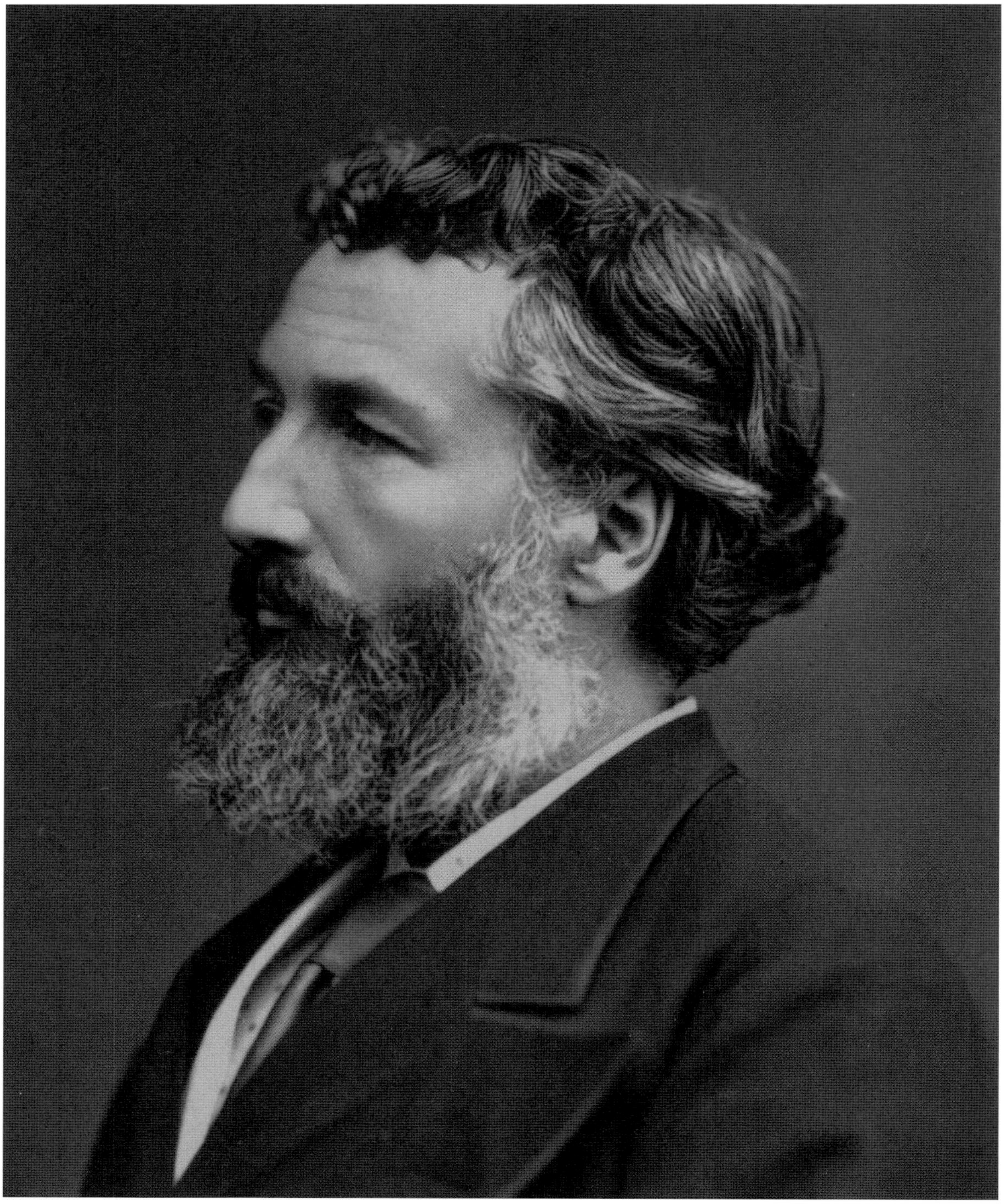

cat. ill. **14.**
A photographic portrait of Frederic Leighton, taken by Samuel Robert Lock and George Carpe Whitfield in 1877.

WORKING AT HOME IN THE STUDIO 1877

...I am very glad to put in a word for that gallant artist, our friend Mr. Leighton, who has certainly come out in a new walk and proved that he deserves fully the encomium which has been passed upon him. (Cheers.)

[His Royal Highness Prince George, Duke of Cambridge, speaking at the Royal Academy, Saturday 5 May 1877.[1]]

In 1877 Leighton was 46 and approaching the pinnacle of his career. His submissions to the Royal Academy were frequently lavished with praise. *The Daphnephoria*, exhibited the previous year, was described by William Holman Hunt as 'the finest, the most beautiful picture in the world',[2] while his bronze, *Athlete Struggling with a Python* (RA 1877), was praised by the sculptor Joseph Edgar Boehm as 'superb... the best statue of modern days'.[3]

Leighton had been a full Royal Academician for almost 10 years, and was a staunch supporter of the institution. He became increasingly involved in Academy affairs, and played a leading role in the Winter Exhibitions of Old Master paintings, doing much of the administration and research, and travelling throughout the UK to visit private collections. He was not only an established figure in the art world but, with the help of friends such as Adelaide Sartoris and the Prince of Wales, also an important member of London society. His success and status had made him something of a celebrity. When his father complained of the frequent requests for his son's photograph, Leighton sympathised: 'I think it preposterous that the ambulant spinsters... should expect you to furnish them with photos of your "celebrated son." I like enthusiasm; but genuine enthusiasm does not halt at a shilling, which is the sum for which my effigy is obtainable in the public market'.[4]

Demonstrating the thoroughness with which he continued to approach his work, in the spring of 1877 Leighton completed a detailed life-size cartoon in preparation for *The Arts of Industry as Applied to War*, his 15-foot wide fresco for the South Kensington Museum (now the Victoria and Albert Museum). In the same year he worked on the designs for several paintings to be exhibited the following spring – including *Elijah in the Wilderness* (*c*.1878, Walker Art Gallery, National Museums Liverpool), *Nausicaa* (*c*.1878, Private Collection) and *Winding the Skein* (*c*.1878, Art Gallery of New South Wales, Sydney) – drawing exhaustively from models in the studio of his home in Holland Park Road.

Leighton continued to alter and extend his house throughout his life, and in the autumn of 1877 building work began on the imposing Arab Hall. The painting studio had been enlarged in 1869–70 to allow models to enter the room from a discrete door behind a screen at the far end of the studio, and undress in privacy before a small fireplace. The model would then pass through the opening in the screen to enter the main studio area where Leighton worked. He spent over seven hours a day in his studio, painting and sketching almost exclusively from the nude, from draped models, or from drapery which he had carefully arranged. In 1877, studies from the model continued to be made with black and white chalk on blue paper. However, sometime towards the end of 1877 or early in 1878, Leighton replaced the blue paper with a thicker, warm brown paper, perhaps reflecting the use of a warmer ground in his paintings.

In the autumn of 1877 Leighton left England for Spain to study paintings in the Prado Museum and elsewhere, although he complained in a letter to his father that the light had been too poor to see the artworks adequately.[5] From Spain he made his first trip to Tangiers in Morocco, with the intention of making sketches of local people (perhaps for a future painting) and to capture the cloud effect he was seeking for the background of the painting *Winding the Skein*. He returned to London in time to make preparations for the Royal Academy Winter Exhibition, which opened shortly after the New Year, and to complete the paintings destined for the Academy's Summer exhibition opening in April 1878.

Leighton's work as an artist, his social and organisational skills and his dedication to the Royal Academy, marked him out as a leading figure of the institution. 1877 would be his last year as a mere Royal Academician. Although he could not have known, studies made for *Elijah in the Wilderness* in this year were in preparation for one of his first works exhibited as President of the Royal Academy. *P.M.*

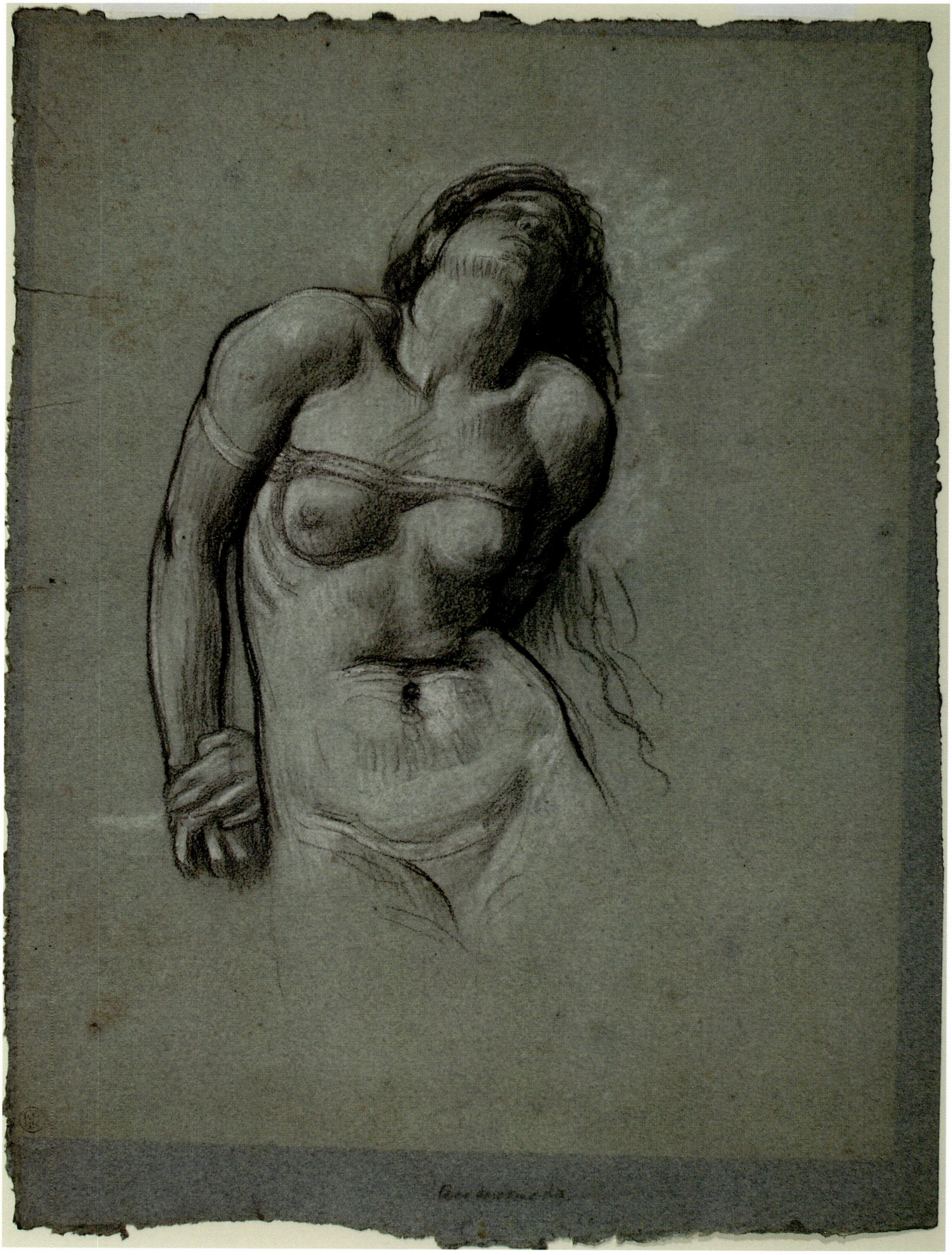

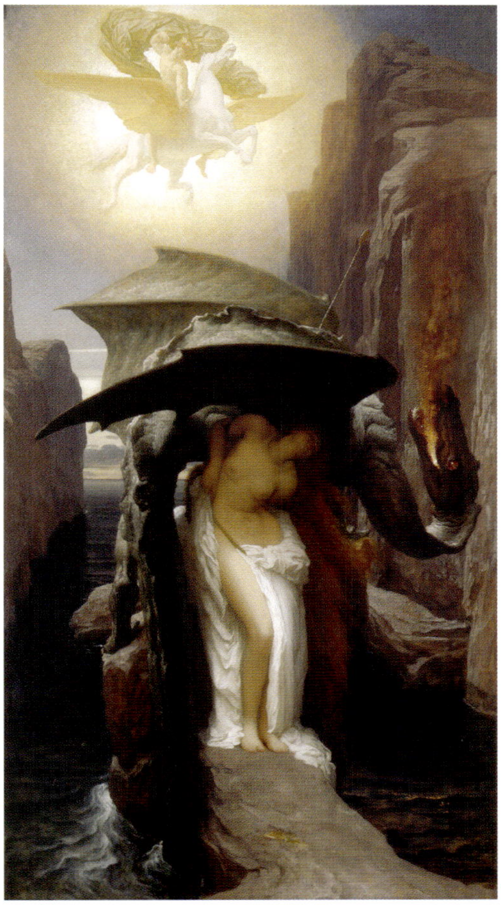

15.

cat. ill. 15. ***Perseus and Andromeda***, RA 1891. Oil on canvas. 235 x 129.3 cm. Walker Art Gallery, Liverpool.

4.1

Study for 'And the Sea Gave Up the Dead Which Were in It', later used for 'Perseus and Andromeda': Female Figure, *c.*1877

Black and white chalk on blue paper
329 x 246 mm
LHO/D/0693

In 1877 Leighton agreed to design eight roundels, for a fee of £600 each, to form part of the new mosaic decorations planned for the interior of the dome of St Paul's Cathedral.[6] The mosaics were to be created in collaboration with Alfred Stevens, Edward Poynter and Hugh Stannus. Leighton began to make sketches for the first roundel in the same year. The subject, *And the Sea Gave Up the Dead Which Were in It*, is a quote from the Old Testament's Book of Revelations, describing a scene from the Last Judgement. A small version of the cartoon for the design was shown at the Royal Academy in 1882. However, much to Leighton's frustration, the project was abandoned in 1885 as a result of objections to the proposed scheme.

It would seem that the figure in this drawing was initially intended for the mosaic roundel, but was discarded as the biblical project evolved. Leighton returned to the composition about 14 years later and, perhaps coming across this drawing, developed the pose for the figure of Andromeda in a completely unrelated painting: *Perseus and Andromeda* (*c.*1891, Walker Art Gallery, Liverpool; cat. ill. 15). The bands restraining the figure and the position of the head, falling back and to the left, indicate that this drawing was almost certainly inspired by Michelangelo's sculpture of the *Dying Slave* (*c.*1513–16, Louvre, Paris). *P.M.*

INSCRIPTIONS

Stamped, lower left, 'LLC' encircled. Inscribed, lower centre, 'Andromeda' in graphite, by the FAS.

PROVENANCE

Bequeathed by the artist to his sisters, Mrs Augusta Matthews and Mrs Alexandra Orr; from whom purchased by the FAS in 1896; from whom probably purchased by Matthews and Orr and presented to the LHC by 1900; transferred to RBK in 1926 (now RBKC).

BIBLIOGRAPHICAL REFERENCES

Studio, vol. ix, 1897, ill. p. 109; Barrington 1906, vol. II, ill. opp. p. 256; Ormond 1975b, p. 171 (listed under cat. no. 358); Simon 1996, p. 38 fig. 11.

EXHIBITION HISTORY

Possibly **LONDON 1900**, no. 140b.

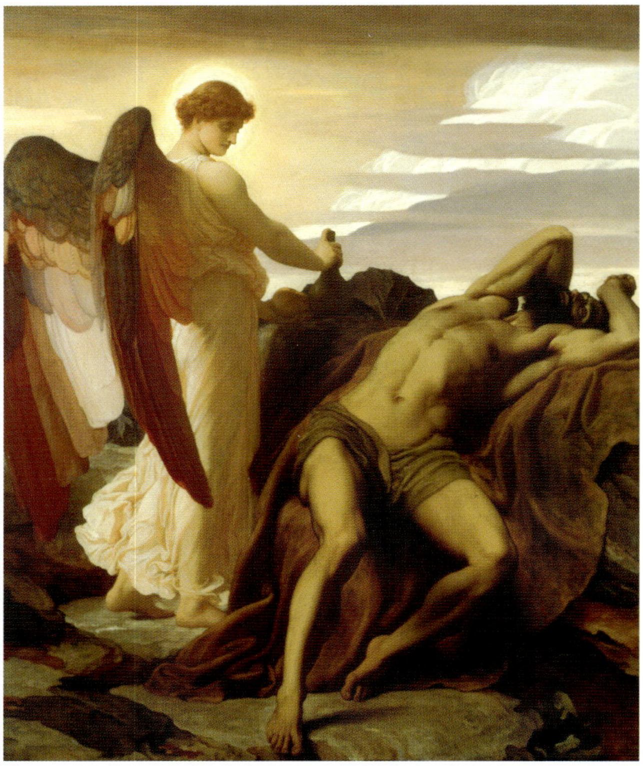

cat. ill. **16.** ***Elijah in the Wilderness***, Paris 1878. Oil on canvas. 235 x 210.2 cm. Walker Art Gallery, Liverpool.

16.

Six Studies for 'Elijah in the Wilderness', *c.*1877
(Cat. nos 4.2, 4.3, 4.4, 4.5, 4.6 and 4.7)

Elijah in the Wilderness (cat. ill. 16), exhibited at the Exposition Universelle in Paris in 1878 and at the Royal Academy the following year, is one of several paintings by Leighton that focus on an heroic male, represented as a powerful, semi-nude figure reminiscent of Greek sculpture. The painting gives a very literal interpretation of the biblical story, showing Elijah contorted with anguish as he pleads 'O Lord, take away my life', and including the image of the angel who brought Elijah 'cake baken on the coals, and a cruse of water'.[7] The choice of subject may have been partly influenced by Mendelssohn's oratorio, based on the story, which was first performed in England in 1846 and became the most popular of all his compositions. However, Elijah as the icon of the prophets of Israel, epitomising the struggle between idolatry and true faith, was a subject which was 'particularly congenial' to Leighton. He expressed his interest in Elijah during work on illustrations for the Dalziels' *Bible Gallery* of 1863–64, and had already depicted the prophet in the painting *Jezebel and Ahab* (*c.*1863).[8]

There are approximately 12 known drawings for the painting, most of which are in the collection at Leighton House Museum. The earlier drawings show Leighton struggling to establish a pose for the central figure of Elijah. He begins with a lethargic, resigned posture, reminiscent of the collapsing figure of Christ in Michelangelo's painting *The Entombment* (*c.*1500–01, purchased by the National Gallery in London in 1868).[9] Leighton made minor changes to the pose of the model for each of the sketches on the sheet, as he struggled to reach a more satisfying arrangement. However, the results lack the drama he was striving for and which he reserved almost exclusively for his biblical subjects. A study at the Ashmolean Museum in Oxford (ref. no. WA1988.332) reveals that Leighton also experimented with a standing figure of Elijah, before turning the seated model to the right, extending the left arm, and drawing him first with his head bowed and then, to heighten the sense of despair, with the head resting on the left arm (cat. no. 4.3). The small drawing at the bottom of this sheet was probably made without a particular purpose, as the model broke from the pose.

A subsequent drawing in which Leighton continues his endeavour to resolve the pose shows the seated figure turned, almost to face the viewer, and includes a version of the pose he would eventually use for the final painting, with the arms of Elijah raised over his head in an exposed and abandoned gesture (cat. no. 4.4). This pose has been likened to the marble, sleeping satyr known as the *Barberini Faun* (early 2nd century BC) in the Staatliche Antikensammlungen in Munich.[10] However, the long process of experimentation that led to the pose indicates that it was not a direct influence.

Having settled on the stance for Elijah, Leighton added drapery and worked out the pose in greater detail. It may have been at this point that he modelled a clay version of the figure 'in the round'. This was the first of several clay models Leighton made as an aid to working out the more problematical poses of figures in his paintings.

The composition of the painting, including the pose for Elijah established through earlier drawings, is sketched on a sheet which also includes a study for the painting *Nausicaa*, and two tentative studies for the angel in the composition. It would seem that Leighton is still striving to resolve the pose of this second figure.

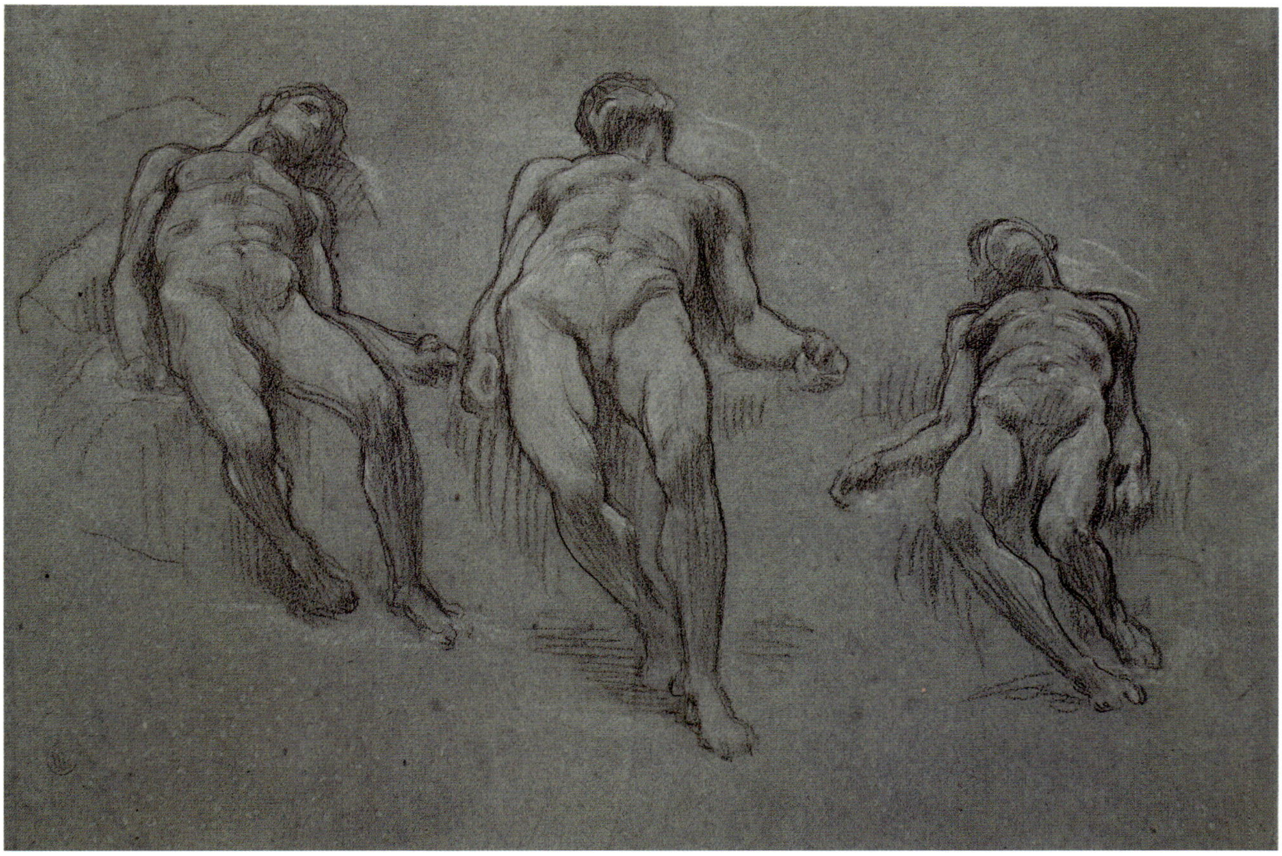

When Leighton described his working method, he maintained that the composition was conceived in his imagination before he began, and the first sketch was to record this idea on paper. It is tempting to assume that this small study for the composition of *Elijah in the Wilderness* is the very first sketch for the painting. However, close inspection of the surviving studies for this project suggests that Leighton's description of his working method is a simplification of what at times could be a complicated process of trial and error. In this case, his initial conception may have been for a single figure of Elijah. Having resolved the pose of Elijah, Leighton apparently remained displeased with the composition and drew a small sketch including a second, contrasting figure of an angel. The pose of the angel had yet to be established. Certainly a more careful study for the angel was made after the aforementioned studies (cat. no. 4.7). It is an unusual drawing, as the same character has been sketched from a female and from a male figure. Male and female models were not commonly employed by artists to pose at the same time for reasons of both expense and modesty, and this drawing was probably made in two separate sessions. In the finished work the figure is androgynous, with hair and arms like that of the male figure, but more feminine facial features. This may have been a deliberate endeavour by Leighton to represent an idealised beauty that is neither male nor female. The pose of the figure on the right of the sheet is virtually identical to the finished work. It is also one of the earliest studies Leighton made on a warm brown paper, which from *c.*1877 replaced the blue paper previously used. He would continue to order quantities of similar brown paper for his studies for the next 15 years, before again altering his choice of drawing paper in about 1892.

Referring to *Elijah in the Wilderness,* Emilie Barrington reported that Leighton claimed he 'had put more of himself into that picture than into any other that he had ever invented'.[11] This may have referred partly to his identification with the character of Elijah, and also to the exertion required to resolve the complexities of the composition. *P.M.*

4.2

Study for 'Elijah in the Wilderness': Elijah, *c.*1877

Black and white chalk on blue paper

202 x 280 mm

LHO/D/0586

INSCRIPTIONS

Stamped, lower left, 'LLC' encircled. Inscribed, lower right, 'Elijah' in graphite, by the FAS.

PROVENANCE

Inherited by the artist's sisters Mrs Augusta Matthews and Mrs Alexandra Orr; from whom purchased by the FAS in 1896; from whom possibly purchased by the LHC; transferred to RBK in 1926 (now RBKC).

BIBLIOGRAPHICAL REFERENCES

Ormond 1975b, p. 164 (listed under cat. no. 251); **LONDON 1996**, p. 222.

EXHIBITION HISTORY

Possibly **LONDON 1897**, no. 1, 2, 3, or 5 ('Elijah in the Wilderness...'); **LONDON 1900**, no. 195a.

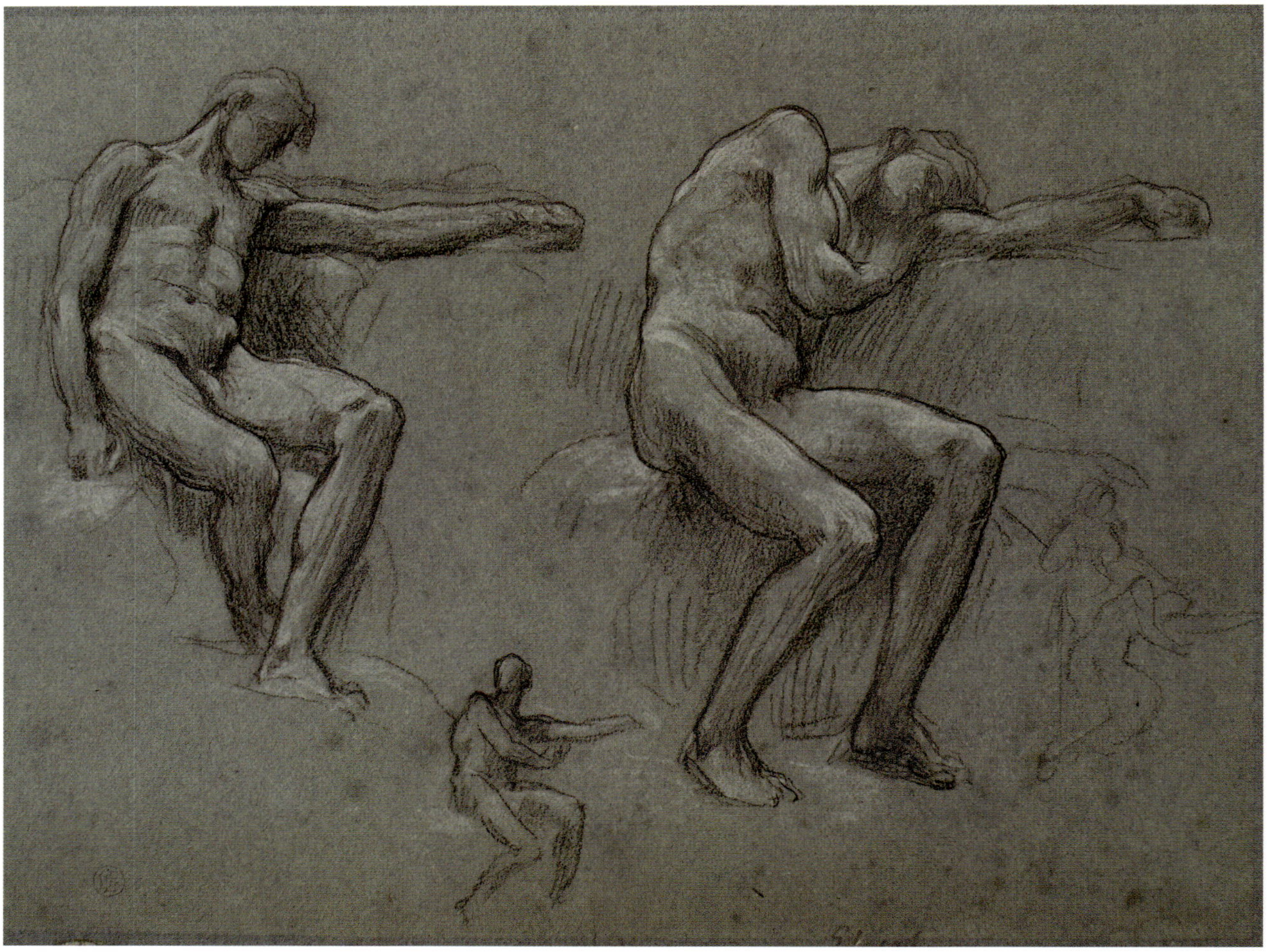

4.3
Study for 'Elijah in the Wilderness': Elijah, *c.*1877
Black and white chalk on blue paper
210 x 281 mm
LHO/D/0587

INSCRIPTIONS
Stamped, lower left, 'LLC' encircled. Inscribed, lower right, 'Elijah' in graphite, by the FAS.

PROVENANCE
Bequeathed by the artist to his sisters, Mrs Augusta Matthews and Mrs Alexandra Orr; from whom purchased by the FAS in 1896; probably acquired by the LHC by 1900; transferred to RBK in 1926 (now RBKC).

BIBLIOGRAPHICAL REFERENCES
Ormond 1975b, p. 164 (listed under cat. no. 251).

EXHIBITION HISTORY
Possibly **LONDON 1897**, no. 1, 2, 3, or 5 ('Elijah in the Wilderness...'); **LONDON 1900**, no. 195a.

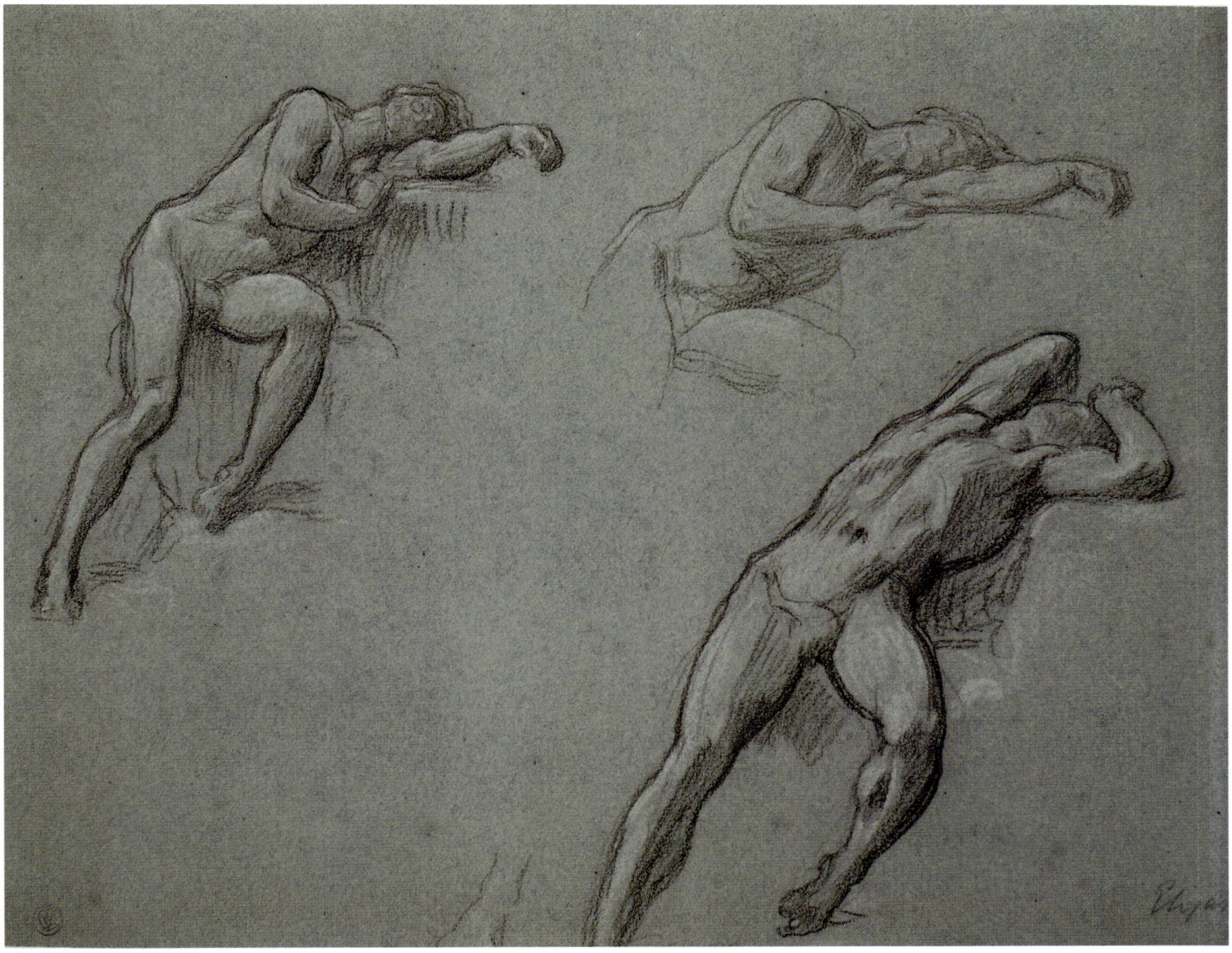

4.4

Study for 'Elijah in the Wilderness': Elijah, *c.*1877

Black and white chalk on blue paper
214 x 313 mm
LHO/D/0585

INSCRIPTIONS

Stamped, lower left, 'LLC' encircled. Inscribed, lower right, 'Elijah' in graphite, by the FAS.

PROVENANCE

Bequeathed by the artist to his sisters, Mrs Augusta Matthews and Mrs Alexandra Orr; from whom purchased by the FAS in 1896; from whom possibly purchased by the LHC by 1897; transferred to RBK in 1926 (now RBKC).

BIBLIOGRAPHICAL REFERENCES

Ormond 1975b, p. 164 (listed under cat. no. 251).

EXHIBITION HISTORY

Possibly **LONDON 1897**, no. 1, 2, 3, or 5 ('Elijah in the Wilderness...'); **LONDON 1900**, no. 195a; **LONDON 1969**, no. 130.

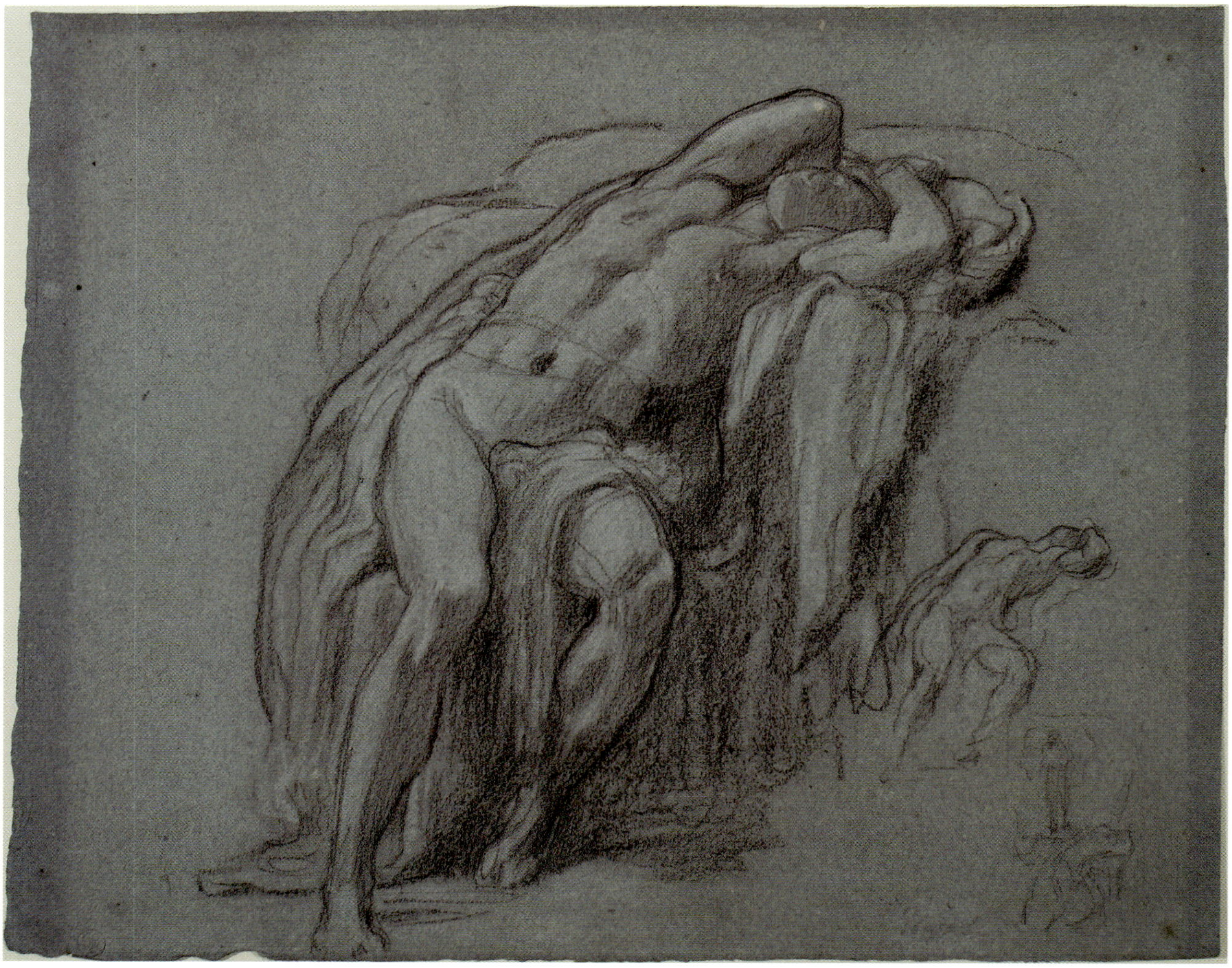

4.5

Study for 'Elijah in the Wilderness': Elijah, *c.*1877

Black and white chalk on blue paper
224 x 283 mm
LHO/D/0588

INSCRIPTIONS

Stamped, lower left, 'LLC' encircled. Inscribed, lower right, 'Elijah' in graphite by the FAS.

PROVENANCE

Bequeathed by the artist to his sisters, Mrs Augusta Matthews and Mrs Alexandra Orr; from whom purchased by the FAS in 1896; from whom probably purchased by Matthews and Orr and presented to the LHC by 1900; transferred to RBK in 1926 (now RBKC).

BIBLIOGRAPHICAL REFERENCES

Barrington 1906, vol. II, ill. opp. p. 255; Ormond 1975b, p. 164 (listed under cat. no. 251); **LONDON 1996**, p. 222; Simon 1996, p. 36.

EXHIBITION HISTORY

Possibly **LONDON 1897**, no. 1, 2, 3, or 5 ('Elijah in the Wilderness...'); **LONDON 1900**, no. 195b.

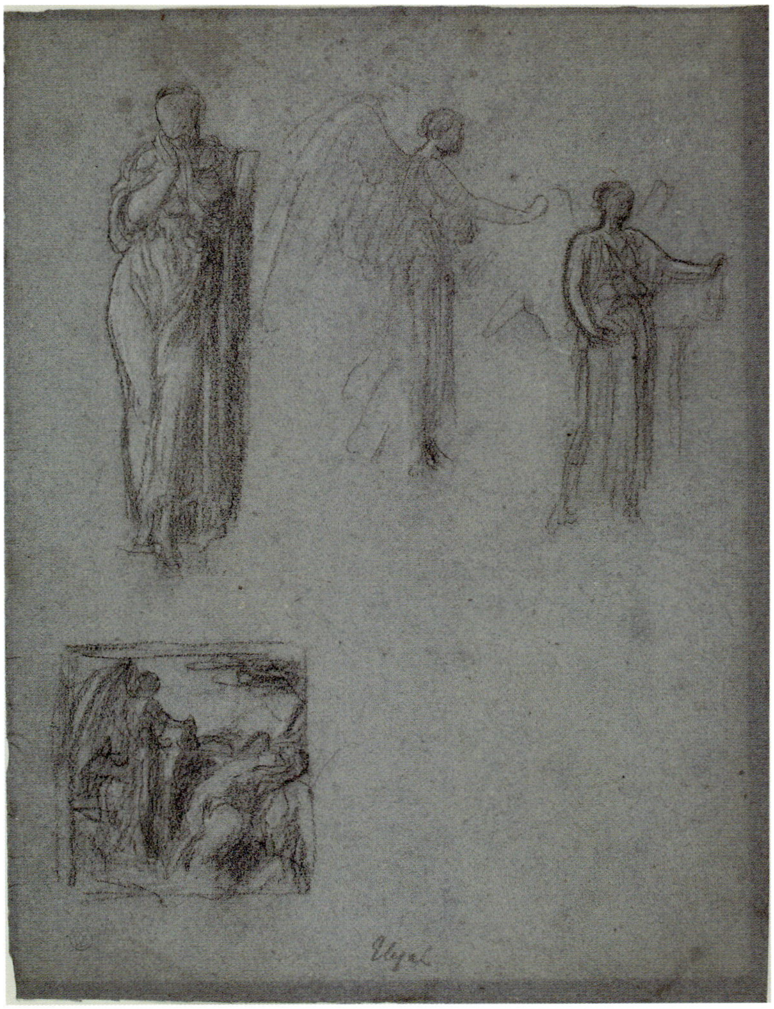

4.6

Studies for 'Nausicaa' and 'Elijah in the Wilderness': Composition, Female Figures, c.1877

Black and white chalk on paper
29.5 x 22.5 mm
LHO/D/0589

INSCRIPTIONS

Stamped, lower left, 'LLC' encircled. Inscribed, lower centre, 'Elijah' in graphite, by the FAS.

PROVENANCE

Inherited by the artist's sisters, Mrs Augusta Matthews and Mrs Alexandra Orr; from whom purchased by the FAS in 1896; from whom purchased by the LHC; transferred to RBK in 1926 (now RBKC).

BIBLIOGRAPHICAL REFERENCES

Rhys 1895, ill. opp. p. xxii; Ormond 1975b, p. 164 (listed under cat. nos 248, 251).

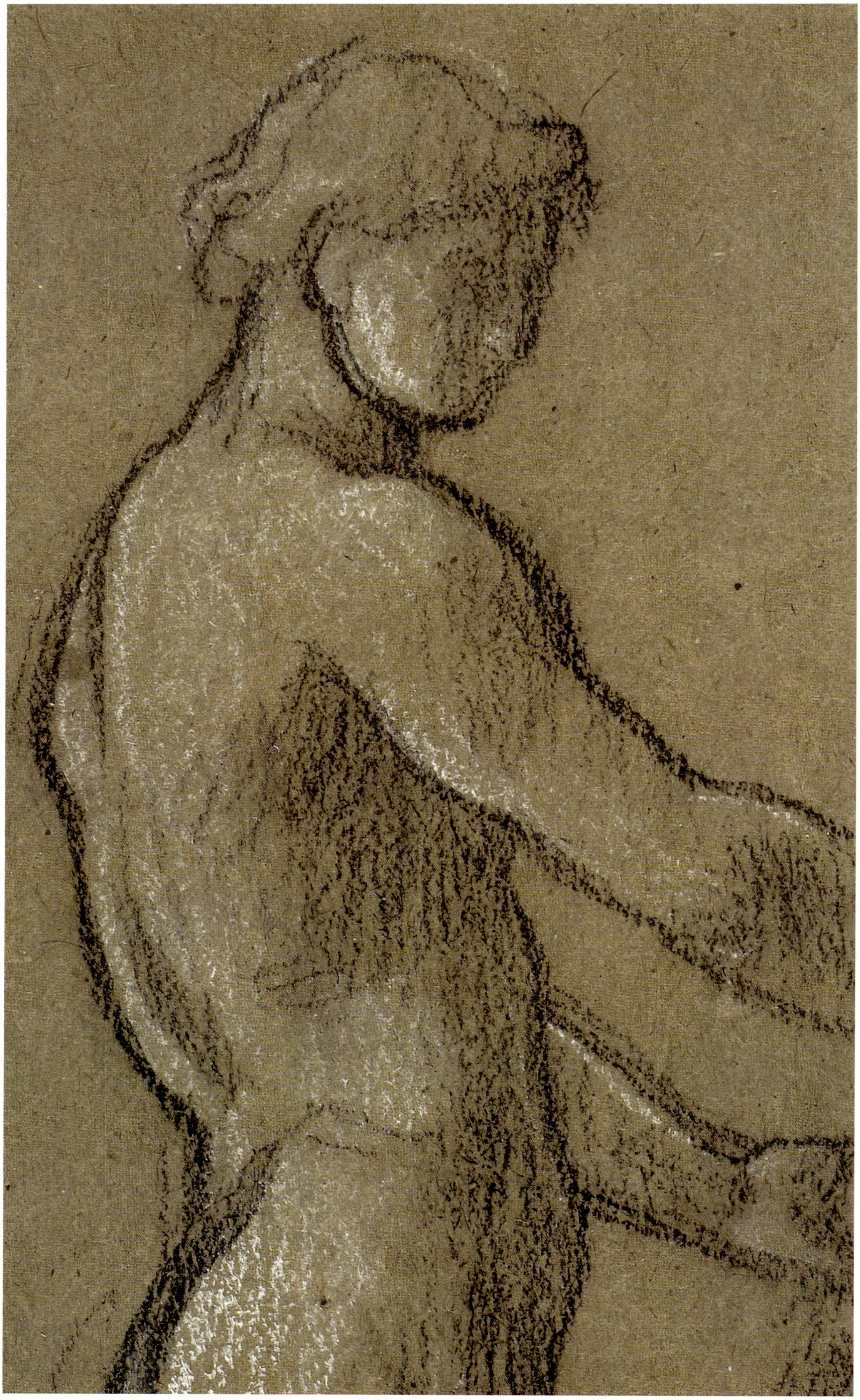

Detail of
cat. no. 4.7.

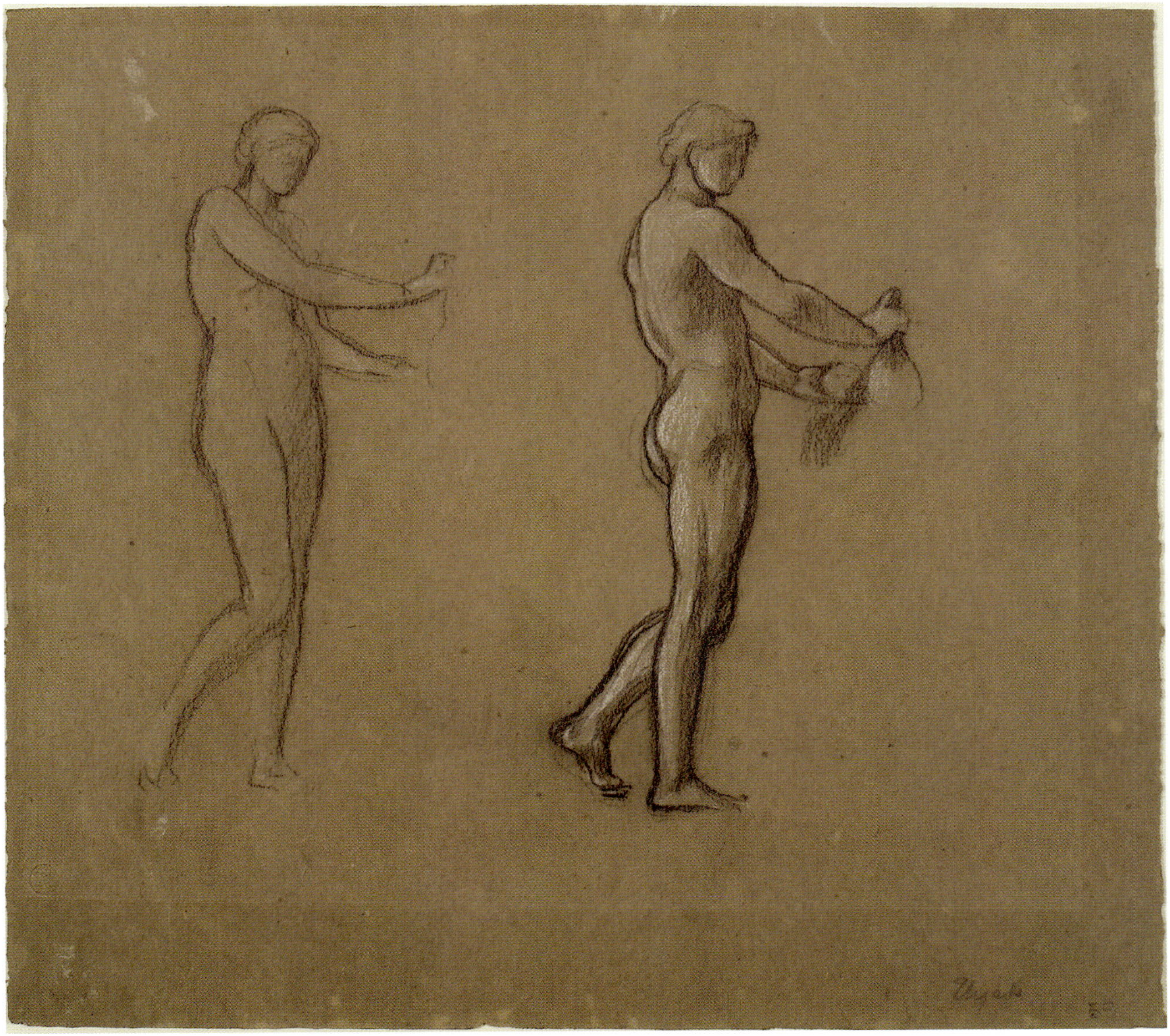

4·7

Study for 'Elijah in the Wilderness': Angel, c.1877

Black and white chalk on brown paper
235 x 265 mm
LHO/D/0591

INSCRIPTIONS

Stamped, lower left, 'LLC' encircled. Inscribed, lower right, 'Elijah' in graphite, by the FAS.

PROVENANCE

Bequeathed by the artist to his sisters, Mrs Augusta Matthews and Mrs Alexandra Orr; from whom purchased by the FAS in 1896; possibly purchased by the LHC by 1897; transferred to RBK in 1926 (now RBKC).

BIBLIOGRAPHICAL REFERENCES

Ormond 1975b, p. 164 (listed under cat. no. 251).

EXHIBITION HISTORY

Possibly **LONDON 1897**, no. 1, 2, 3, or 5 ('Elijah in the Wilderness...').

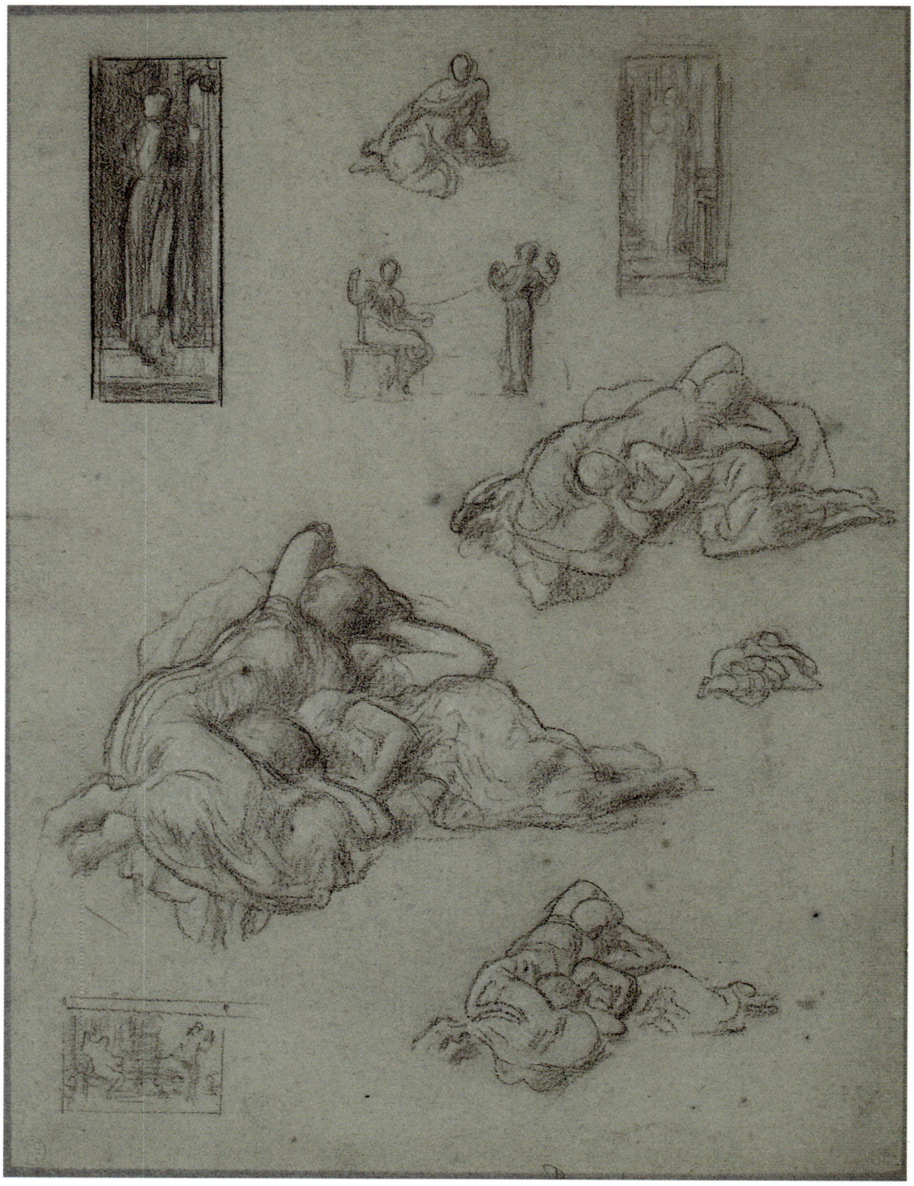

4.8

Studies for 'Nausicaa' and 'Winding the Skein': Compositions, Female Figures, *c.*1877

Black and white chalk on blue paper
290 x 222 mm
LHO/D/0582

On occasion Leighton would put down ideas for different paintings on a single sheet like this one. The compositions seen at the top left and top right would later become the painting *Nausicaa* (*c.*1878; cat. ill. 17). Those just above the centre of the sheet, and to the lower left, are for the painting *Winding the Skein* (*c.*1878; cat. ill. 18).

Four similar studies of the reclining figures of a woman and girl, curled up together, are reminiscent of the two female figures to the lower left of the painting *Cymon and Iphigenia* (*c.*1884; cat. ill. 22), painted about six years after this drawing was made. These studies are almost certainly the origin for the two sleeping attendants, seen to the lower right of the painting. It may be that Leighton referred back to this drawing several years later, whilst working on *Cymon and Iphigenia*. However, he continued to rework the poses several times before settling on a satisfactory arrangement, producing at least 15 drawings of these figures alone. *P.M.*

INSCRIPTIONS

Stamped, lower left, 'LLC' encircled. Inscribed, lower centre, 'Project' in graphite, by the FAS.

PROVENANCE

Bequeathed by the artist to his sisters, Mrs Augusta Matthews and Mrs Alexandra Orr; from whom purchased by the FAS in 1896; acquired by the LHC by 1900; transferred to RBK in 1926 (now RBKC).

BIBLIOGRAPHICAL REFERENCES

LONDON 1969, p. 33; cat. no. 144; Ormond 1975b, p. 164 (listed under cat. nos 248, 249).

EXHIBITION HISTORY

LONDON 1900, no. 276C; **LONDON 1969**, no. 144.

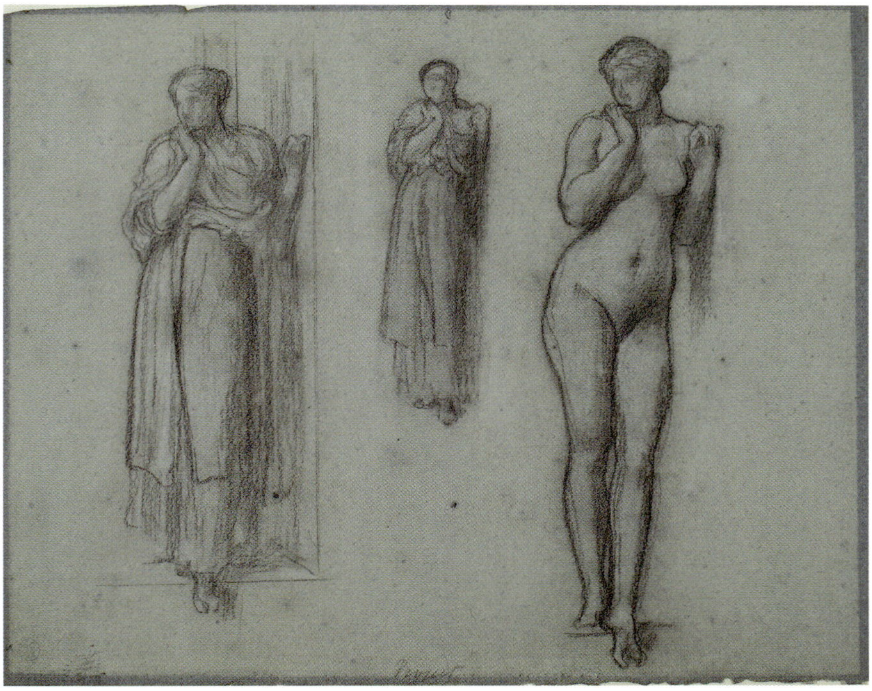

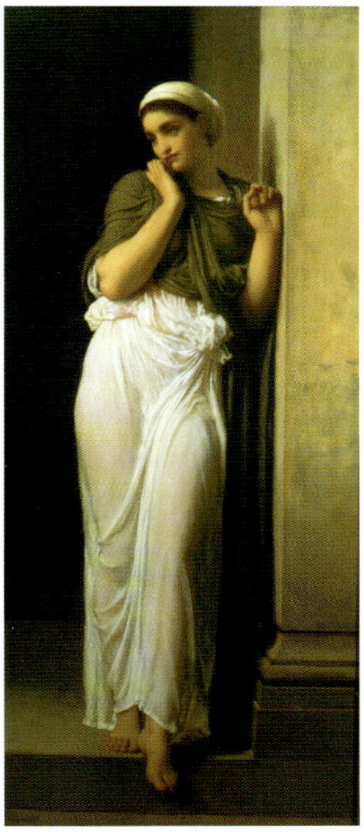

cat. ill. 17. ***Nausicaa***, RA 1878. Oil on canvas. 145 x 67 cm. Private Collection.

17.

4.9

Studies for 'Nausicaa': Female Figure, *c*.1877

Black and white chalk on blue paper
218 x 292 mm
LHO/D/0581

Nausicaa is one of several paintings in which Leighton used an incidental event from classical mythology as the pretext for a painting of a beautiful young woman. Nonetheless the design conforms closely to the narrative of Homer's *Odyssey*, and illustrates the moment when the two lovers, Nausicaa and Odysseus, are parted:

> *...Nausikaa, having a God-given beauty,*
> *marveled standing there by a post of the well-built*
> *hall as her eyes regarded Odysseus closely.*[12]

Leighton's *Nausicaa* was first exhibited at the Royal Academy in 1878 and has been described as 'a symphony of cool, silvery tones and delicate passages of paint'.[13] There are just four studies known to exist, three of which are in the collection at Leighton House Museum. As there are relatively few studies, each showing little variation in the pose of the central figure, it would seem Leighton settled on the pose and composition quickly and with ease. A slight alteration was made from this early study in which a length of apparently darker fabric is wrapped around Nausicaa's waist. In the finished work, the fabric was rearranged and worn as a shawl. In addition to these quick studies of the model, both clothed and nude, Leighton made more detailed drapery studies. *P.M.*

INSCRIPTIONS

Stamped, lower left, 'LLC' encircled. Inscribed, lower centre, 'Project' in graphite, by the FAS.

PROVENANCE

Bequeathed by the artist to his sisters, Mrs Augusta Matthews and Mrs Alexandra Orr; from whom purchased by the FAS in 1896; from whom probably purchased by Matthews and Orr and presented to the LHC by 1900; transferred to RBK in 1926 (now RBKC).

BIBLIOGRAPHICAL REFERENCES

Ormond 1975b, p. 164 (listed under cat. no. 248).

EXHIBITION HISTORY

LONDON 1900, no. 276b.

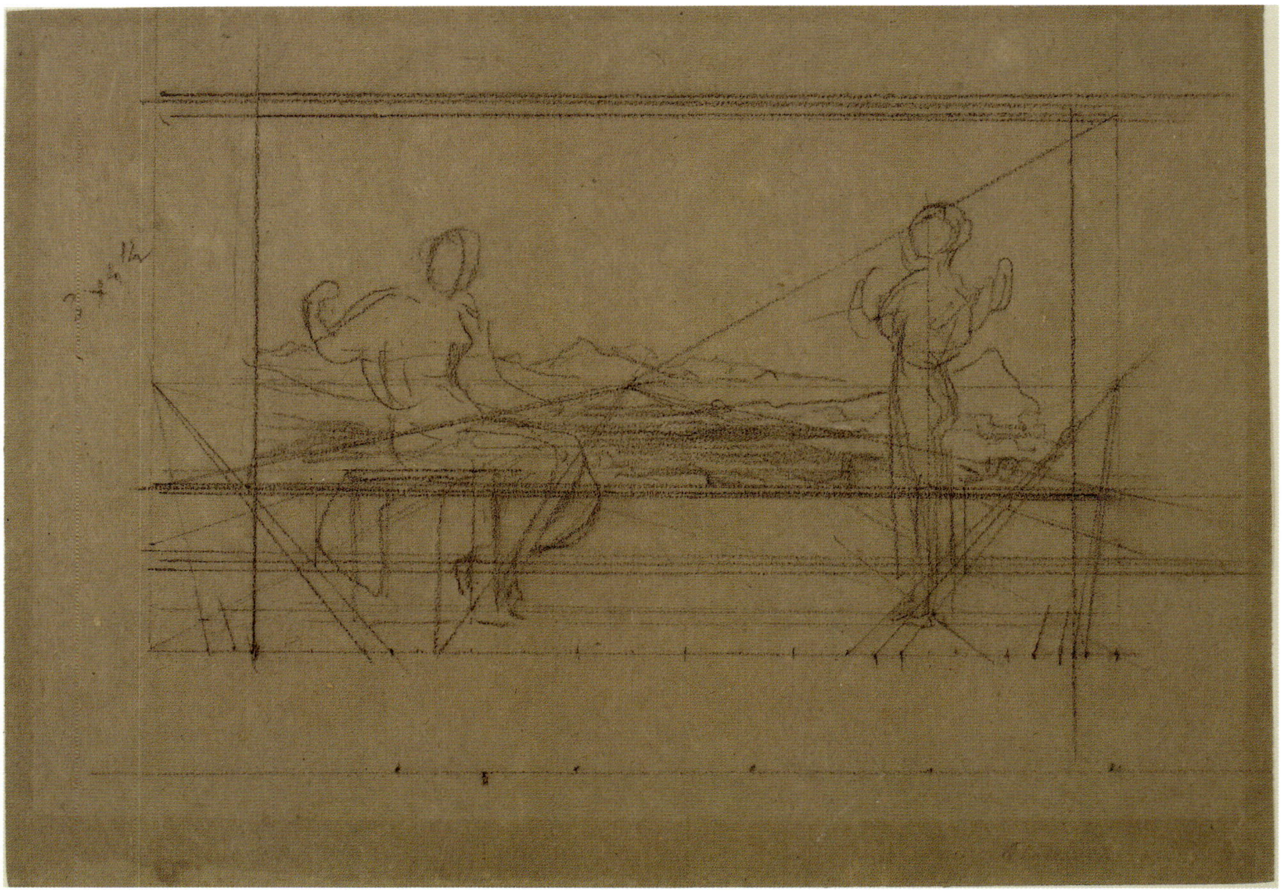

4.10

Study for 'Winding the Skein': Composition, *c.* 1877

Black and white chalk on brown paper
212 x 299 mm
LHO/D/0583

This study was developed into a relatively unremarkable genre painting (cat. ill. 18) depicting a 'classicised' domestic activity exemplifying the type of decorative picture for which the Victorian public had a particular fondness. Leighton may have been attempting to capture the light and mood of the eastern Mediterranean – appreciated many times during his travels – within a commercially successful painting. Whilst favourably received at the time, later critics have been less well disposed to the work, commenting on the lack of a convincing relationship between the figures and the background.

This is one of the last drawings Leighton made for the painting, the earlier studies for this work being on blue paper. The drawing shows Leighton establishing the lines of perspective and 'vanishing point'. These would be valuable in marking out the terrace on which the figures stand.

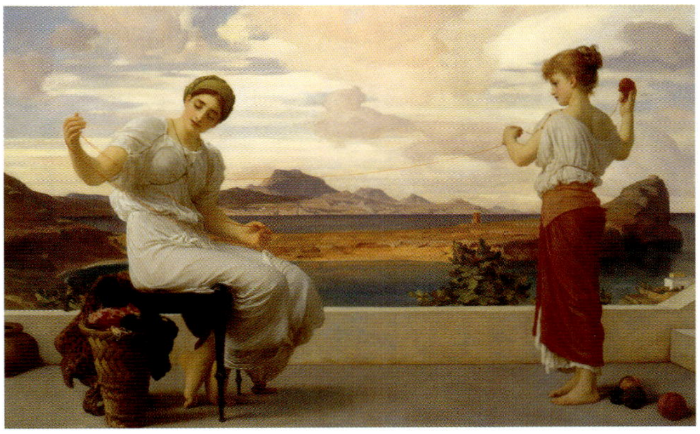

18.

cat. ill. 18. ***Winding the Skein***, RA 1878. Oil on canvas. 100.3 x 161.3 cm. Art Gallery of New South Wales, Sydney.

Of further interest is that the sketches of the child are the last occasion in which Connie Gilchrist – model for the paintings *The Daphnephoria, Moorish Garden* and many more besides – was asked to pose for Leighton. Her increasing age marked a loss of the particular sense of innocence that Leighton required. *R.S.*

INSCRIPTIONS

Inscribed, upper left, '3 x 4½' in black chalk, in the artist's hand. Inscribed, lower right, 'Winding the Skein' in graphite, by the FAS.

PROVENANCE

Bequeathed by the artist to his sisters, Mrs Augusta Matthews and Mrs Alexandra Orr; from whom purchased by the FAS in 1896; presented to the LHC by Lady Nicholson by 1900; transferred to RBK in 1926 (now RBKC).

BIBLIOGRAPHICAL REFERENCES

Ormond 1975b, p. 164 (listed under cat. no. 249), pl. 122.

EXHIBITION HISTORY

LONDON 1900, no. 198b.

NOTES

1. Speech made during the dinner to inaugurate the opening of the annual summer exhibition at the Royal Academy, as reported in *The Times*, Monday 7 May 1877, p. 10. Leighton had received much praise for his bronze statue entitled *An Athlete Struggling with a Python*, first exhibited in this exhibition.
2. Ash 1995, opp. pl. 17.
3. Barrington 1906, vol. II, p. 200.
4. Letter from Leighton to his father, written in Granada, 19 October 1877, Barrington 1906, vol. II, p. 211.
5. Barrington 1906, vol. II, p. 210.
6. See Ormond 1975b, pp 123–24.
7. *Kings*, Chapter 19, verses 1 to 9 (Authorised Version).
8. George and Edward Dalziel, *The Brothers Dalziel: A Record of Fifty Years Work, 1840–1890*, Metheun & Co., London, 1901, p. 238.
9. LONDON 1996, p. 222.
10. LONDON 1996, p. 185.
11. Barrington 1906, vol. II, p. 188.
12. Homer, *The Odyssey*, John Hopkins University Press, Baltimore, 2004, p. 114.
13. Ormond 1975b, p. 10.

5

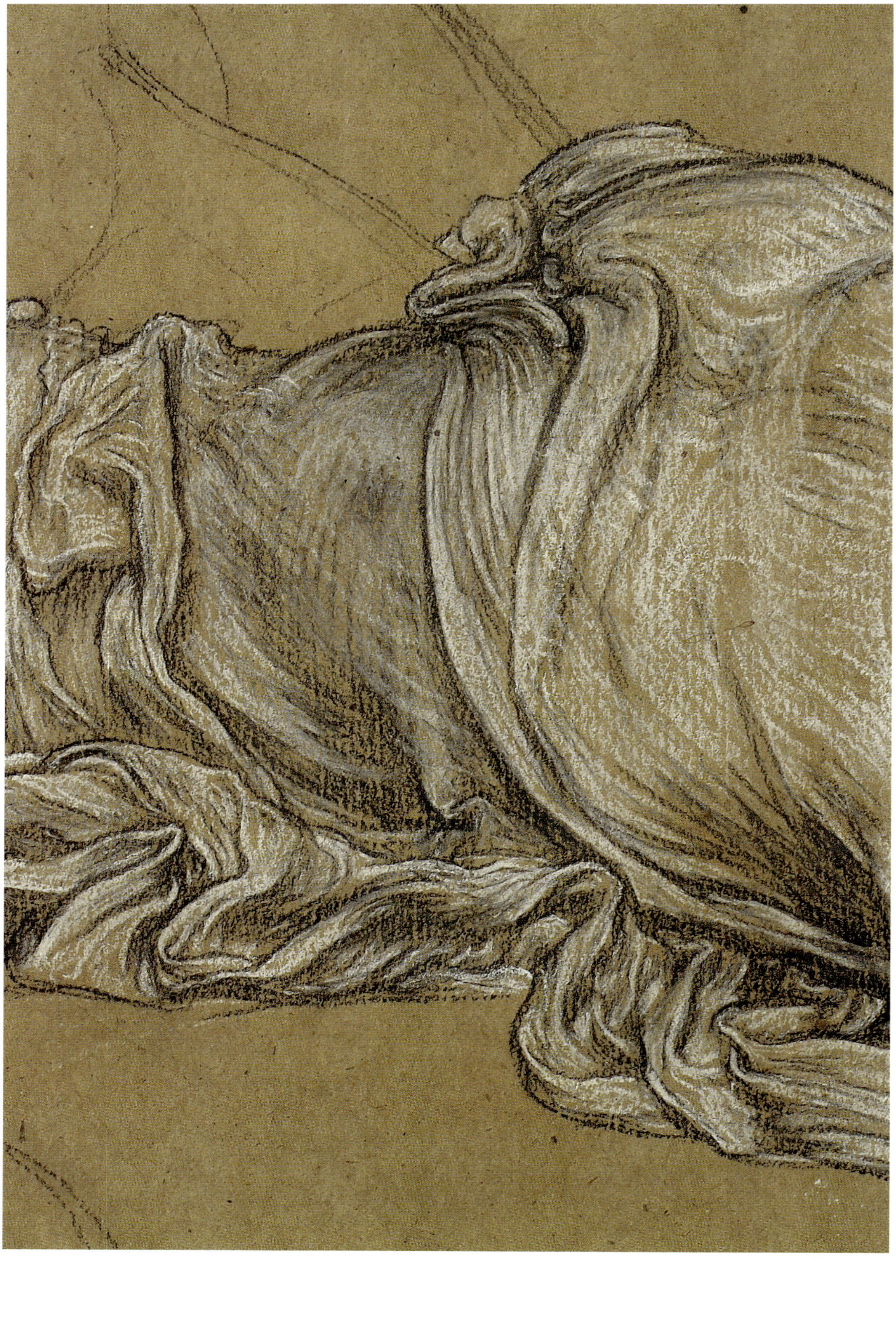

Detail of
cat. no. 6.10.

PRESIDENTIAL EMINENCE 1878–1893

...herein, at the most anxious period of the Academy's history, has Sir Frederick Leighton proved his power and his finesse, not only with credit, but with triumph.

[Marion Harry Spielmann: 'Painters in Their Studios, I. – Sir Frederick Leighton, P.R.A.', *Graphic*, 2 June 1888.]

Sir Francis Grant was the President of the Royal Academy from 1866. After his death on 5 October 1878, an election was held for a new president. Leighton received 31 votes, far exceeding all other candidates.[1] He was in Lerici in Italy, with his artist friend Giovanni Costa, when a telegram arrived with the good news. Although Leighton was confident that he had 'every possibility of being elected', he was delighted when it happened. His long-standing friend Adelaide Sartoris recalled how he took up the post 'with a natural sort of schoolboy delight'.[2]

Leighton proved to be an exceptional president. He coped with his administrative duties with efficiency and discipline, and was known for his scrupulous time keeping. He took his bi-annual address to the Academy very seriously, and went to great lengths to research the subjects of art and architectural history on which he spoke. He also continued to arrange the Academy's Winter Exhibition of works by Old Masters, and maintained a busy itinerary of social engagements. In 1888 Marion Harry Spielmann, in an article on Leighton for the *Graphic*, remarked on the impressive array of 'personal talents and acquirements' that he brought to the position, including the several languages he spoke, his great capacity for 'learning and research' and his polished social graces.[3]

Leighton's new position had a positive effect on his already flourishing career. From 1878 he built on his artistic achievements with large-scale classical paintings such as *Captive Andromache* (*c*.1888) and *Cymon and Iphigenia* (1884), both well received. Leighton also produced large-scale works designed to compliment schemes of interior decoration. He worked with George Aitchison on the decoration of several London houses (see cat. nos 5.3, 5.4) and designed the ceiling for a private residence in New York (*The Marquand Ceiling*, *c*.1886, possibly Private Collections, cat. ills 23, 24). In the late 1880s and early '90s his Royal Academy submissions included several paintings of female allegorical figures including *Sibyl* (cat. ill. 26), *Solitude* (*c*.1890, Maryhill Museum of Art, Washington) and *Tragic Poetess* (*c*.1890, Private Collection). Each represents a classical image of a powerful and apparently melancholic woman, and demonstrate Leighton's now renowned skill in capturing the effect of elaborate ripples of delicate drapery, inspiring one writer to refer to him as 'the great English master of drapery'.[4]

Leighton had always made regular trips through Europe, but his position as president meant that his journeys had to be fitted in after the closure of the Summer Exhibition (in the first week of August) and before arrangements for the opening of the Winter Exhibition the following January. From the time he was made president he developed a habit of always visiting Scotland in September, and then travelling on to Perugia in Italy. In Perugia he would stay at the Brufani Hotel, his 'second home', where guests included aristocrats from across Europe. He continued this pattern for the rest of his life, adding visits to other destinations around the UK, France, Italy and elsewhere along the way.

From the early 1880s, publications such as the *Magazine of Art* and the *Art Journal* were able to reproduce photographs of paintings and drawings, rather than engravings. As a result drawings could be more accurately copied, and were used with more frequency. It was also during this decade that the *Graphic* and the *Magazine of Art* published articles detailing Leighton's working method, based on interviews with the artist. Increased interest in Leighton's drawings and methods coincided with his production of several large-scale, highly finished, drapery studies in black and white chalk for paintings such as *Captive Andromache* (cat. ill. 25), *The Return of Persephone* (*c*.1891, City Art Gallery, Leeds) and *Cymon and Iphigenia* (cat. ill. 22), perhaps intended to be reproduced or exhibited at the Royal Academy.

Leighton's explanation of his working method describes a consistent and rigorous approach. He would begin by deciding on the composition and fixing the image in his imagination or 'minds eye'. He would then set this composition down on paper. Next he drew each figure, from the nude model. The composition would be transferred onto the canvas, and painted with all figures in the nude and in monochrome. Drawings were then made from the draped model or from a draped lay figure (or mannequin). Finally, colour and drapery would be added to the nude painted figures on the canvas. Drawings were used for reference throughout the painting process and would be pinned to a stand positioned alongside the canvas.

According to the popular writer on art Emilia, Lady Dilkie (née Emily Francis Strong) Leighton worked with a 'nervous and resolute energy', bringing 'an attention equally punctilious and exact' to his paintings and to his role as president.[5] This rigorous discipline and thorough approach to both his painting and his official duties, and the workload required for each role, meant his schedule was relentless. Spielmann concluded his 1888 article on Leighton with a warning: 'It will be an evil day for the Academy when the stress of work begins to tell, and he feels the time has come for him to lay aside his chain of office, and seek well-earned repose in the evening of his life'.[6] *P.M.*

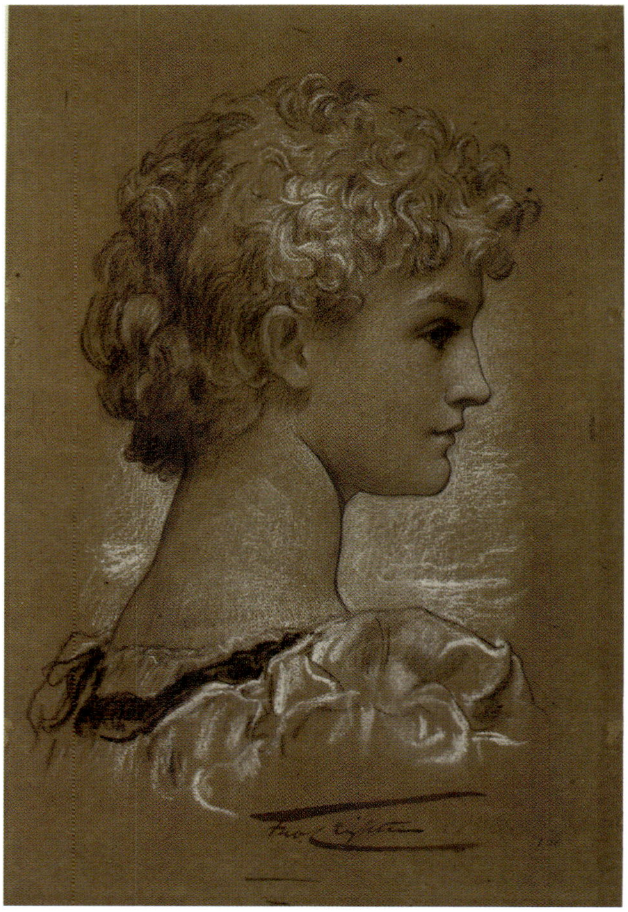

5.1

Portrait of Dorothy Dene, *c.*1880

Black and white chalk on brown paper
293 x 200 mm
LHO/D/0758

This portrait of Dorothy Dene shows Leighton's favourite model and muse from the later part of his career. She was born Ada Alice Pullan, in 1859, but adopted the name of Dorothy Dene for her stage career. The story of her discovery in 1879 by Emilie Barrington is told in the latter's biography of the artist.[7] Dorothy became Leighton's closest female friend and confidante, and at one point it even seemed as if his anxious care for her health and happiness might be a prelude to marriage. He supported Dorothy's ambition to go on the stage, although he was dubious of her chances of success.

This drawing is unusual on a number of counts. It is signed, suggesting that Leighton may have intended to part with it, either by selling it or as a gift. Alternatively it may have been destined for reproduction. It is much more highly finished than other studies of this period; it has the look of a 'presentation' drawing, perhaps inspired by Michelangelo's portrait drawings. The pose in profile and the strongly emphasized outline give it the appearance of a cameo portrait or bas relief, a sculptural form which very much interested Leighton. Unlike the majority of drawings of this period, it is not directly connected with a painting, except obliquely with one of the first of his studies of Dene – the fancy portrait *Bianca* (*c.*1881, Leighton House Museum), where she is shown half-length, dressed in white with velvet ribbon trim and posed against a gold damask curtain. Dene looks much younger than her actual age of about 22. She kept her real age a secret, and it was incorrectly given on her death certificate as 33 when she was in fact 40. The drawing was formerly dated to 1885 through its known connection with *Serenely Wandering in a Trance of Sober Thought* (exhibited 1885).[8] Following the signature there appears to be a faint date – possibly 1880, written in the artist's hand, which has subsequently been erased. On the basis of this, and of its likeness to *Bianca* – the arrangement of the hair is precisely the same and she is wearing the same dress – it might alternatively be dated to around 1880.

There are subtle differences between Leighton's studies of professional models and his preparatory studies for portraits of friends and patrons (often in Leighton's case, the same thing). Dorothy is a special case in being both model and close friend. This is an 'ideal' portrait and so tends in the direction of the formal study of a model, but it is lovingly and perceptively executed. In 1881 Leighton contributed to a series running in the *Graphic* entitled 'Types of Beauty'. His example was published on 24 December 1881 and this drawing may have been an early idea for the painting, which shows a similar view of Dene, although not in profile. *C.G.*

INSCRIPTIONS

Signed, lower right, 'Fred Leighton' in brown ink.

PROVENANCE

Probably acquired by the LHC before 1926.

EXHIBITION HISTORY

LONDON 1969, no. 7; **YORK, LONDON, NOTTINGHAM** 1999, no. 70.

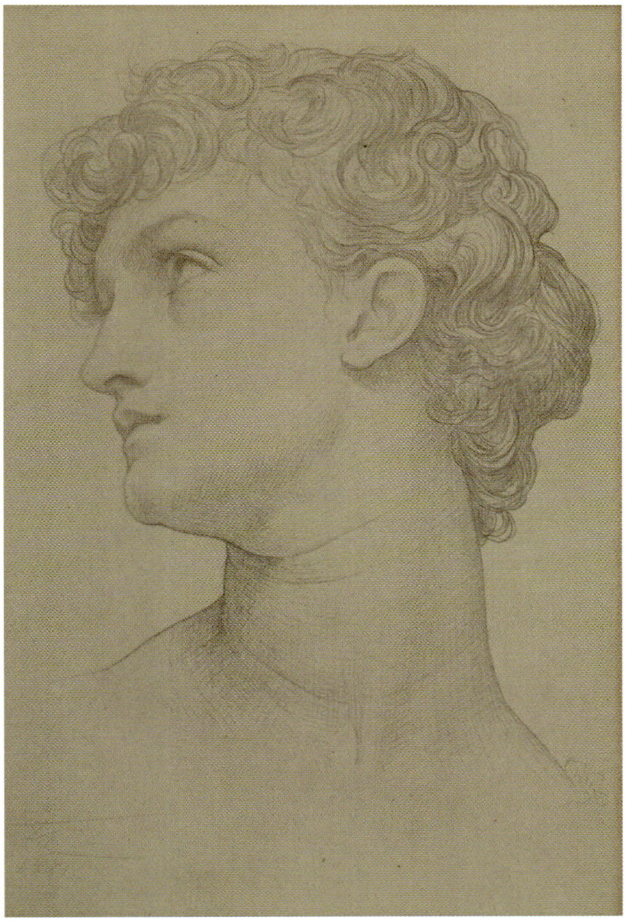

5.2

Head of Dorothy Dene, 1881

Graphite on white paper
228mm x 174 mm
LHO/D/1039

Essentially a portrait, this drawing is something of an oddity from later in the artist's career. Not only is it initialled and dated, but it is also drawn in pencil on white paper. By 1881, excluding drawings in sketchbooks made during his travels, Leighton almost exclusively worked in black and white chalk on brown paper, and rarely signed or dated his work. However, this is almost certainly a copy of a study for the painting *Antigone* (c.1882, Private Collection) for which Dorothy Dene posed.

There is another example of Leighton making a pencil copy of a chalk drawing in this way, now in the Royal Collection (ref. no. 3339). A drawing within an album compiled by Alexandra, Princess of Wales, is a copy of a study at Leighton House Museum (ref. no. LHO/D/0670) made in connection with the painting *Captive Andromache*. The drawing was presented as a gift to Princess Alexandra by the artist. This study was almost certainly made for a similar purpose, although the recipient is unknown. Calculations inscribed along the lower edge are probably measurements for a frame and mount. The drawing demonstrates the value Leighton placed upon his preparatory studies. When required to produce a drawing as a gift, he would select one of the studies that were carefully preserved in his studio and make a copy, to avoid parting with the actual study that represented a part of his creative process.

Although Dene and Leighton were undoubtedly close, the extent of their relationship has never been established with any certainty. As an artist's model, Dene would not have been regarded as a suitable companion for Leighton, and his position required him to be guarded when referring to her. However, a letter to Charles Pooley, chairman of the exhibitions committee at Manchester Art Gallery (where the paintings *Last Watch of Hero*, c.1887 and *Captive Andromache*, c.1888 are held) provides an unusual insight into his ardent support of her as an aspiring actress:

> I know that apart from your love for what is beautiful & poetic it will interest you to see the source of the excursion of 'Hero' and 'Andromache'. – I owe those excursions entirely to the kindness of that very gifted young actress Miss Dorothy Dene... Miss Dene and her sisters are great friends of mine & very many of my friends; – I have known them since she was well back in her teens & like all her friends have a very high regard for her.[9] *P.M.*

INSCRIPTIONS

Signed and dated, lower left, 'FL / 1881' in graphite. Inscribed, lower left, 'x 7½ s of frame' in graphite, possibly in the artist's hand. Inscribed, lower centre, '7¾ x 5⅛ / 2½ 2' in graphite, possibly in the artist's hand. Inscribed, lower right, '9⅞ x 7⅜' in graphite, possibly in the artist's hand.

PROVENANCE

Acquired by RBKC, probably after 1926.

BIBLIOGRAPHICAL REFERENCES

Rhys 1895, ill. opp. p. 34.

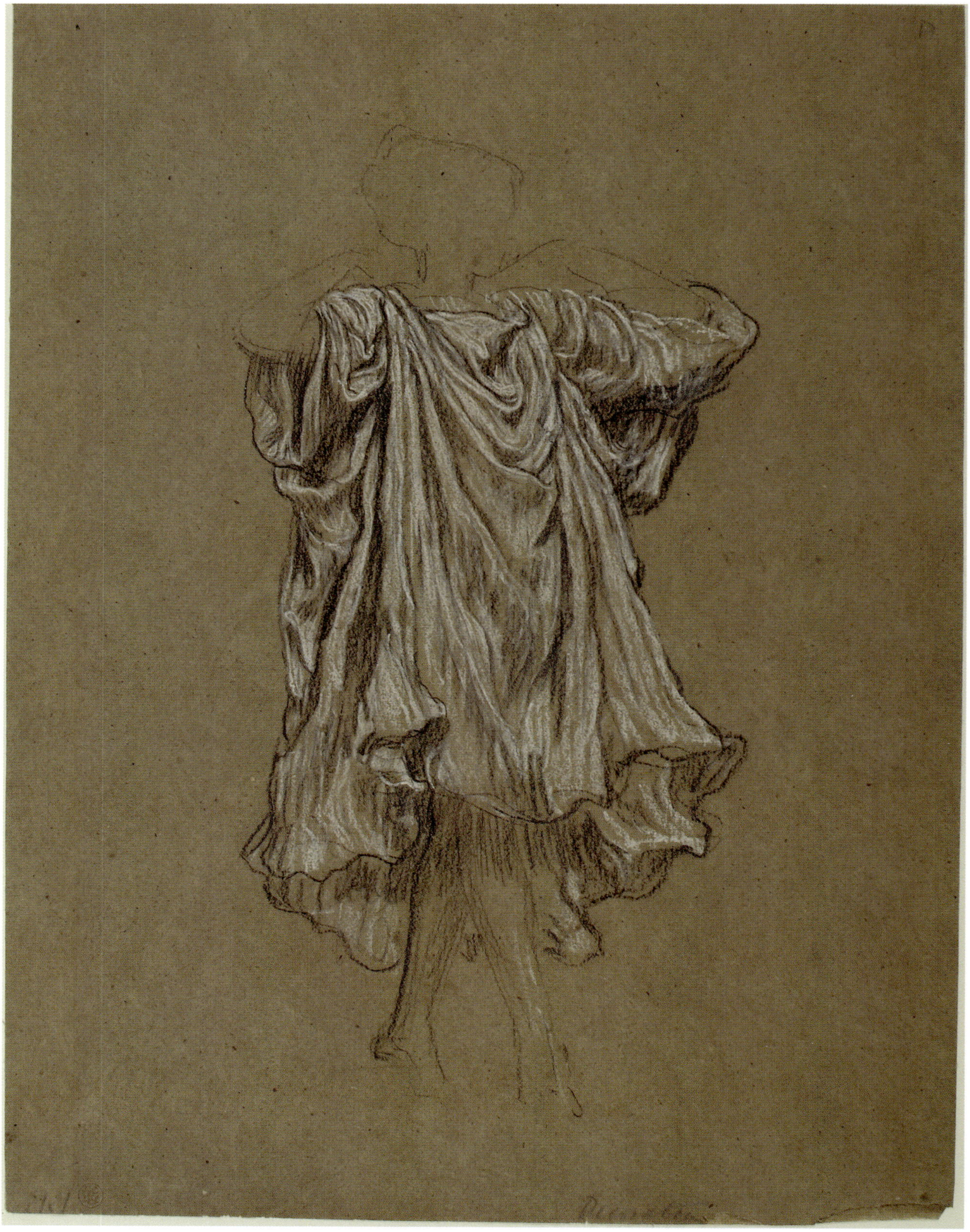

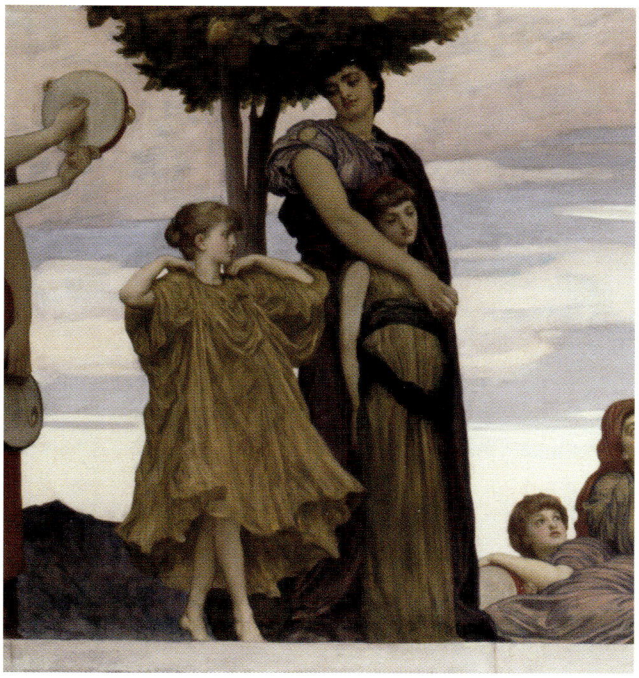

cat. ill. **19.** ***The Dance***, RA 1883.
Oil on canvas. 89 x 292 cm.
Leighton House Museum, London.

cat. ill. **19a.** Detail of ***The Dance***.

19a.

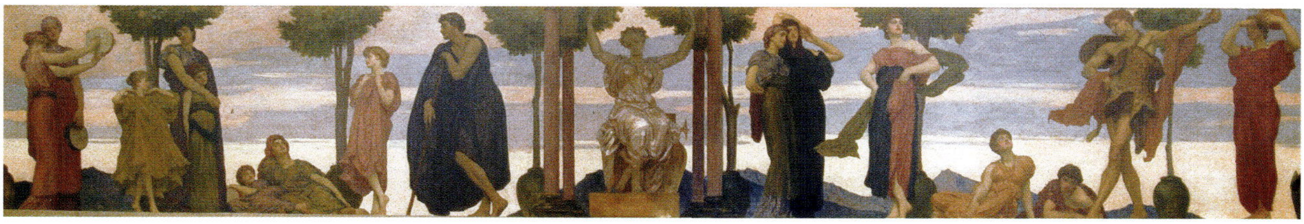

19.

5.3

Study for 'The Dance': Drapery for Girl, *c.*1882

Black and white chalk on brown paper
330 x 257 mm
LHO/D/0620

This dancing child, essentially a drapery study, shows the figure on the left of a decorative frieze, *The Dance* (cat. ill. 19). The frieze was started around 1881 for the London house of James Stewart Hodgson (a wealthy patron of the arts and banker) at No. 1 South Audley Street, Mayfair. *The Dance* was matched by another frieze, *Music* (cat. ill. 20) on the other side of the drawing room. The model for the dancing child was Lena Pullan (Isabell Helena), one of five sisters of whom three modelled for Leighton.[10] Her older sister Dorothy was the most important to him (see cat. nos 5.1, 5.2), but Lena may have been the first to sit for the artist. She was the one most used in Leighton's earliest acquaintance with the family, taking on the childish roles that had been played in the 1870s by Connie Gilchrist (who modelled for the singing girls in The *Daphnephoria*, also owned by James Stewart Hodgson). Lena sat for a number of Leighton's most popular child subjects, including *Kittens* (1881–83, Private Collection) and *Letty* (*c.*1884, Private Collection). She would have been eight or nine years old at the date of this study. *C.G.*

INSCRIPTIONS

Stamped, lower left, 'LLC' encircled. Inscribed, lower left, 'i/i/' in graphite. Inscribed, lower right, 'Decoration' in graphite, by the FAS.

PROVENANCE

Bequeathed by the artist to his sisters, Mrs Augusta Matthews and Mrs Alexandra Orr; from whom purchased by the FAS in 1896; from whom purchased by the LHC by 1897; transferred to RBK in 1926 (now RBKC).

BIBLIOGRAPHICAL REFERENCES

Ormond 1975b, p. 166 (listed under cat. no. 292).

EXHIBITION HISTORY

LONDON 1897, no. 6 ('Studies for Two Friezes'); **LONDON 1900**, no. 224a; **LONDON 2005**.

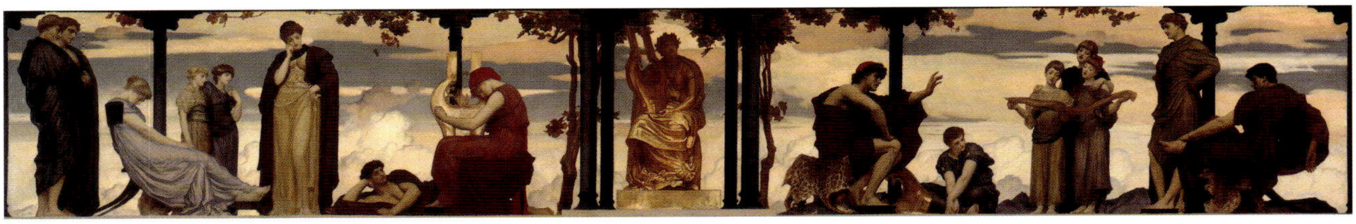

20.

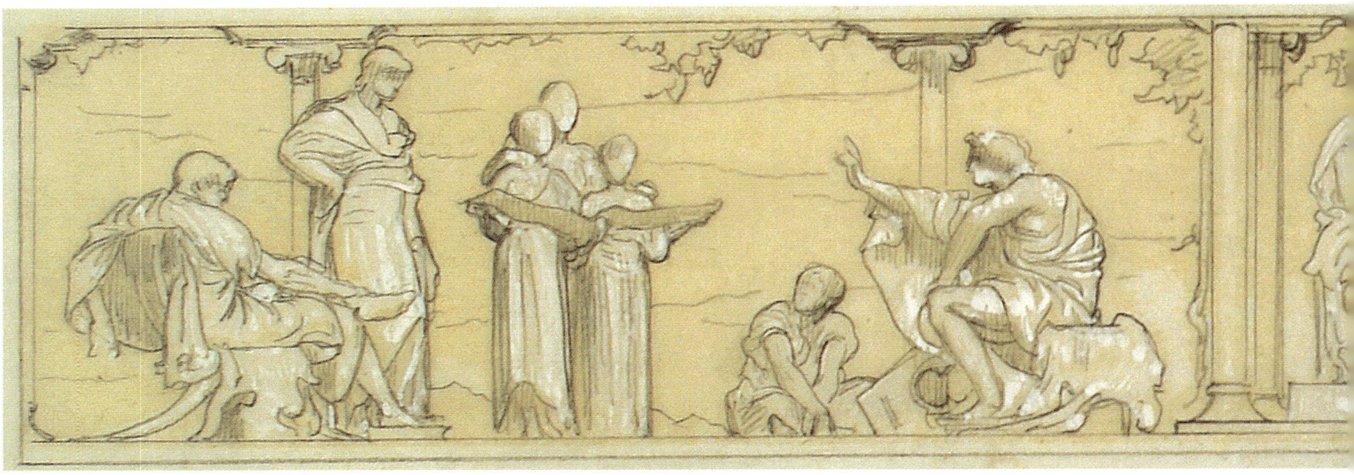

5.4

Study for 'Music': Composition, *c.*1884

Graphite and bodycolour on tracing paper
87 x 456 mm
LHO/D/3003

Music (cat. ill. 20) is carefully matched to *The Dance*; both feature a procession of figures in a shallow plane performing actions symbolizing the titles. This drawing is a tracing for the composition of *Music*, with highlights added in white bodyco our. The decoration of Hodgson's South Audley Street house was undertaken by George Aitchison in 1881, and his designs for the drawing room survive in the RIBA Library's Drawings Collection. It is one of four designs for interior decoration by Aitchison for which Leighton produced painted panels. Aitchison's drawings for the decoration of the drawing room include rough versions of the friezes, which strongly relate to Leighton's designs, suggesting that the two friends worked closely together on the project.[11]

Hodgson had been a valued friend since the late 1850s and a loyal patron of Leighton's, owning several important works including *Lieder Ohne Worte* (1861) and *The Daphnephoria* (*c.*1874–76) which hung in his country house, Lythe Hill at Haslemere in Surrey, as well as a long-lost portrait of his two daughters (1888). Rediscovered in Evansville, Indiana, it is now in a private collection, and was lent for exhibition at Leighton House in 2001.[12] He also had a number of oil sketches relating to other important works. Letters from the artist to Hodgson plot the progress of the two friezes, which was slow, partly owing to their size. Each was as long as *The Daphnephoria*, as Leighton pointed out,[13] but this was somewhat disingenuous as the height was much less. The requirements of a decorative frieze are very different from that of an easel painting – thus, the figures in *The Dance* and *Music* are fewer, more static and more simply

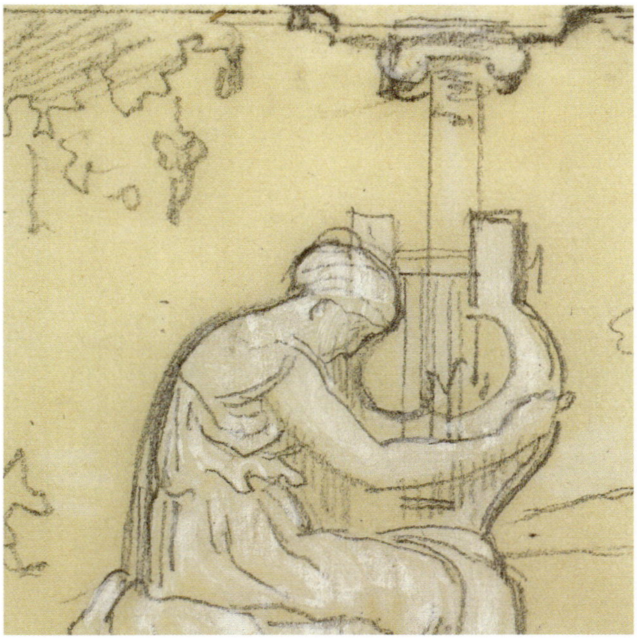

20a.

cat. ill. **20.** ***'Music'***, RA 1885.
Oil on canvas. 84 x 231 cm.
Leighton House Museum, London.

cat. ill. **20a.** Detail of cat. no. 5.4.

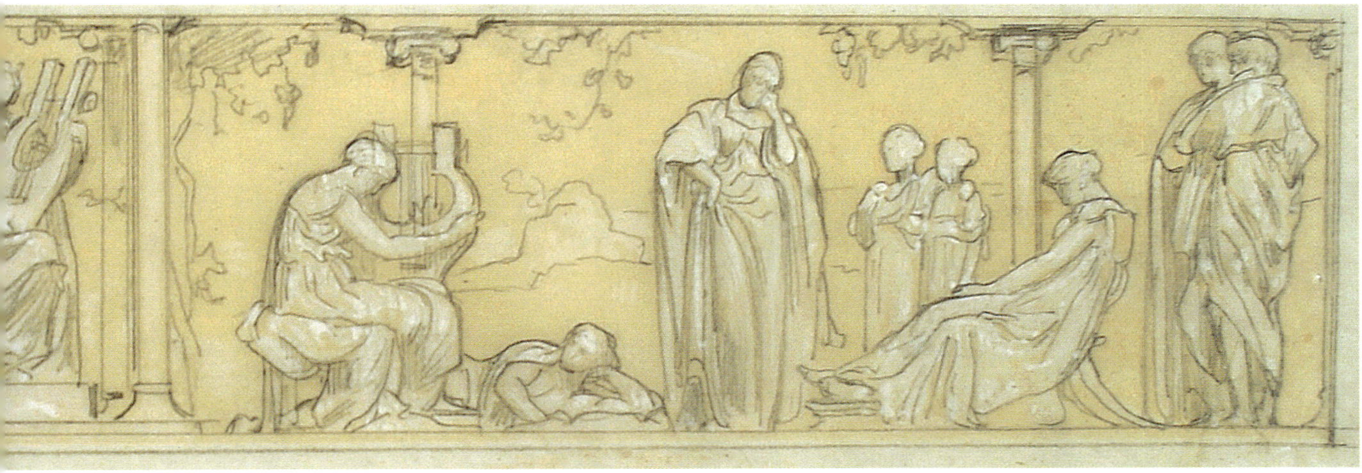

modelled, in a style reminiscent of Greek vase painting. In spite of further delays – caused by work on the South Kensington frescoes, the casting of Leighton's bronze sculpture, *An Athlete Struggling with a Python*, and the designs for St Paul's Cathedral (see cat. nos 4.1, 5.5) – *The Dance* was completed in time to be exhibited at the Royal Academy in 1883. *Music* was completed by 1885. There are studies at Leighton House for both *The Dance* (ref. nos LHO/D/0619–24) and *Music* (ref. nos LHO/D/0626–34 and 0804); Hodgson owned a colour sketch for *Music*, which was shown in the Royal Academy Winter Exhibition in 1897. The scheme was one of three undertaken by Leighton in collaboration with Aitchison in the early 1880s. *C.G.*

INSCRIPTIONS

Signed and inscribed on a fragment of paper, formerly part of original mount, 'Fred Leighton / design for frieze in drawing / room / Music' in brown ink.

PROVENANCE

Bequeathed by the artist to his sisters, Mrs Augusta Matthews and Mrs Alexandra Orr; from whom purchased by the FAS in 1896; from whom purchased by Harry W. Birks in 1897; Sotheby's, London, *Victorian Pictures*, 3 November 1993; Christopher Wood Gallery (formerly part of Mallett); from whom purchased by a private collector in Manchester in *c.*1994; from whom purchased by Christopher Wood Gallery in 2005; from whom purchased by Leighton House Museum in 2006.

BIBLIOGRAPHICAL REFERENCES

Ormond 1975a, p. 167.

EXHIBITION HISTORY

LONDON 1896, no. 134; **NEW YORK 2005**, no. 28.

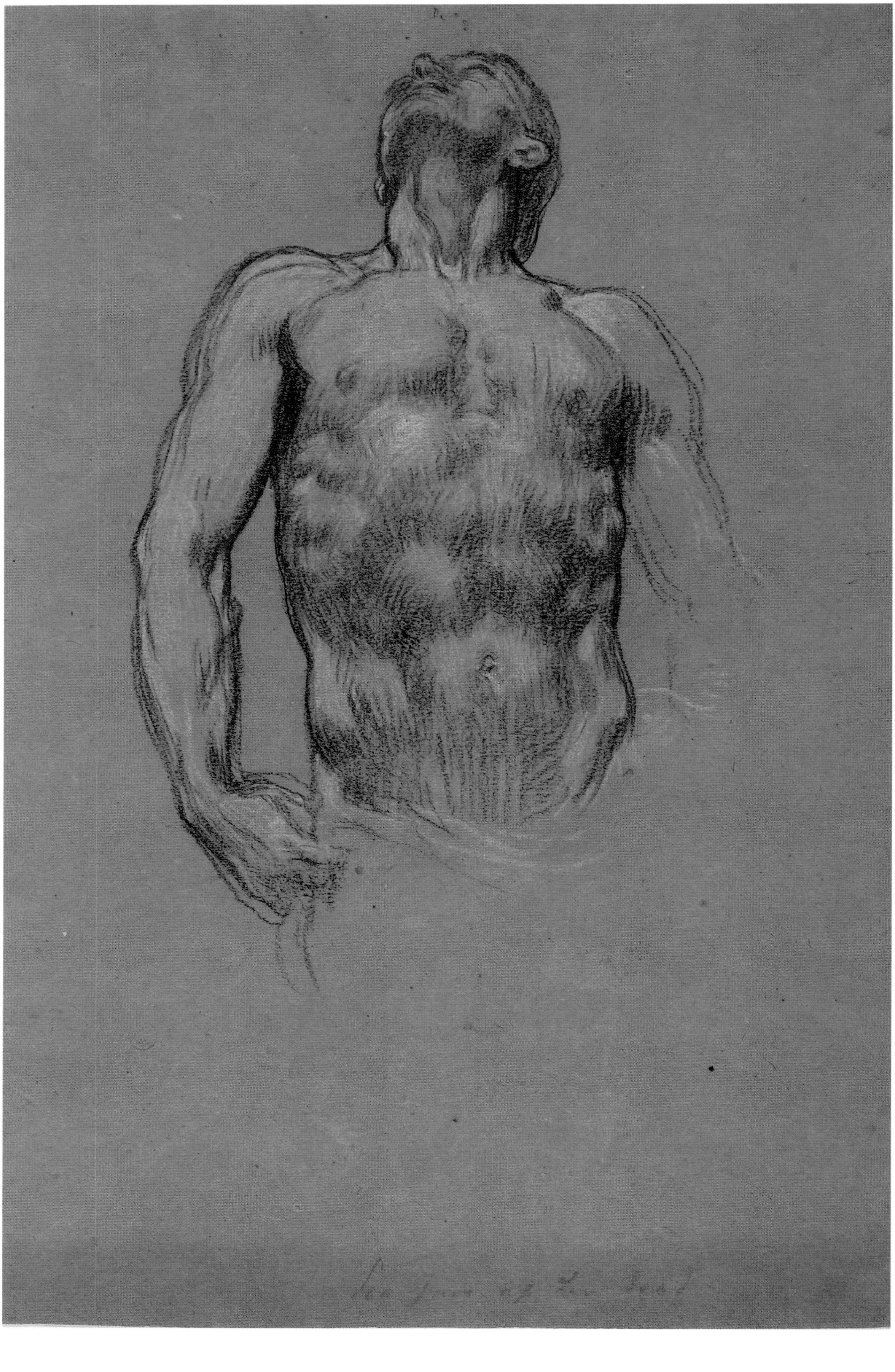

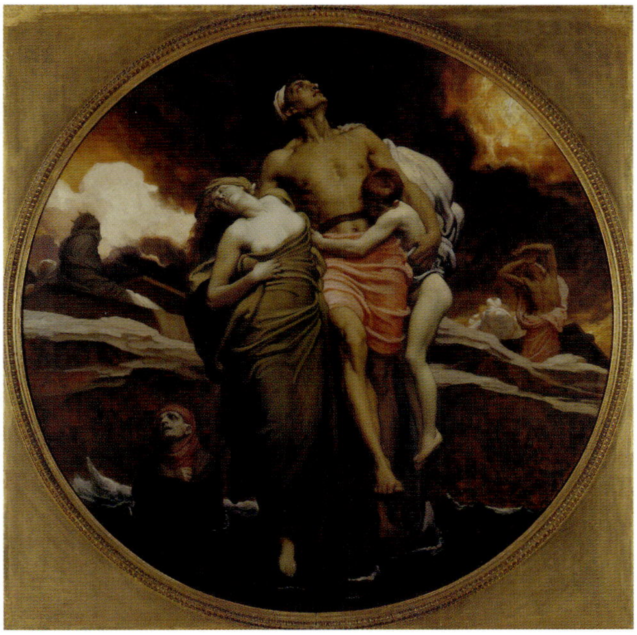

21.

cat. ill. 21. ***And the Sea Gave Up the Dead Which Were in It***, RA 1892. Oil on canvas. 228.5 cm diameter. Tate Britain, London.

5.5

Study for 'And the Sea Gave Up the Dead Which Were in It': Male Figure, *c.*1881

Black and white chalk on brown paper
321 x 220 mm
LHO/D/0615

This powerful study from life of a male nude torso is for the central figure in *And the Sea Gave Up the Dead Which Were in It* (cat. ill. 21), one of the most Michelangelesque of Leighton's late works. Among the very large number of figure studies for the painting, this is probably the one that comes closest to an actual Michelangelo drawing.

The composition of the painting was first created for a project to decorate the interior of the dome of St Paul's Cathedral, abandoned in 1885 (see cat. no. 4.1). In 1891 Leighton heard that Henry Tate, the sugar magnate and donor of the National Gallery of British Art (now the Tate), was forming a public collection of works for his new gallery on Millbank. The artist wrote to him, urging him to commission an oil painting based on the design. 'Mr. Tate somewhat reluctantly selected [the composition] at his urgent request: for Leighton believed that this was the finest of all his purposeful imaginative works', and the painting was completed in 1892.[14] Tate's collection formed the core of the National Collection of British Art and the painting has been in the Tate Gallery since 1894, soon after its completion.

The group of drawings preparatory to this work in the Leighton House Museum collection was analysed in detail for the centenary exhibition at the Royal Academy in 1996.[15] It is apparent that these examples were chosen with care to demonstrate Leighton's drawing technique and his painstaking approach to planning a complex figure group. Leighton tried a number of variations of the central figure supporting dead bodies as they arise from the sea, using the same model. A number of figures were explored in detail and then not used in the final resolution of the group. The drawings often demonstrate a dramatic intensity that could not be sustained in the painting, in spite of its monumentality and apocalyptic character. *C.G.*

INSCRIPTIONS

Stamped, lower left, 'LLC' encircled. Inscribed, lower centre, 'Sea gave up its dead' in graphite, by the FAS.

PROVENANCE

Bequeathed by the artist to his sisters, Mrs Augusta Matthews and Mrs Alexandra Orr; purchased by the FAS in 1896; from whom purchased by the LHC by 1897; transferred to RBK in 1926 (now RBKC).

BIBLIOGRAPHICAL REFERENCES

Ormond 1975b, p. 170 (listed under cat. no. 354); **LONDON 1996**, p. 220, cat. no. 115f, ill. p. 222, p. 224.

EXHIBITION HISTORY

LONDON 1897, no. 7 ('And the sea...'); **LONDON 1900**, no. 222e; **LONDON 1996**, no. 115f.

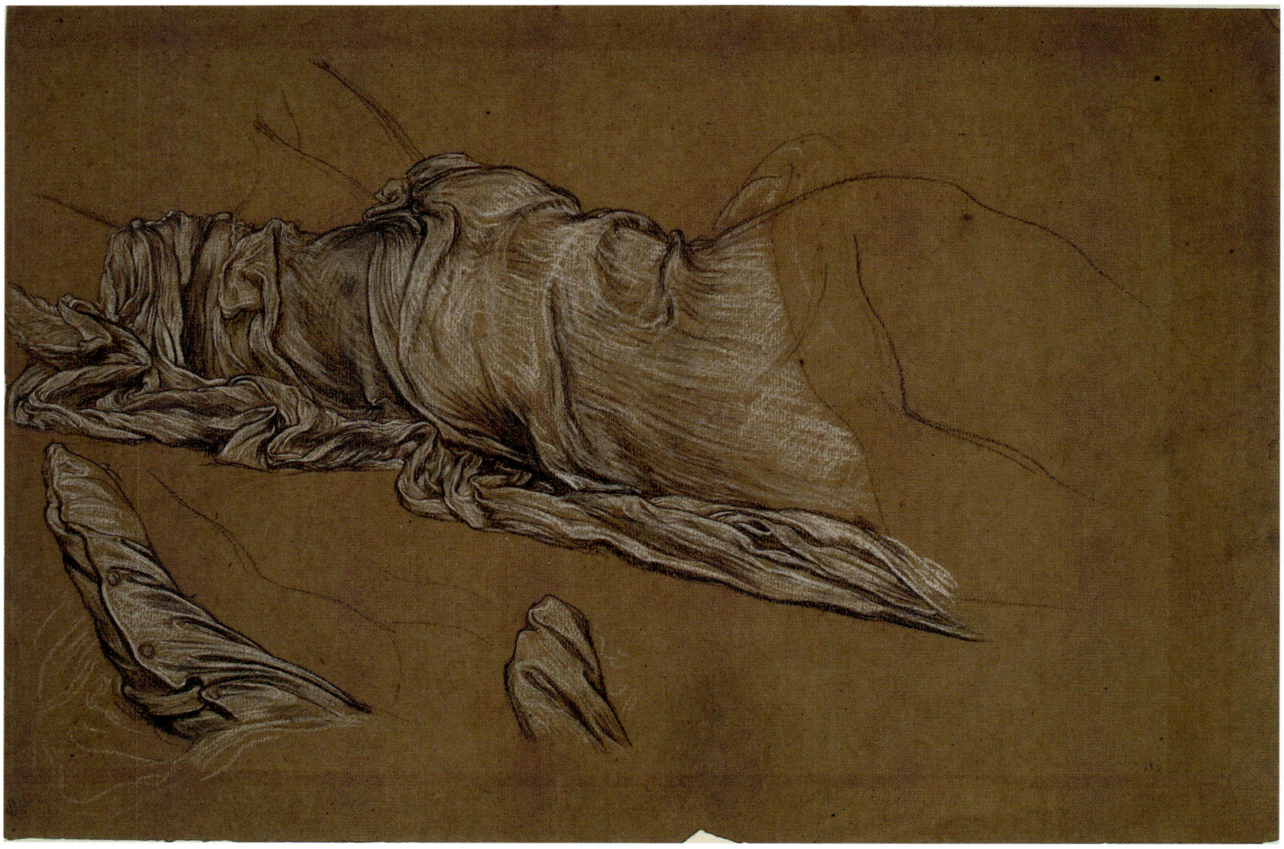

5.6

Study for 'Cymon and Iphigenia': Drapery for Iphigenia, *c.*1883

Black and white chalk on brown paper
369 x 561 mm
LHO/D/0830

This is a study for the sleeping figure of Iphigenia in the painting of *Cymon and Iphigenia* (exhibited at the Royal Academy in 1884; cat. ill. 22). The subject is taken from Boccaccio's *Decameron* (Fifth Day, novel I). The shepherd Cymon discovers the sleeping Iphigenia with her companions, and is transformed from his rustic simplicity by this vision of beauty and the power of love. Emilie Barrington thought that the painting embodied Leighton's 'creed of creeds... the ennobling and elevating influence of beauty in the lives of men and women'.[16] This drapery study for the sleeping Iphigenia reveals the nude figure beneath the semi-transparent material more explicitly than is usual with Leighton's drawings of this type. The painting itself is less revealing but still unashamedly

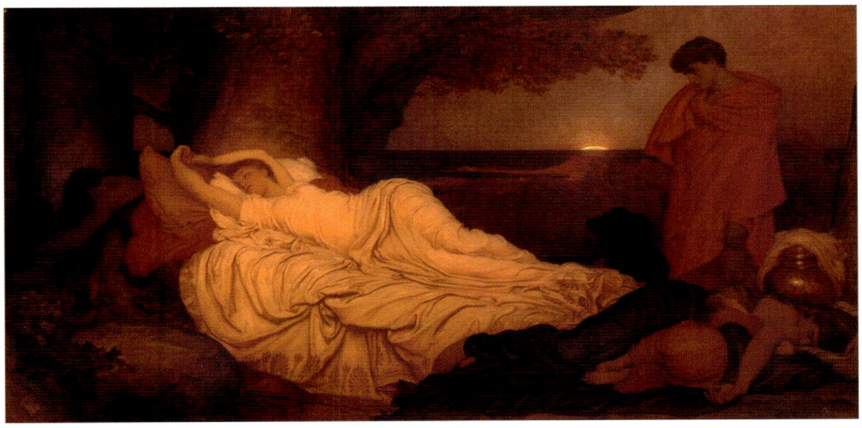

cat. ill. **22.**
Cymon and Iphigenia,
RA 1884. Oil on canvas.
162.5 x 327.6 cm.
Art Gallery of
New South Wales, Sydney.

22.

sensuous, reflecting the description of Iphigenia in a contemporary translation of Boccaccio: 'a beautiful damsel asleep... [her] mantle so exceedingly fine and delicate, as scarcely to conceal underneath the exquisite whiteness of her skin'.[17] The painting was bought by the Fine Art Society, who put it on exhibition accompanied by an elaborate, fully illustrated catalogue, including material from all stages of its execution.[18] Amidst the flowery language relating to the subject matter, the text provides a detailed exposition of Leighton's methods in building the finished work. The inspiration for Iphigenia's pose is *Odalisque and Slave*, by Ingres (two versions, painted in 1839 and 1842); the figure of Iphigenia is in reverse to Ingres's Odalisque. Leighton had acquired in the 1860s a fine draped study by Ingres for the figure of the Odalisque, an instance – among many – of his collecting influencing his own work. There are several studies for the painting in the Leighton House Museum collection.

The setting and beautifully twilit background in the painting refer directly to Leighton's botanical studies and landscape sketches. He told Barrington that he wanted to capture the moment of the day which is 'the most mysteriously beautiful in the whole twenty-four hours, when the merest lip of the moon has risen from behind the sea horizon, and the air is haunted still with the flush of the after-glow from the sun already hidden in the west'.[19] A colour sketch for the painting was owned by James Stewart Hodgson. *C.G.*

INSCRIPTIONS
Stamped, lower left, 'LLC' encircled.

PROVENANCE
Bequeathed by the artist to his sisters, Mrs Augusta Matthews and Mrs Alexandra Orr; from whom purchased by the FAS in 1896; from whom probably purchased by Matthews and Orr and presented to the LHC by 1900; transferred to RBK in 1926 (now RBKC).

BIBLIOGRAPHICAL REFERENCES
Ormond 1975b, p. 168 (listed under cat. no. 313).

EXHIBITION HISTORY
Possibly LONDON 1900, no. 52Ac; LONDON 1969, no. 6.

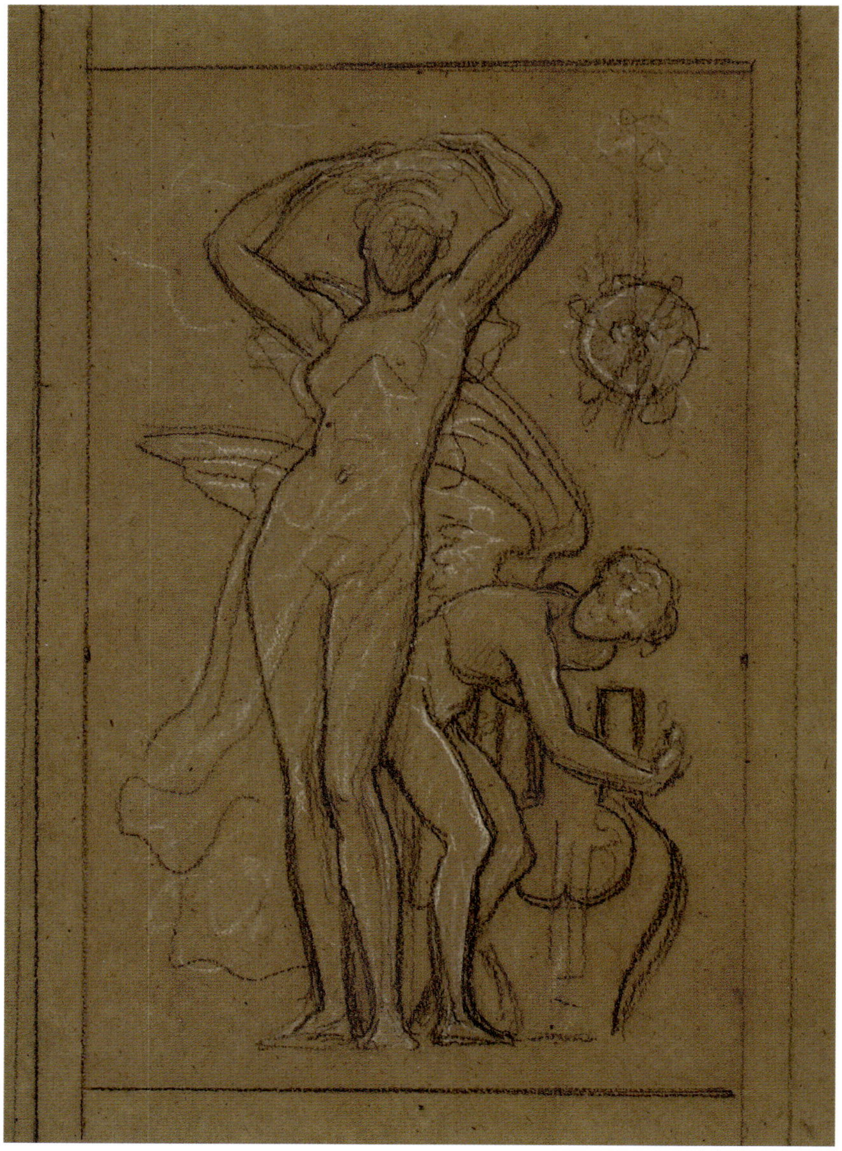

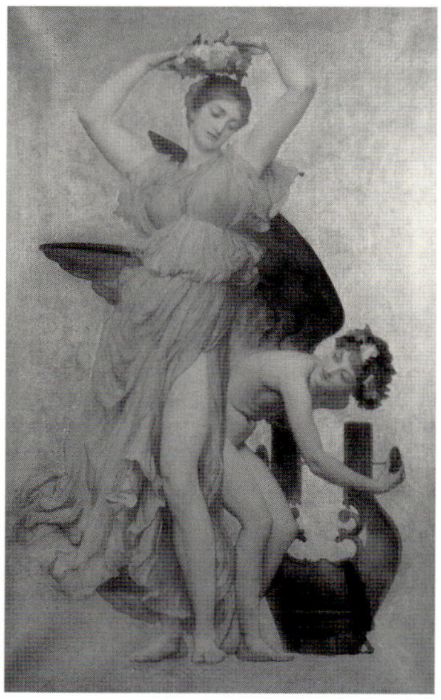

23.

Two Studies for 'The Marquand Ceiling', *c.*1885
(Cat. nos 5.7 and 5.8)

In 1884 – while he was still immersed in planning vastly complex and large-scale decorative schemes for the South Kensington lunettes and the dome of St Paul's Cathedral (see cat. nos 4.1, 5.5) – Leighton was approached by Lawrence Alma-Tadema to contribute to the decoration of the Greek Parlor, or Music Room, in a magnificent New York mansion for the multi-millionaire Henry Marquand.[20] Although very different from his collaborations with George Aitchison for patrons like James Stewart Hodgson, this was nonetheless a commission of considerable prestige, with exotic and luxurious furnishings by Alma-Tadema and contributions from Edward Poynter and Edward Onslow Ford, all executed entirely regardless of cost. Leighton's ceiling panels were exhibited at the Royal Academy in 1886, and the room was all but complete by 1887.

These two studies are for the dancing figures of Erato and Terpsichore, who flank the central tableau featuring the muses Melpomene, Mnemosyne and Thalia. These three are identified in Greek characters above the heads of the principal figures. Leighton did not name the dancing figures, simply describing the left-hand figure as emblematic of 'the poetry of love' and the right-hand dancer with the tambourine as 'a Bacchante'. The names by which they are now known were given subsequently.[21] Erato and Terpsichore frame and contrast with the static poses of the three statuesque central figures. With their fluttering draperies, they offer a suggestion of movement. The nude figure of a boy beside Erato is tuning a lyre. Leighton owned such an instrument, and first explored the motif of a lyre when designing the tomb in Florence of the poet Elizabeth Barrett Browning in 1863. He used it again in *Music* (cat. ill. 21).[22] The dancing nude boy beside Terpsichore is playing a double flute. In about 1886 Leighton made a colour sketch showing the three panels in their relative positions.[23]

Henry Marquand died in 1902, and the Marquand Mansion was demolished ten years later. The decorations were thought to have been dispersed or destroyed. However, works sold as replicas of the design may in fact be parts of the original ceiling. The finished ceiling is known from a contemporary photograph of the central panel[24] and versions of the side panels (cat. ills 23, 24). C.G.

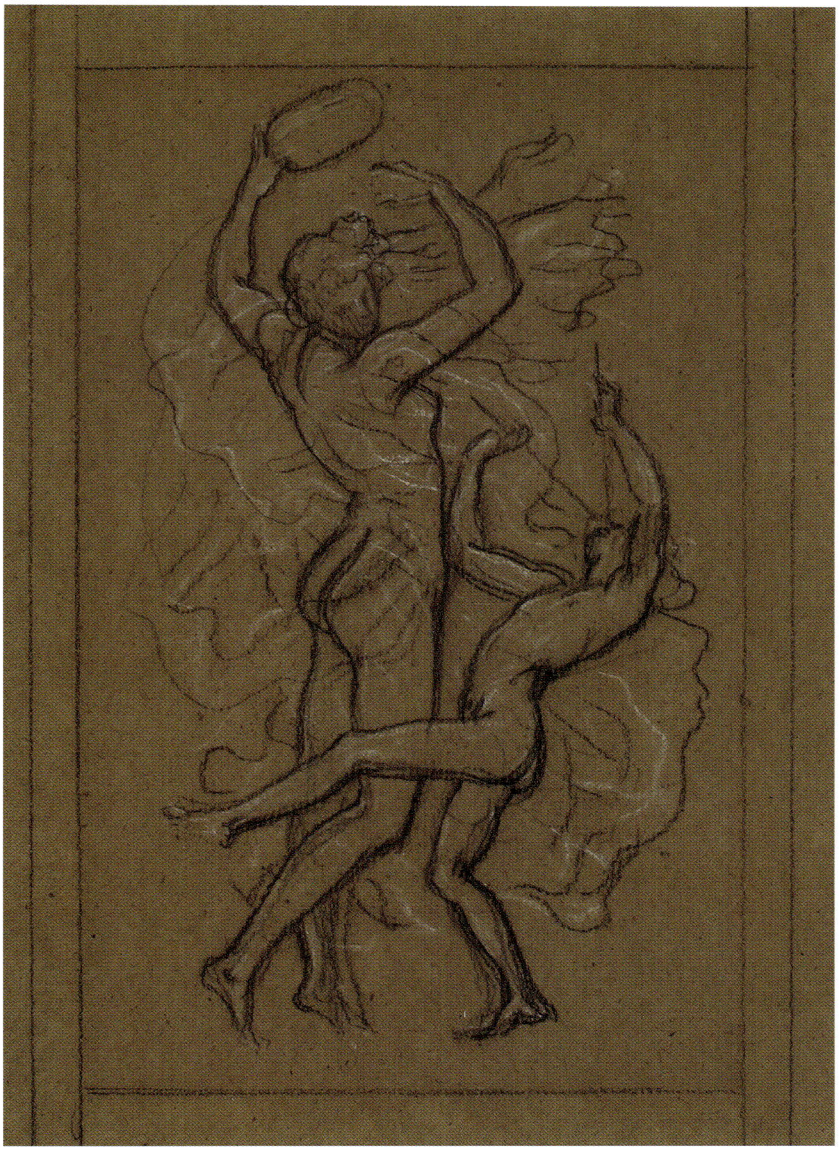

cat. ill. 23. ***The Marquand Ceiling, left panel (Erato)***, RA 1886. Oil on canvas. 163 x 111 cm. Previously thought to be a replica of the panel, this may in fact be the original work, removed from the ceiling of Henry Marquand's New York house. Private Collection.

cat. ill. 24. ***The Marquand Ceiling, right panel (Terpsichore)***, RA 1886. Oil on canvas. 163 x 111 cm. Previously thought to be a replica. Private Collection.

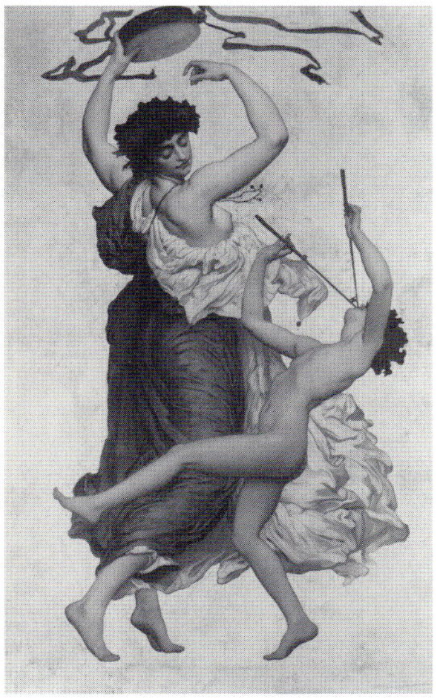

24.

5.7

Study for 'The Marquand Ceiling': Composition of Left Panel, *c.*1885

Black and white chalk on brown paper

367 x 254 mm

LHO/D/0655

INSCRIPTIONS

Inscribed, lower right, 'Marquand Ceiling' in graphite, by the FAS.

PROVENANCE

Bequeathed by the artist to his sisters, Mrs Augusta Matthews and Mrs Alexandra Orr; from whom purchased by the FAS in 1896; presented to the LHC by Mrs Charles Fowler by 1897; transferred to RBK in 1926 (now RBKC).

BIBLIOGRAPHICAL REFERENCES

Anon. 1897, p. 25, cat. no. 4; Barrington 1900, p. 179, cat. no. 161b; Ormond 1975b, p. 168 (listed under cat. no. 323).

EXHIBITION HISTORY

LONDON 1897, no. 4 ('Studies for Decorative Work'); **LONDON 1900**, no. 161b.

5.8

Study for 'The Marquand Ceiling': Composition of Right Panel, *c.*1885

Black and white chalk on brown paper

357 x 259 mm

LHO/D/0652

INSCRIPTIONS

Inscribed, lower right, 'Marquand Ceiling' in graphite, by the FAS, partially erased.

PROVENANCE

Bequeathed by the artist to his sisters, Mrs Augusta Matthews and Mrs Alexandra Orr; from whom purchased by the FAS in 1896; presented to the LHC by Mrs Charles Fowler by 1897; transferred to RBK in 1926 (now RBKC).

BIBLIOGRAPHICAL REFERENCES

Barrington 1906, vol. I, ill. opp. p. 276; Ormond 1975b, p. 168 (listed under cat. no. 323); Yellow Book 1894.

EXHIBITION HISTORY

LONDON 1897, no. 3 ('Studies for Decorative Work'); **LONDON 1900**, no. 161b.

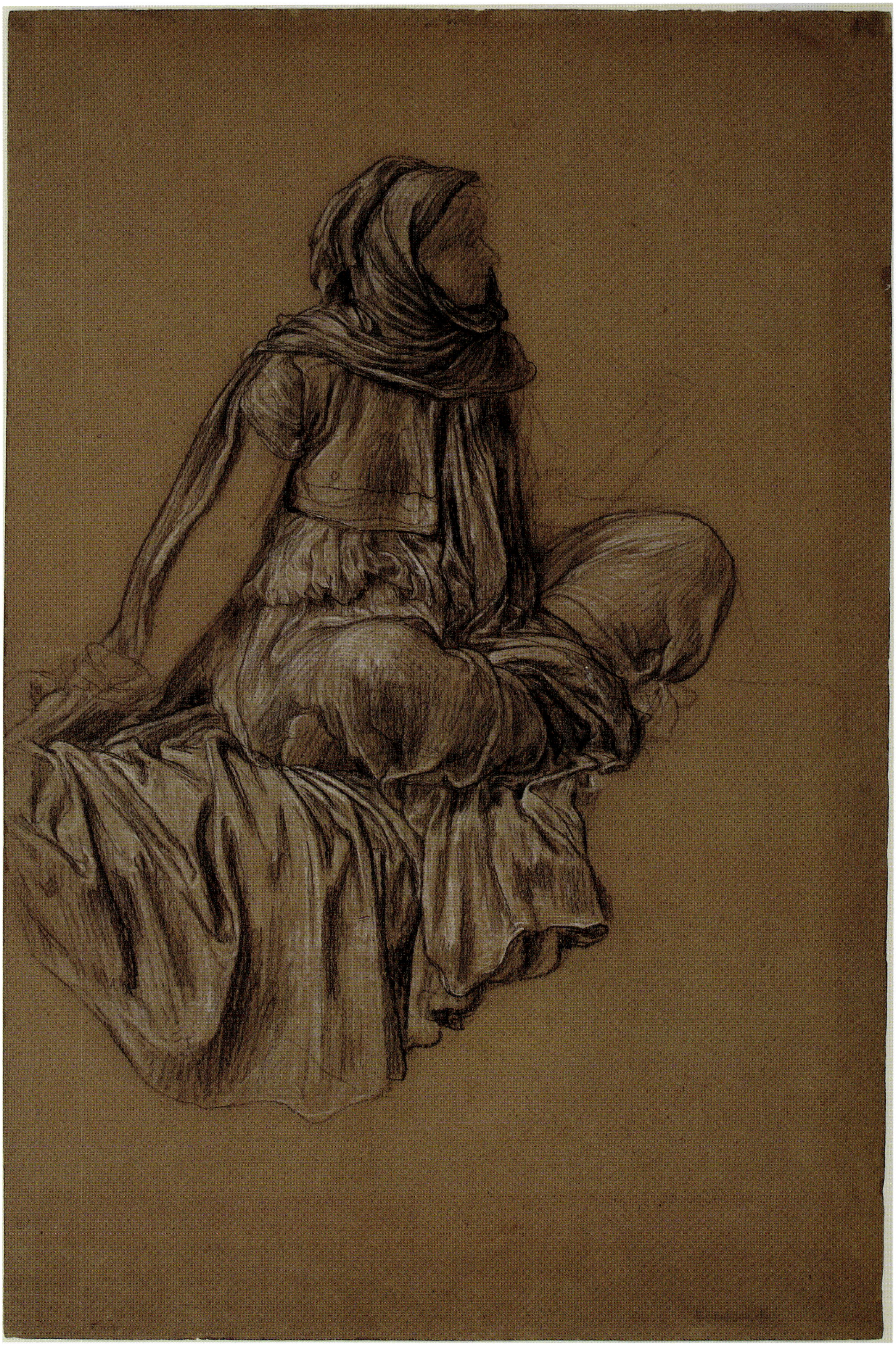

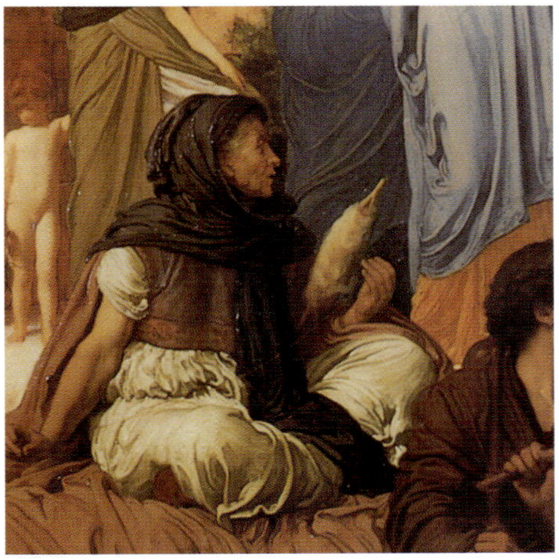

25a.

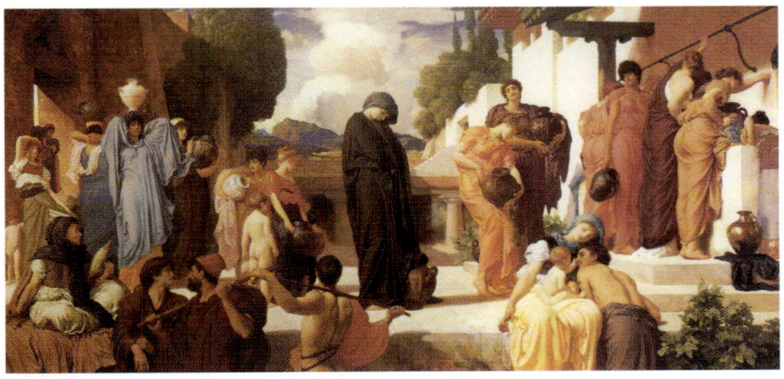

25.

cat. ill. 25. ***Captive Andromache***, RA 1888. Oil on canvas. 197 x 407 cm. Manchester Art Gallery.

cat. ill. 25a. Detail of ***Captive Andromache***.

5.9

Study for 'Captive Andromache': Drapery for Seated Female Figure, *c*.1887

Black and white chalk on brown paper

556 x 369 mm

LHO/D/0677

With its Homeric subject of Andromache enslaved in Argos, fetching water for her captors, *Captive Andromache* (cat. ill. 25) was the last of Leighton's vast processional works, which had commenced with his first great public success, *Cimabue's Celebrated Madonna*. The later painting demonstrated Leighton's continuing mastery of large-scale works embodying the ideals expected of 'high' art in the nineteenth century. The gestation period for this extraordinarily ambitious painting was long.[25] His first thoughts on the subject emerged in the early 1870s, when he made a thumbnail-sized sketch of the whole composition. Successive larger drawings of the whole subject show how the work evolved.[26] The final version of the painting was probably in hand for at least a year. It was exhibited at the Royal Academy in 1888, and after prolonged negotiations with collectors and institutions it was bought by Manchester Art Gallery.

This study is for the figure of the girl immediately to the right of Andromache (who was modelled by Dorothy Dene; her sister Lena is just behind her). The girl holds a hydria, a large three-handled jar used as a water-pitcher in the ancient world. Most of the women carry pitchers to fill with water at the well on the right of the painting. Leighton researched the shapes diligently at the British Museum and in books, and the painting includes a fascinating array of Antique types.[27] Leighton made large-scale drapery studies, like this one, for a limited number of projects, including: *Cymon and Iphigenia* (cat. no. 5.6), *Captive Andromache* and *The Return of Persephone*. The largest number was for *Captive Andromache*, of which 21 are at Leighton House Museum. These are exquisite works of art in themselves, and go far beyond the practical requirements of studies for paintings. One of the finest and most highly finished, a virtuoso study of drapery made for the figure of Andromache, was given by Leighton to the Luxembourg Museum in Paris (the French national collection of modern art). It is now in the Louvre.[28] Leighton must have regarded this as a significant honour, since he rarely parted with his drawings. It may be more than just coincidence that at this time the technology had developed to reproduce coloured chalk drawings with truth to the original. Leighton's drawings were among those featured in the *Magazine of Art* and the *Art Journal*. A colour sketch in oil of the whole composition was owned by James Stewart Hodgson.[29] The painting sold for £4,000 (although Leighton had at one point put its worth at £8,000) and was his greatest financial success. *C.G.*

INSCRIPTIONS

Stamped, lower left, 'LLC' encircled. Inscribed, lower right, 'Andromache' in graphite, by the FAS.

PROVENANCE

Bequeathed by the artist to his sisters, Mrs Augusta Matthews and Mrs Alexandra Orr; from whom purchased by the FAS in 1896; collection of Miss Helen Squire; by whom presented to RBKC in 1937.

BIBLIOGRAPHICAL REFERENCES

Staley 1906, p. 213; Ormond 1975b, p. 169 (listed under cat. no. 334); Simon 1996, ill. p. 70.

EXHIBITION HISTORY

LONDON 1900, no. 21C; **LONDON 1969**, cat. no. 41.

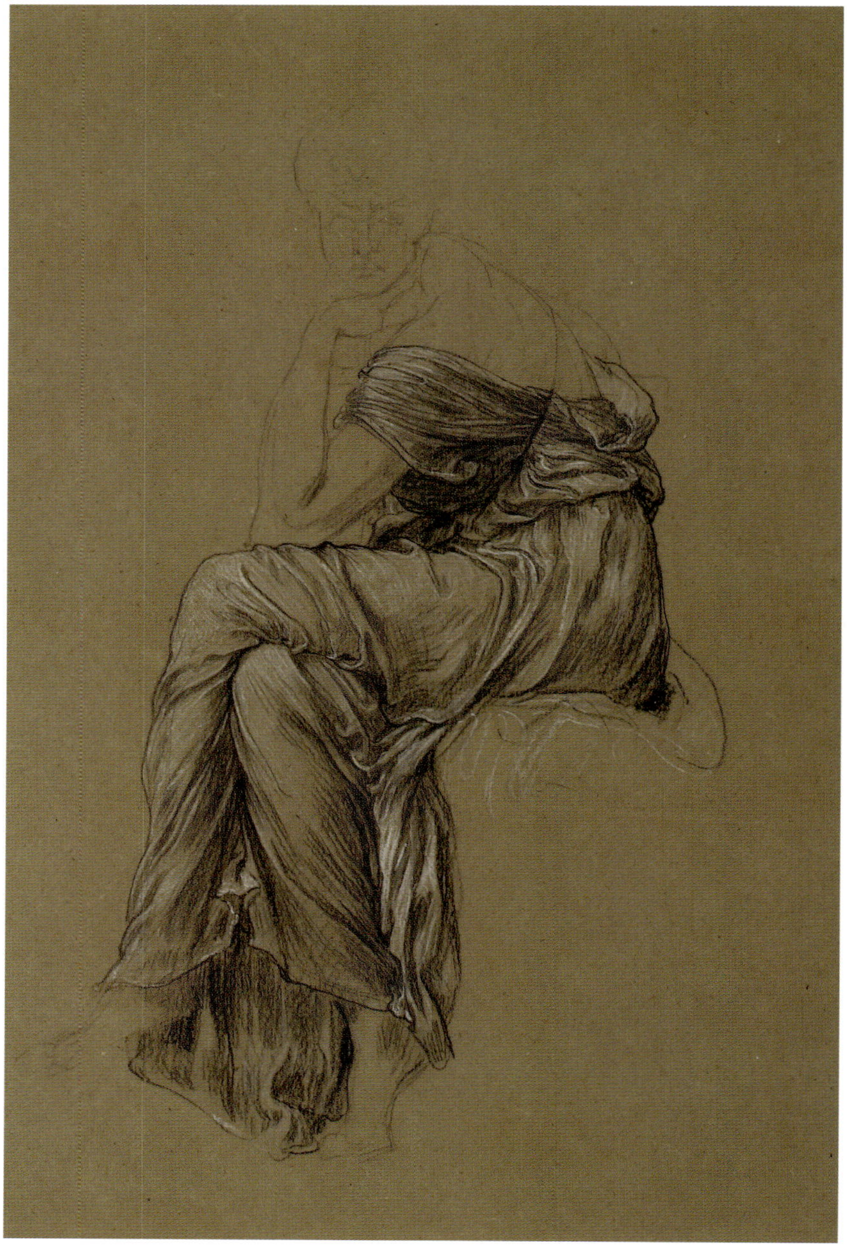

cat. ill. **26.** ***Sibyl***, RA 1889.
Oil on canvas. 152 x 89.5 cm.
Private Collection.

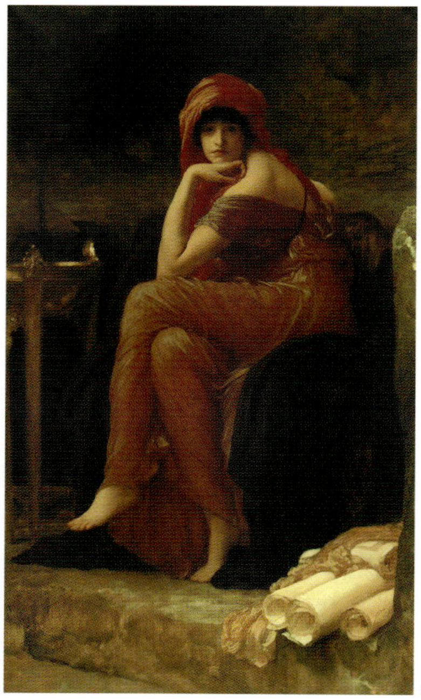

26.

5.10

Study for 'Sibyl': Drapery for Female Figure, *c.*1889

Black and white chalk on brown paper
556 x 370 mm
LHO/D/0841

This very complete drapery study is for *Sibyl* (cat. ill. 26), exhibited at the Royal Academy in 1889. The swiftly sketched head, arm and torso contrast with the carefully described folds covering solidly present limbs beneath. The painting is one of a series dating from the last decade of the artist's life, of monumental female single figures with soulful or enigmatic expressions, possibly Leighton's response to Continental Symbolism. They represent a mood or a personification of an idea. The standing muses in the central panel of the Marquand music room ceiling and the still, dark figure of Andromache in *Captive Andromache* are obvious precedents. One of this group of subjects without narrative content, *Corinna of Tanagra* (exhibited 1893), is in Leighton House Museum (purchased 1908). The Museum also owns a study for *Solitude* (1890, now in the Maryhill Museum of Art, Washington, USA), which is another seated and draped single figure of this type, close in size and mood to *Sibyl*. It has been noted that the darkness of mood and brooding spirit were new to Leighton, perhaps reflecting the pervasive spirit of Symbolism.[30] *C.G.*

INSCRIPTIONS
Stamped, lower left, 'LLC' encircled.

PROVENANCE
Bequeathed by the artist to his sisters, Mrs Augusta Matthews and Mrs Alexandra Orr; from whom purchased by the FAS in 1896.

BIBLIOGRAPHICAL REFERENCES
Spielmann 1889, ill. p. 225; Rhys 1895, ill. opp. p. xxvi; **LONDON 1969**, p. 33, cat. no. 147.

EXHIBITION HISTORY
LONDON 1969, no. 147.

NOTES

1. Sidney C. Hutchinson, *The History of the Royal Academy, 1768–1968*, Rupert Royce, London, 1986, p. 119.
2. Costa 1897, p. 378; Ormond 1975b, p. 102.
3. Spielmann 1888, p. 590.
4. Williams 1889, p. 61.
5. F.G. Dumas, *Illustrated Biographies of Modern Artists*, Chapman & Hall, London, 1882, p. 23.
6. Speilman 1888, p. 590.
7. Barrington 1906, vol. II, p. 267; see also Ormond 1975b, pp 134–38.
8. Ormond 1975b, p. 135; YORK, LONDON, NOTTINGHAM 1999, no. 70.
9. Ref. no. 25, John Ryland's Library, Manchester.
10. The story of the discovery of the Pullan girls and part they played in Leighton's life is told in Barrington 1906, vol. II, p. 267, and in Ormond 1975b, pp 133–38.
11. RIBA Library Drawings Collection, London, ref. no. SB95/1(3-4).
12. The portrait was sold to a Mrs Boink in the 1970s and inherited by her heirs, who first thought it by an artist named 'Bart' (it was signed 'Frederic Leighton, Bart'). On being shown to a fine art dealer the artist's true identity was discovered. The painting was sold on-line through Sotheby's in 2001 for a record $550,750.
13. The two letters referring specifically to the frieze are nos 12640 and 12612A in the Leighton archive.
14. M.H. Spielmann, 'The National British Gallery', *Graphic*, 17 July 1897.
15. LONDON 1996, pp 115–17.
16. Barrington 1906, vol. II, p. 258.
17. From Giovanni Boccaccio (introduction by Thomas Wright), *The Decameron or Ten Days' Entertainment of Boccaccio*, Chatto & Windus, London, 1874, p. 263.
18. *Cymon and Iphigenia, Painted by Sir F Leighton, PRA, The Story of the Picture Illustrated*, The Fine Art Society, London, 1884.
19. Barrington 1906, vol. II, p. 258.
20. See Danièlle O. Kisluk-Grosheide, 'The Marquand Mansion', *Metropolitan Museum Journal*, 29, 1994.
21. Leighton, in correspondence with Marquand, quoted by Kisluk-Grosheide, *ibid.*, pp 161–62. Their identities as Erato and Terpsichore are given in Ormond 1975b, pls 158–59, and by Newall 1990, p. 108.
22. For a page of studies of different forms of lyre, see Leighton's notebook, ref. no. LEI/35, in the Library of the Royal Academy.
23. Now in a New York private collection, repr. Ormond 1975b, pl. 157.
24. *ibid.*, fig. 20, showing a photo from the *Illustrated Catalogue of the Art and Literary Property Collected by the Late Henry G. Marquand*, New York, 1903.
25. The literature on this painting is extensive. See LONDON 1996, cat. no. 95, which includes a comprehensive bibliography.
26. See Newall 1990, fig. 47; Ian Jenkins, 'Frederic Lord Leighton and Greek Vases', *The Burlington Magazine*, no. 967, vol. CXXV, October 1983, fig. 17.
27. Ian Jenkins, *ibid.*, pp 597–605.
28. See *De Burne-Jones à Bonnard: dessins provenant du muse national d'art moderne*, Musée du Louvre, Paris, 1977, cat. no. 67.
29. Ormond 1975b, pl. II.
30. See Robert Upstone and Andrew Wilton (eds): *The Age of Rossetti, Burne-Jones and Watts, Symbolism in Britain 1860–1910*, Tate Gallery, London, 1997.

6

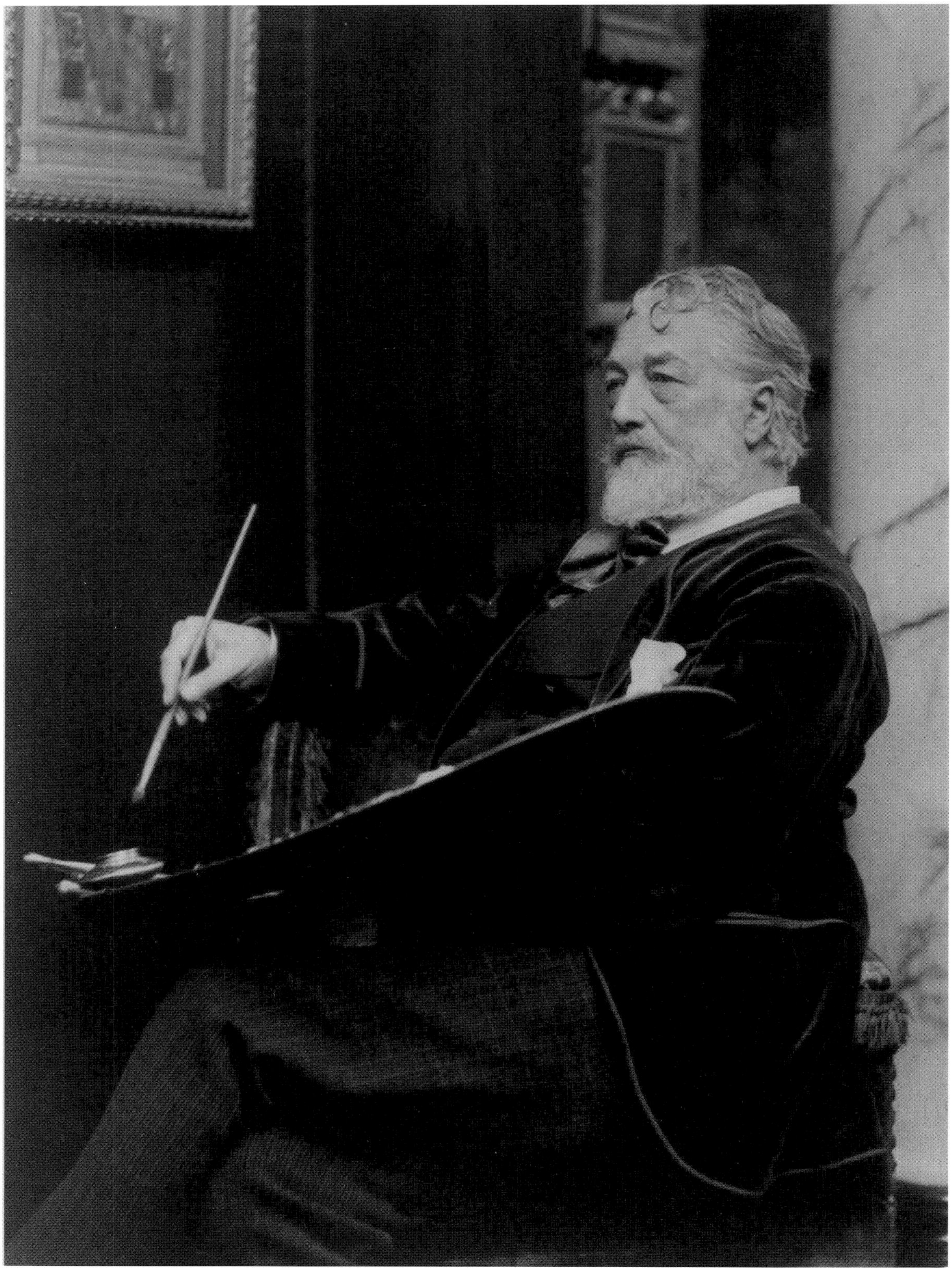

cat. ill. **27.** Photograph of Frederic Leighton, 1895. Leighton House Museum, London.

THE FINAL YEARS
1894–1896

Quick to resent, vehement in temper – as many even of his friends could testify – prompt in rebuffing any unwarranted familiarity, he was singularly ready to unbend to those in whom he could place confidence.

[Anon., *St James's Budget*, no. 814, vol. xxxii, Friday 31 January 1896, p. 6.]

By 1894 Leighton had been President of the Royal Academy for 12 years. He was a man of enormous influence and social status, and was soon to be raised to the peerage. However, he was finding the extent of his Royal Academy duties a burden. The quantity of his correspondence meant he was increasingly 'forced to use the hand of [his] secretary'.[1] He had also become something of a loner, and admitted to having a quick temper. Keen to escape from public engagements, and rigorous in guarding his private life, at times he appeared aloof and remote, leading William Powell Frith to comment: 'I've known Leighton for more than thirty years... and I don't know him yet!'.[2] In August 1894 he travelled to Germany with his younger sister Augusta for the annual Wagner festival. Later that month he visited Lindisfarne on the north east coast of England, before making his regular trips to Scotland and then to Italy.

He was becoming increasingly troubled by a heart condition, and throughout 1894 and '95 angina attacks grew more frequent. Perhaps for the first time, Leighton's travels of 1895 were not made with the primary intention of researching his Royal Academy address, sketching or visiting friends and associates, but in the hope that relaxation, warmer climates and fresh air would improve his health. In the spring he sailed from London, destined for Morocco. An onlooker described his departure 'in search of the health which his intimates knew would never be restored', a lone figure 'on the huge vessel, with not even a servant to minister to his wants'.[3] In North Africa he engaged in 'a little quiet, unconventional, but *most* enjoyable *sketching* (landscape bits) from nature'. He also made sketches of mountain ranges and local people, not with any particular purpose but, as he explained, 'it is the most irresponsible *restful* thing I can do and *fills time* delightfully'.[4] He journeyed back through France and continued to make 'a few very tidy little sketches', returning to his home in Kensington in June. Despite his health problems, Leighton worked on paintings throughout the summer, including *Perseus on Pegasus Hastening to the Rescue of Andromeda* (*c*.1895–96, Museum and Art Gallery, Leicester) and *Clytie* (*c*.1895–96, Private Collection). His drawings for them were in black and white chalk on a heavy, textured, grey-brown paper, considerably darker than the warm brown paper he had used throughout the 1880s, as though reflecting a more sombre attitude. The subjects of his final paintings are similarly darker and more emotive. The drawings of the mid-1890s are also amongst his most confident studies, and were described by Emilie Barrington as displaying 'more freedom and power of touch'.[5]

Throughout his career, Leighton was at times denigrated by the art critics. He had achieved enormous success through his art, and many of his paintings and sculptures were well received, but he also bore intense criticism, which was not diminished by his professional success. By the end of his career, condemnation of his work was so commonplace that his art could be said to have 'never received unanimous praise, or gained attachment from the general public'.[6] Despite this, Leighton remained passionate about his work and whilst engaged on *Clytie*, his last painting, he was reported to have said 'I have never had a better appetite for work; nor done better work'.[7]

In the autumn of 1895 Leighton travelled to Ireland, and made landscape and botanical studies. He then went to Italy once more, for what was to be his final tour of his most beloved country. He spent much of his time viewing works of art and enjoying the countryside, but his main purpose was to recuperate. In a letter from Paris he enthused: 'the love of what is beautiful & noble in Nature & art does not become blunter with year [sic] but rather grows & gathers warmth & glow'.[8] In November he returned to Kensington to begin a new project to paint decorative panels of the four seasons for a house in Stretford, Greater Manchester (cat. nos 6.4, 6.5), and to continue work on *Clytie*. Just two months later, on 25 January 1896, he died at his home in Holland Park Road.

When Leighton's home first opened as a museum, in 1900, A.G. Temple wrote of the display of drawings for *Clytie*: 'It is well that he left this example behind him for it shows that he had what he was least suspected of having in any marked degree, and which with singular reticence he seldom showed.'[9] As a passionate expression of emotion, the painting *Clytie* is virtually unique in his oeuvre. Passion and emotion are not qualities the artist or his paintings were known for. However, in this instance Leighton's death prevented him from covering the under painting and applying his usual high level of finish. With the strokes of the artist's brush still evident, the tragic figure of *Clytie* pleading with the sun came to symbolise the artist's own demise, and the painting remains as Leighton's one unashamedly expressive work. *P.M.*

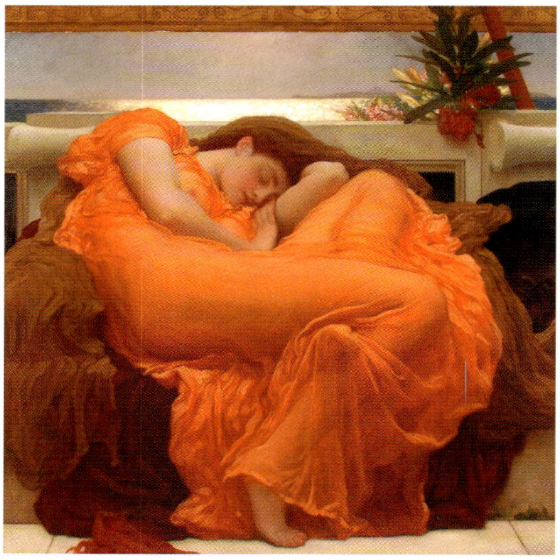

27.

cat. ill. 28. ***Flaming June***, RA 1895.
Oil on canvas. 119 x 119 cm.
Museo de Arte de Ponce, Puerto Rico.

Two Studies for 'Flaming June', *c.*1894

(Cat. 6.1 and 6.2)

The painting *Flaming June* (*c.*1895–96, Museo de Arte de Ponce, Puerto Rico; cat. ill. 28) depicts the highly saleable subject of a beautiful woman in repose, positioned within an idealised setting. She wears fiery orange, semi-transparent drapery, and is curled into a curious posture. Her body forms an almost circular shape with her left knee raised towards her bowed head. In the background, sunlight glistens on the surface of the sea, and the mood is warm and serene. The pose used for *Flaming June* probably developed from that of the central figure in Leighton's painting *The Garden of the Hesperides* (*c.*1892, Lady Lever Art Gallery, Port Sunlight), although the actual composition was first used as the design for a sculpted relief on the side of a marble bath seen in the painting *Summer Slumber* (*c.*1894, Private Collection). It has been suggested that *Flaming June* followed *Summer Slumber* as a sequel, as each deal with the same themes of sleep and serenity. Leighton claimed to have first seen the pose 'in the chance attitude of a weary model who had a peculiarly supple figure,'[10] and several of Leighton's drawings demonstrate that it was not uncommon for him to continue sketching as the model broke from a pose. However, an early study for the work (cat. no. 6.1) shows him experimenting with minor alterations to the posture, indicating that the process was rather less spontaneous than his account suggests. These may have been made before the stone relief version in *Summer Slumber* was painted.

Today, the painting has become a symbol of High Victorian Art and is widely reproduced. However, when it was exhibited at the Royal Academy in 1895 it was met with a torrent of criticism. The pose was described as 'impossible' and the anatomy of the figure thought to be incorrect – in particular, the right thigh was criticised as 'too long'. Even Leighton's biographer and staunch supporter Emilie Barrington found fault with the painting, claiming that it lacked 'direct simplicity'. However, she did admire a study in which 'the pose is better explained than in the picture, the foreshortened line of the back and shoulder being confused somewhat by the drapery in the painting'.[11] Another of Leighton's biographers, Edgcumbe Staley, felt compelled to defend the work: 'Her position has been called in question by captious critics. She is disposed, on the contrary, naturally and easily. She has merely yielded to the natural relaxation of alert muscles in repose.'[12]

The model for *Flaming June* was traditionally thought to be Leighton's close friend, Dorothy Dene, but in 1996 an article in *Apollo* magazine by Martin Postle suggested that Mary Lloyd may have been the model. Lloyd began modelling in 1893 and was used by Leighton for several paintings in his final years, including *Lachrymae* (*c.*1895, Metropolitan Museum of Art, New York) and *Twixt Hope and Fear* (*c.*1895, Private Collection). The head of the figure of *Flaming June* is similar to that of Lloyd, with her thick wavy hair and prominent jaw, although the colouring is somewhat fairer. If we are to believe that Lloyd, coming from a respectable middle-class background, would 'only pose draped or for head studies',[13] then nude studies for the painting may well have been modelled by Dene, and therefore the resulting figure could represent a combination of features from both women. *P.M.*

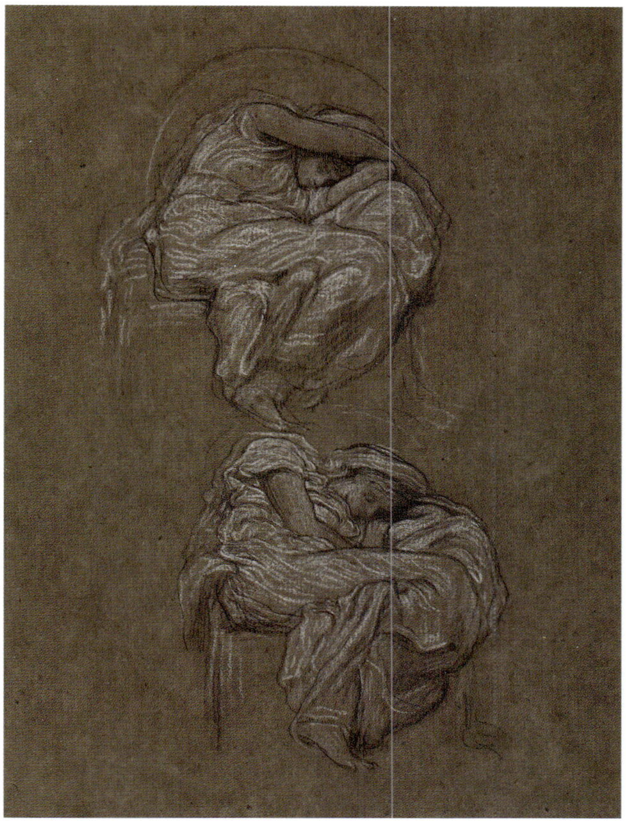

6.1

Studies for 'Flaming June': Female Figure, *c*.1894

Black and white chalk on brown paper
367 x 278 mm
LHO/D/0743

INSCRIPTIONS
Stamped, lower left, 'LLC' encircled.

PROVENANCE
Bequeathed by the artist to his sisters, Mrs Augusta Matthews and Mrs Alexandra Orr; from whom purchased by the FAS in 1896; from whom probably purchased by Matthews and Orr and presented to the LHC by 1900; transferred to RBK in 1926 (now RBKC).

BIBLIOGRAPHICAL REFERENCES
Barrington 1900, p. 161, cat. no. 1b; Ormond 1975b, p. 172 (listed under cat. no. 388) ; Staley 1906, p. 212.

EXHIBITION HISTORY
LONDON 1900, no. 1b.

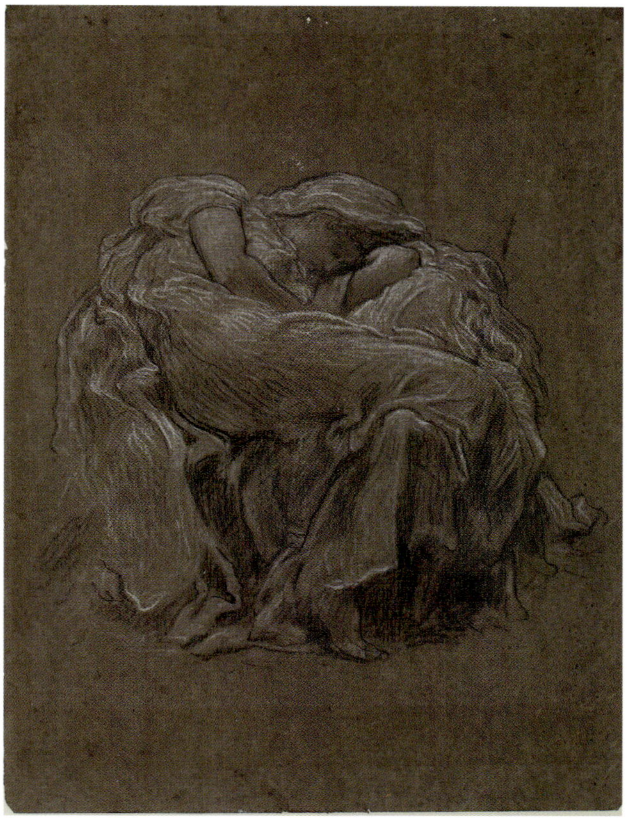

6.2

Study for 'Flaming June': Female Figure, *c*.1894

Black and white chalk on brown paper
367 x 281 mm
LHO/D/0742

INSCRIPTIONS
Stamped, lower left, 'LLC' encircled.

PROVENANCE
Bequeathed by the artist to his sisters, Mrs Augusta Matthews and Mrs Alexandra Orr; from whom purchased by the FAS in 1896; from whom purchased by Henry Percy Horne in 1897; by whom presented to the LHC by 1900; transferred to RBK in 1926 (now RBKC).

BIBLIOGRAPHICAL REFERENCES
Cockerell, 1898, pl. xxxviii; Staley 1906, p. 212; Ormond 1975b, p. 172 (listed under cat. no. 388); Simon 1996, p. 21.

EXHIBITION HISTORY
LONDON 1896, no. 200; **LONDON 1900**, no. 1c.

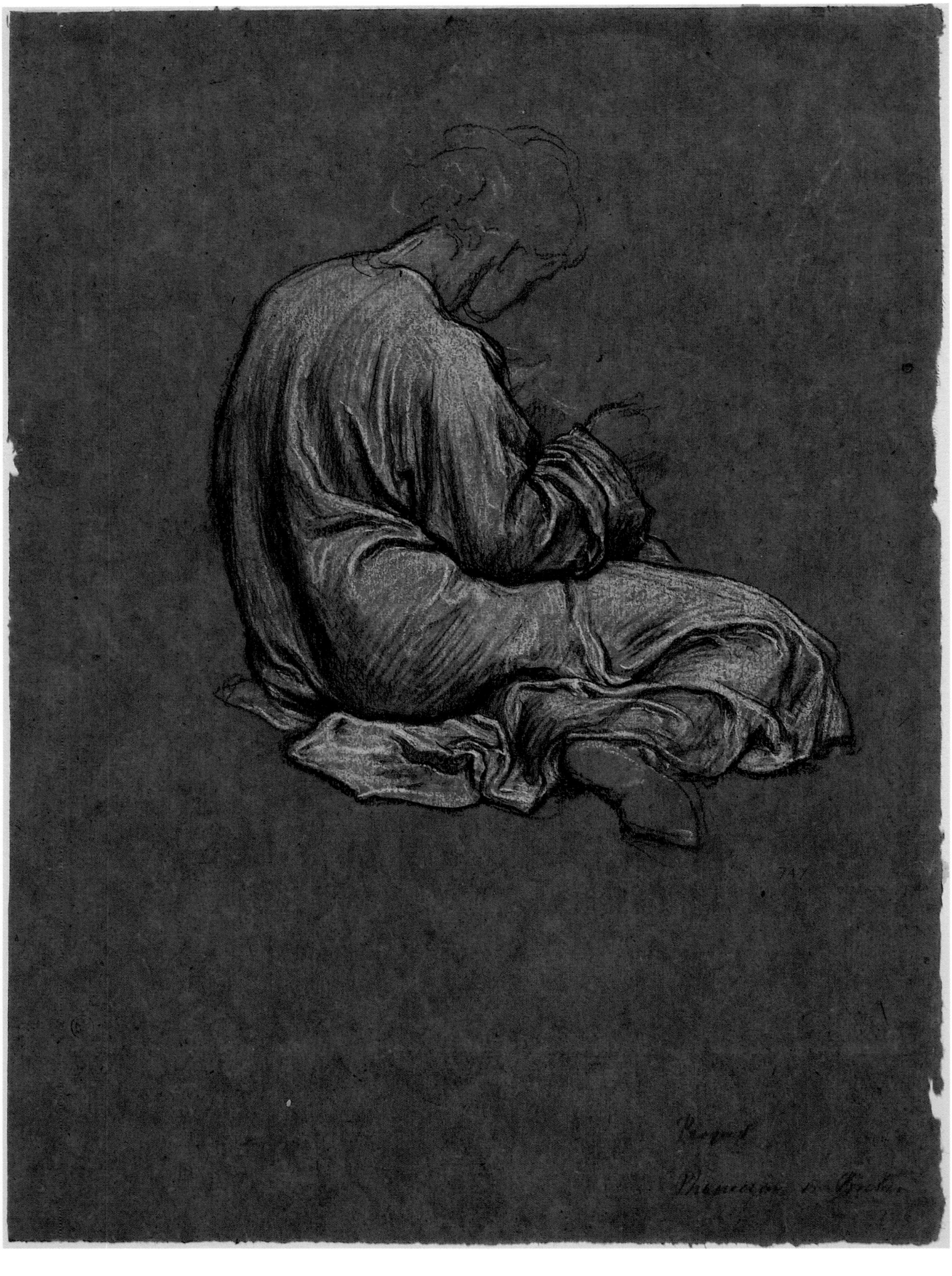

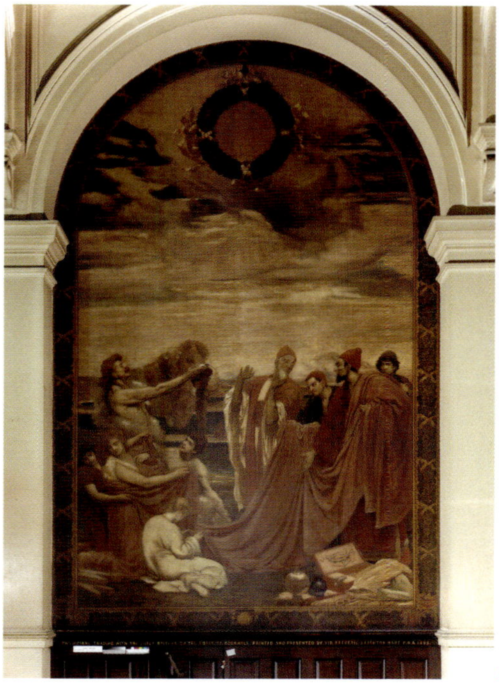

29.

cat. ill. 29. ***Phoenicians Bartering with Ancient Britons***, 1894–95.
Spirit fresco on canvas. 197 x 407 cm.
Royal Exchange, London.

cat. ill. 29a. Detail of ***Phoenicians Bartering with Ancient Britons***.

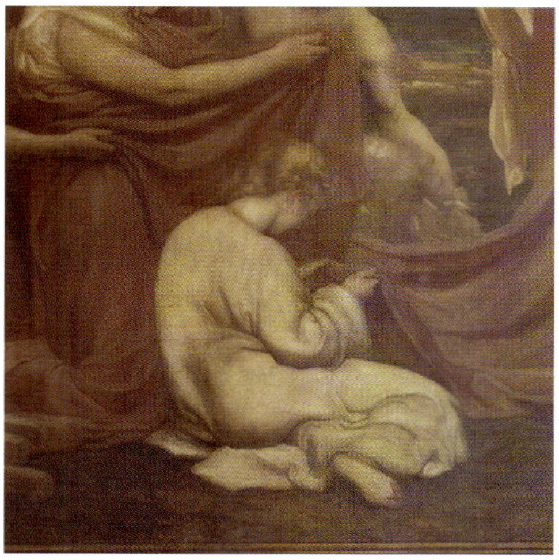

29a.

6.3

Study for 'Phoenicians Bartering with Ancient Britons': Drapery for Female Figure, *c*.1894

Black and white chalk on grey-brown paper
365 x 280 mm
LHO/D/0747

In 1891 the Mercers Company approached Leighton with the idea of commissioning paintings to decorate 24 blank panels in the corridor running around the quadrangle of London's Royal Exchange. Each panel measured approximately 22 feet high by 11 feet wide. Leighton was keen to support the proposal, and when asked to recommend artists, he offered to paint one of the panels himself for the cost of materials alone. Artists or donors were to select a subject from a list drawn up by the Gresham Committee (which manages the affairs of the Royal Exchange), based on incidents in London's history and 'the triumphs of commerce, education and liberty'.[14] Leighton chose to illustrate the triumph of commerce through the subject of the *Phoenicians Bartering with Ancient Britons* (cat. ill. 29). The painting was made onto a canvas using a specialised spirit fresco technique, attached to slate and then to the wall of the Royal Exchange.

To the left of the canvas are the British traders, with the Phoenicians on the right. A Briton holds up the animal skins he wishes to trade, and four British women inspect and wrap themselves in the fabric that the Phoenicians offer. In the centre, an elderly Phoenician raises both hands to reject the price requested for the skins. The Phoenicians were traders noted for their purple dye, and a great length of purple fabric sweeps across the lower part of the painting, connecting the Phoenicians and the Britons. The painting was also known as 'Phoenician merchants Bartering with Ancient Britons on the Coast of Cornwall' and the background is based on the Cornish coast, which Leighton had visited in 1882.

At least 20 drawings are known to have been made for the project, and almost all of these are now in the collection at Leighton House Museum. After seeing the drawings, artist William Blake Richmond remarked that 'perhaps none finer were ever made in England'.[15] The example included here is a drapery study for one of the ancient Briton women, seated on the ground, inspecting fabric.

Author and journalist Wilfred Meynell was impressed by Leighton's fervour for the project, commenting that he 'entered upon his labours with an enthusiasm and verve not often exhibited by those who have suffered the assaults and the disillusions of threescore years'. Meynell visited Leighton's studio in Holland Park Road at the time he was working on the painting, and later described the scene: 'I remember [the painting] upon its mammoth easel in the great studio... drawings and studies, done in chalk upon brown paper, lay about in dozens.'[16]

Scaffolding was built within the studio to allow Leighton to reach the top of the canvas. At this time he was suffering regular attacks of angina, which would ordinarily be worsened by physical exertion. However, Meynell recorded that Leighton continued to work with ease and, reflecting on the irony of his condition, said: 'I can work at that picture like an athlete, but when I lift a right hand to brush my hair in a hurry, I sometimes turn faint.'[17] *P.M.*

INSCRIPTIONS

Stamped, lower left, 'LLC' encircled. Inscribed, lower right, 'Project / Phoenicians & Britons' in graphite, by the FAS.

PROVENANCE

Bequeathed by the artist to his sisters, Mrs Augusta Matthews and Mrs Alexandra Orr; from whom purchased by the FAS in 1896; presented to the LHC by the Rt. Hon. Lord Loch by 1897; transferred to RBK in 1926 (now RBKC).

BIBLIOGRAPHICAL REFERENCES

Barrington 1906, vol. II, ill. opp. p. 256; Staley 1906, p. 214; Ormond 1975b, p. 172 (listed under cat. no. 381).

EXHIBITION HISTORY

LONDON 1897, no. 2 ('Studies for Panel...'); **LONDON 1900**, no. 56e; **LONDON 1969**, no. 70.

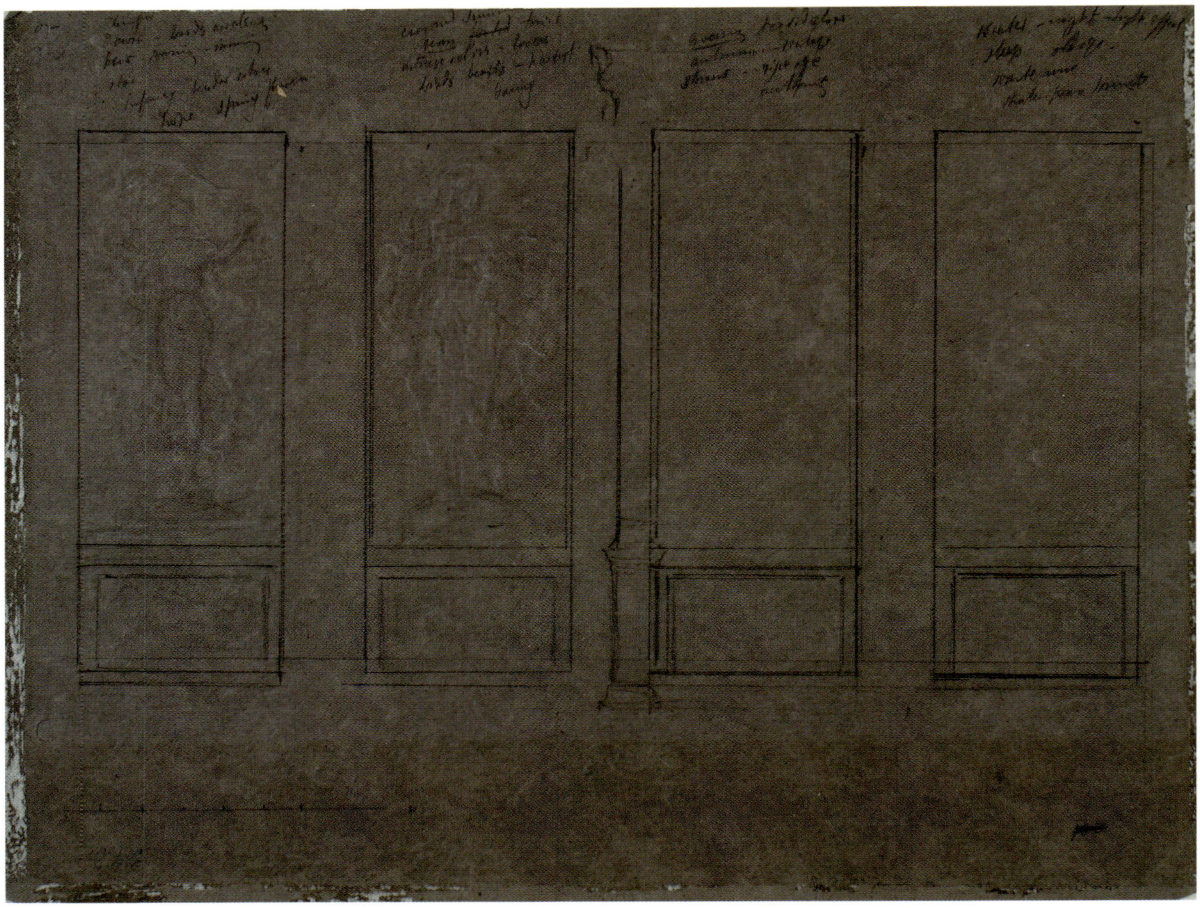

Two Studies for Decorative Panels for Longford Hall, Stretford, *c.*1895

(Cat. nos 6.4 and 6.5)

Mrs Enriqueta Rylands was the widow of the Manchester based cotton manufacturer, John Rylands. She lived at Longford Hall, Stretford, in Greater Manchester. Her husband had taken over the firm of Rylands & Sons, established by his father, and by 1873 it was the largest textile manufacturer in the country. When John Rylands died in 1888 he had no heirs, and his multi-million pound fortune was left to his wife.

On 4 August 1895 Enriqueta wrote to Leighton to enquire if he would accept a commission to paint a series of 'single symbol figures', for four blank panels at Longford Hall. Leighton's dismissive reply is dictated to a secretary and written in the third person: 'He is, as a rule, extremely unwilling to accept commissions, as he finds himself entirely unable to work satisfactorily in lines laid down for him by anybody else.'[18] However, he concluded the letter with a request for information on the dimensions of the panels and the desired subject for them. Enriqueta's reply gave the dimensions as ten feet six inches high and four feet four inches wide, and explained that she had considered the four seasons or four virtues as the subject, but was willing to leave the decision to Leighton, asserting one stipulation: 'that the figures shall be draped'.[19]

The freedom that she offered Leighton reassured him, and a fee of £1,200 each – including copyright – for four canvases representing the four seasons was agreed. Leighton requested that all the works be exhibited together at the Royal Academy in 1897. In November, after returning from a leisurely tour of Italy, taken in the vain hope of improving his health, Leighton began work on the designs. They would be the last drawings he ever made.

John Cassidy, a sculptor working on a statue of Mrs Rylands at the time, remembered her disappointment that Leighton had died having 'never got beyond making two large drawings or sketches, which had met with her approval.'[20] This suggests that she carried out her offer to visit Leighton's studio for 'an interview', and was shown the early drawings for thedesign. In fact Leighton completed at least six drawings for the panels before his death in January 1896, many of which are now in private collections.

A drawing showing the panels at Longford Hall, including a column that stands between them, was probably made by Leighton from a photograph sent to him by Enriqueta (cat. no. 6.4). Leighton has delicately sketched initial ideas for two of the figures into the panels, and has also made notes of words or phrases that evoke each of the seasons. A second sheet of studies shows three female figures believed to represent autumn (on the left) and summer (cat. no. 6.5). *P.M.*

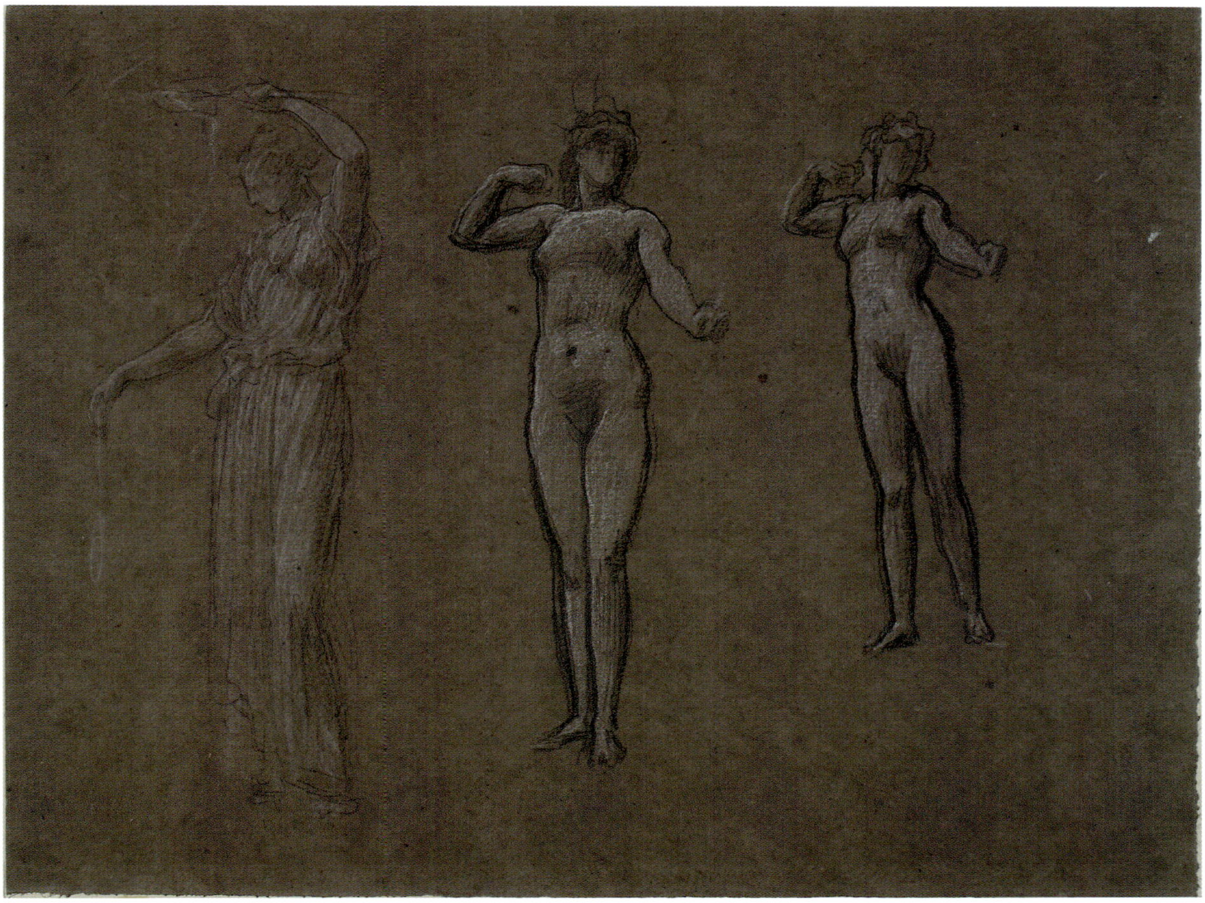

6.4

Study for Decorative Panels for Longford Hall, Stretford: Rough Compositions within Architectural Setting, *c.*1895

Black and white chalk on grey-brown paper
280 x 368 mm
LHO/D/0846

INSCRIPTIONS

Inscribed, upper left, '[illegible] / Dawn – birds awakening / Dew – morning – morning / star / infancy tender colours / hope spring flowers' in black chalk, in the artist's hand. Upper centre, left, 'crossed Summer / Noon [illegible] [illegible] / intense colours – lovers / birds beasts – harvest / dancing' and, upper centre, right, 'Evening [illegible] g ow / autumn – vintage / straw ripe age / [illegible]' in black chalk, in the artist's hand. Upper right, 'Winter – night – light effect / sleep old age – / Dante [illegible] / Shakespeare Sonnet' in black chalk, in the artist's hand. Stamped, lower left, 'LLC' encircled.

PROVENANCE

Bequeathed by the artist to his sisters, Mrs Augusta Matthews and Mrs Alexandra Orr; from whom purchased by the FAS in 1896; from whom probably purchased by Matthews and Orr and presented to the LHC by 1900; transferred to RBK in 1926 (now RBKC).

BIBLIOGRAPHICAL REFERENCES

Staley 1906, p. 223.

EXHIBITION HISTORY

LONDON 1900, no. 336.

6.5

Studies for Decorative Panels for Longford Hall, Stretford: Female Figures, *c.*1895

Black and white chalk on grey-brown paper
279 x 371 mm
LHO/D/0787

INSCRIPTIONS

Stamped, lower left, 'LLC' encircled.

PROVENANCE

Bequeathed by the artist to his sisters, Mrs Augusta Matthews and Mrs Alexandra Orr; from whom purchased by the FAS in 1896; from whom purchased by Douglas Freshfield in 1897; presented to the LHC by Freshfield by 1900; transferred to RBK in 1926 (now RBKC).

BIBLIOGRAPHICAL REFERENCES

LONDON 1896, p. 30, cat. no. 239; Barrington 1900, p. 190, cat. no. 268; Corkran 1904, ill. opp. p. 163.

EXHIBITION HISTORY

LONDON 1896, no. 239; **LONDON 1900**, no. 268.

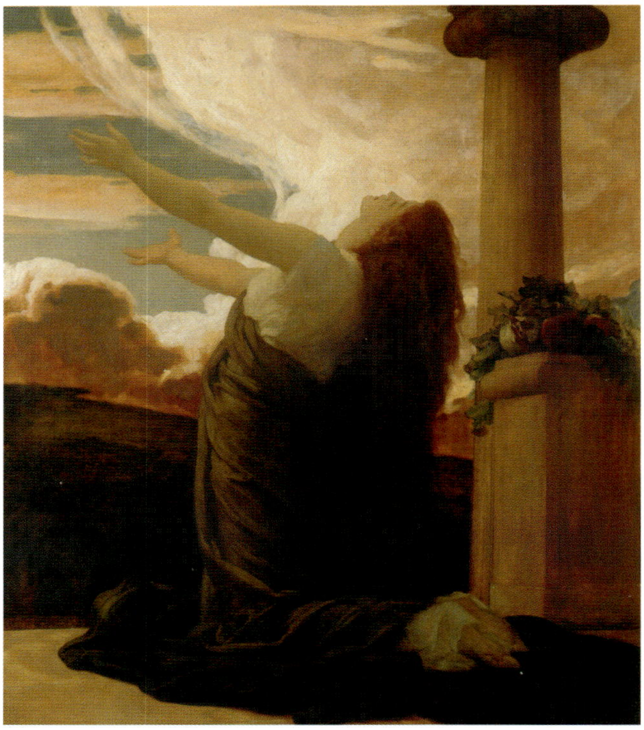

30.

cat. ill. 30. ***Clytie***, RA 1896.
Oil on canvas. 156 x 137 cm.
Private Collection.

Five Studies for 'Clytie'
(Cat. nos 6.6, 6.7, 6.8, 6.9 and 6.10)

Leighton painted two works entitled *Clytie*. Both represent the story of the Roman mythological figure of Clytie (Clytia) taken from Ovid's *Metamorphoses*. Having been scorned by her former love, Apollo, god of the sun, she gazed at the sun in grief for nine days, without food or drink. Eventually the gods took pity on her and transformed her into a flower (in some accounts a sunflower), which turned to face the sun each day.

Leighton chose to represent the tragic figure kneeling and looking up at the sun, with arms stretched out before her in a gesture of pleading. Beside her is a plinth laden with fruit and a column. The first version of *Clytie*, essentially a skyscape with a small depiction of the figure and including a statue of Apollo surmounting the column, was exhibited at the Royal Academy in 1892 and was still in Leighton's possession when he died. There are at least 12 surviving studies for the two projects, although which drawing relates to which version of the painting is not easy to establish. A sheet of studies undoubtedly for the earlier painting show Leighton experimenting with alternative poses for the figure (cat. no. 6.6). The larger sketch shows the model kneeling, with outstretched arms, and was probably the first on the sheet to be made. However, Leighton continued to experiment with the pose before settling on this one. The warm brown paper used for this study was replaced in *c.*1892 by a darker grey-brown paper, another indicator that the drawing relates to the earlier painting.

In 1895 Leighton began work on a second version of the painting, this time focusing on the figure of Clytie herself. The same pose for the figure was adopted, and the composition is essentially an enlargement of a detail from the lower right corner of the earlier work. However, for such a large-scale painting with the figure as the main focus, further studies from the model were required including a nude study for Clytie (cat. no. 6.7). These were made on the grey-brown paper Leighton began using in *c.*1892. The model for this painting (and probably for the earlier version) was Dorothy Dene.

It is entirely appropriate that Dene should have modelled for this, Leighton's last major painting. When the drawings were made Dene was 36 years old, 30 years younger than the artist. She had been Leighton's model and a close friend for about 16 years, and would later be one of a select group of people permitted to visit the artist on his deathbed. After Leighton's death £5,000 was presented to Dene by his sisters, and a further £5,000 was used to set up a Trust to support her and her siblings, according to Leighton's last wishes.

In the later painting, Leighton depicted Dene as a red-head. He rarely felt the necessity to make studies of hair, but in this case the long, red hair of Clytie is one of the most important features of the painting (see cat. no. 6.9). The drawing was exhibited by the Fine Art Society in 1896 after Leighton's death, and was one of 40 plates in a volume of reproductions of Leighton drawings published by the Society.[21]

Occasionally during Leighton's career the pose of a single figure troubled the artist and numerous studies were made (for example the many studies of the figure of Elijah for *Elijah in the Wilderness*, cat. nos 4.2–4.7). In this case Leighton struggled with the position of the head and neck of Clytie. There are four studies at Leighton House for this detail alone. In the completed painting the head of Clytie is tilted even further back than in this example, intensifying the sense of her resignation (cat. no. 6.8). Leighton's final study for the painting was a drawing of the complete design, which was then traced and squared up in order to transfer the composition

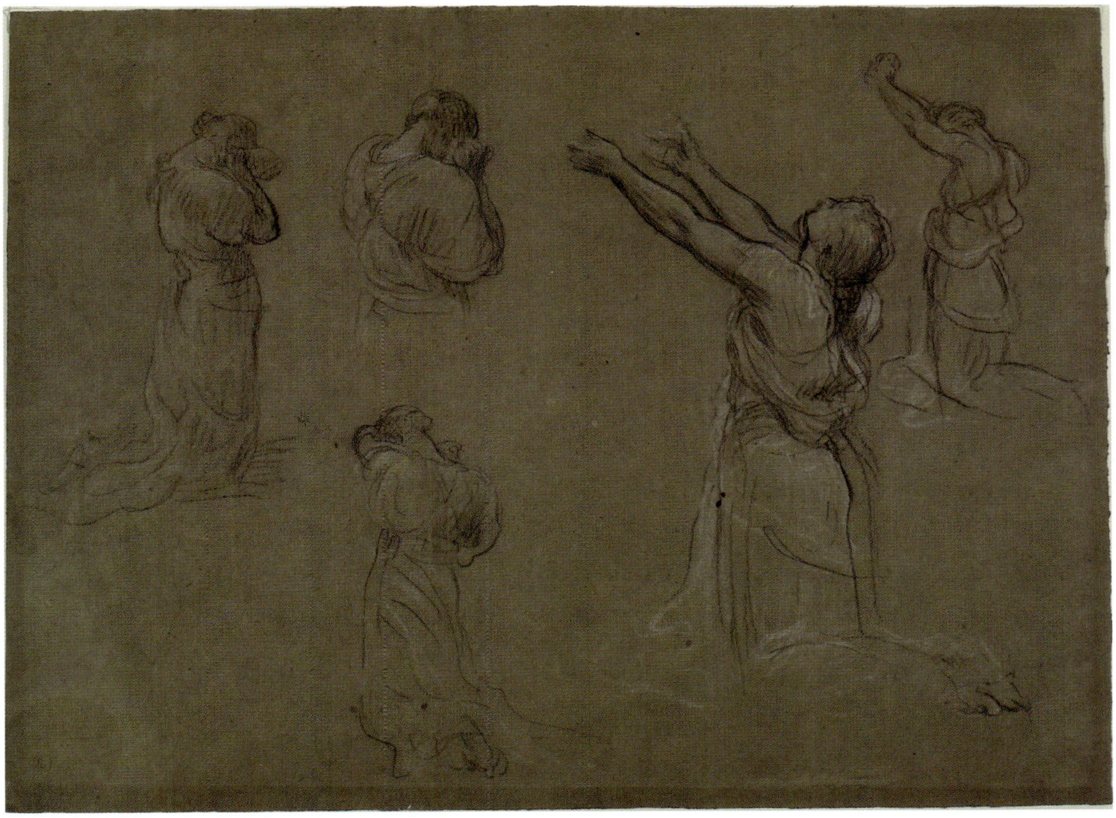

onto the canvas (cat. no. 6.10). The tracing is now in the collection of the Royal Academy (ref. no. 04/709).

The pose of Clytie and the entire composition of the painting are strikingly similar to Leighton's earliest design for an illustration to Elizabeth Barrett Browning's *Ariadne in Naxos*, made in 1860 (published in the *Cornhill Magazine*). At least two drawings for his illustration of Ariadne were in his possession when he died and, as Leighton frequently referred to his own earlier drawings as inspiration for new works, Clytie may have been partly inspired by the Ariadne design.[22]

To his relief, despite his heart condition, Leighton was able to remain productive throughout 1894 and 1895, commenting: 'Thank God, I have neither the distaste nor inability to work'.[23] He remained determined not to be swayed from his chosen path by the critics, and Joseph Comyns Carr noted the 'courage and devotion which he exhibited in his life as an artist'.[24] However, assaults from critics – levelled at his work and his abilities – had rocked his confidence. When asked if he would consider halting work on a painting in preference for its unfinished state, Leighton's reply was astonishingly self-deprecating: 'I shall certainly try to finish it, and shall probably spoil it. I am not a great painter… and it is seldom that I do not fail.'[25] Negative comments from the critics must have been all the more debasing for a public figurehead in such an esteemed position in the art world, who had achieved and continued to achieve enormous success. Despite his defiant devotion to his own ideals in art, and his long established method of working, they affected him deeply.

After his death Emilie Barrington compared the 'passionate appealing figure of Clytie' to Leighton's design for *Giotto as a Shepherd Boy* drawn almost 50 years earlier (cat. no. 1.1). She argued that whilst the earlier drawing represents 'the dreamy half conscious of the awakening artist-nature', the final painting of *Clytie*, made at the end of his life, after Leighton was fully aware of the serious nature of his heart complaint, represents a 'passionate longing to remain in the rich existence' of his profession.[26] *P.M.*

6.6

Studies for 'Clytie': Early Poses, c.1891

Black and white chalk on brown paper
236 x 325 mm
LHO/D/0762

INSCRIPTIONS

Stamped, lower left, 'LLC' encircled. Inscribed, lower right, 'Clytie' in graphite, by the FAS.

PROVENANCE

Bequeathed by the artist to his sisters, Mrs Augusta Matthews and Mrs Alexandra Orr; from whom purchased by the FAS in 1896, possibly acquired by the LHC by 1897; transferred to RBK in 1926 (now RBKC).

BIBLIOGRAPHICAL REFERENCES

Barrington 1906, vol. II, ill. opp. p. 268.

EXHIBITION HISTORY

Possibly **LONDON 1897**, no. 5 ('Drawings of Clytie'); **LONDON 1900**, no. 27c.

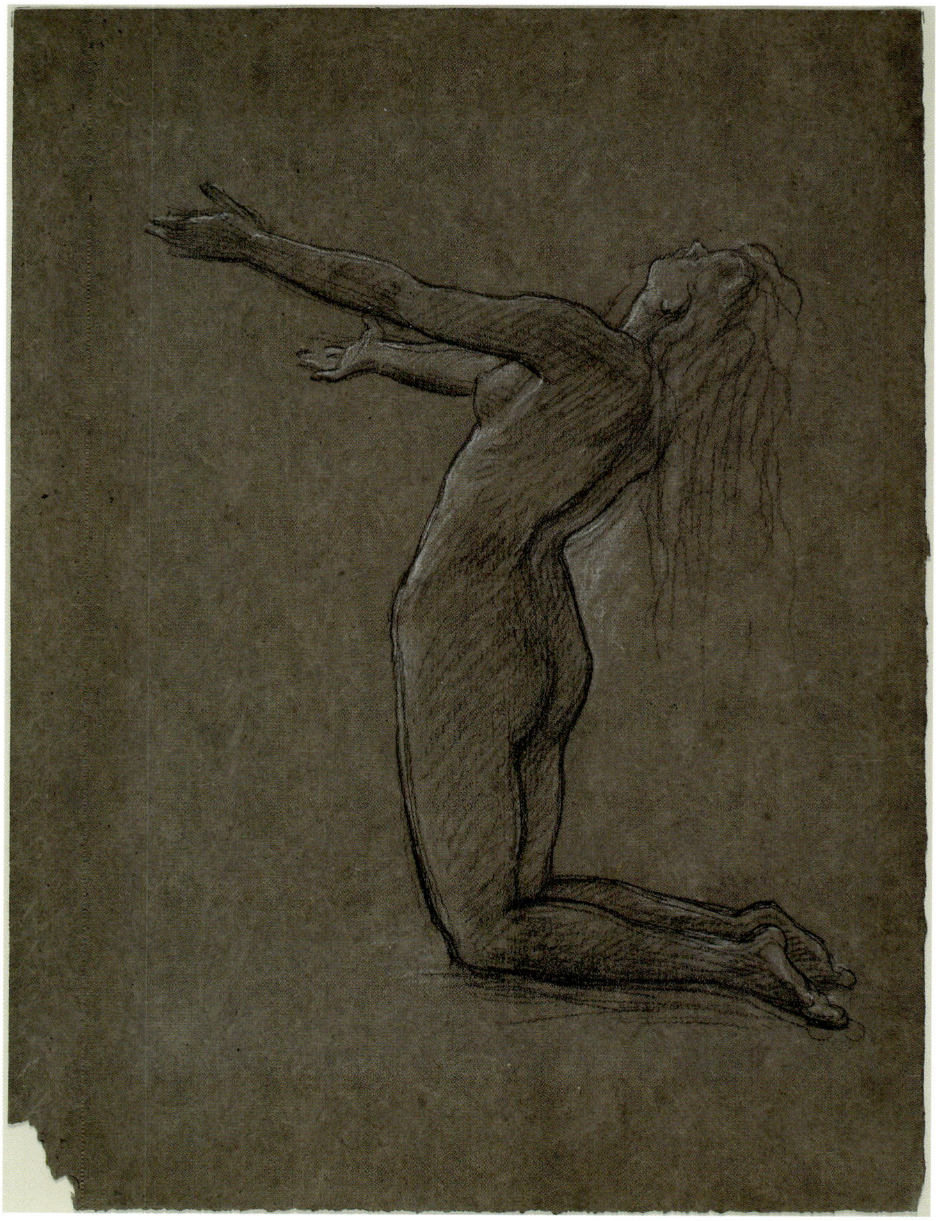

6.7

Study for 'Clytie': Nude Figure, *c.*1895

Black and white chalk on grey-brown paper
365 x 277 mm
LHO/D/0706

INSCRIPTIONS
Stamped, lower left, 'LLC' encircled.

PROVENANCE
Bequeathed by the artist to his sisters, Mrs Augusta Matthews and Mrs Alexandra Orr; from whom purchased by the FAS in 1896; acquired by the LHC by 1897; transferred to RBK in 1926 (now RBKC).

BIBLIOGRAPHICAL REFERENCES
Staley 1906, p. 213; **LONDON 1969**, p. 30, cat. no. 132; Ormond 1975b, p. 173 (listed under cat. no. 396).

EXHIBITION HISTORY
Possibly **LONDON 1897**, no. 3 ('Drawings of Clytie'); **LONDON 1900**, no. 27d; **LONDON 1969**, no. 132.

6.8

Study for 'Clytie': Head, *c.*1895

Black and white chalk on grey-brown paper
264 x 225 mm
LHO/D/0707

PROVENANCE
Possibly acquired by the LHC by 1897, or possibly presented to RBKC by T.C. Sandercock in 1958.

BIBLIOGRAPHICAL REFERENCES
Ormond 1975b, p. 173 (listed under cat. no. 396).

EXHIBITION HISTORY
Possibly **LONDON 1897**, p. 24 no. 2 (Drawings for 'Clytie')

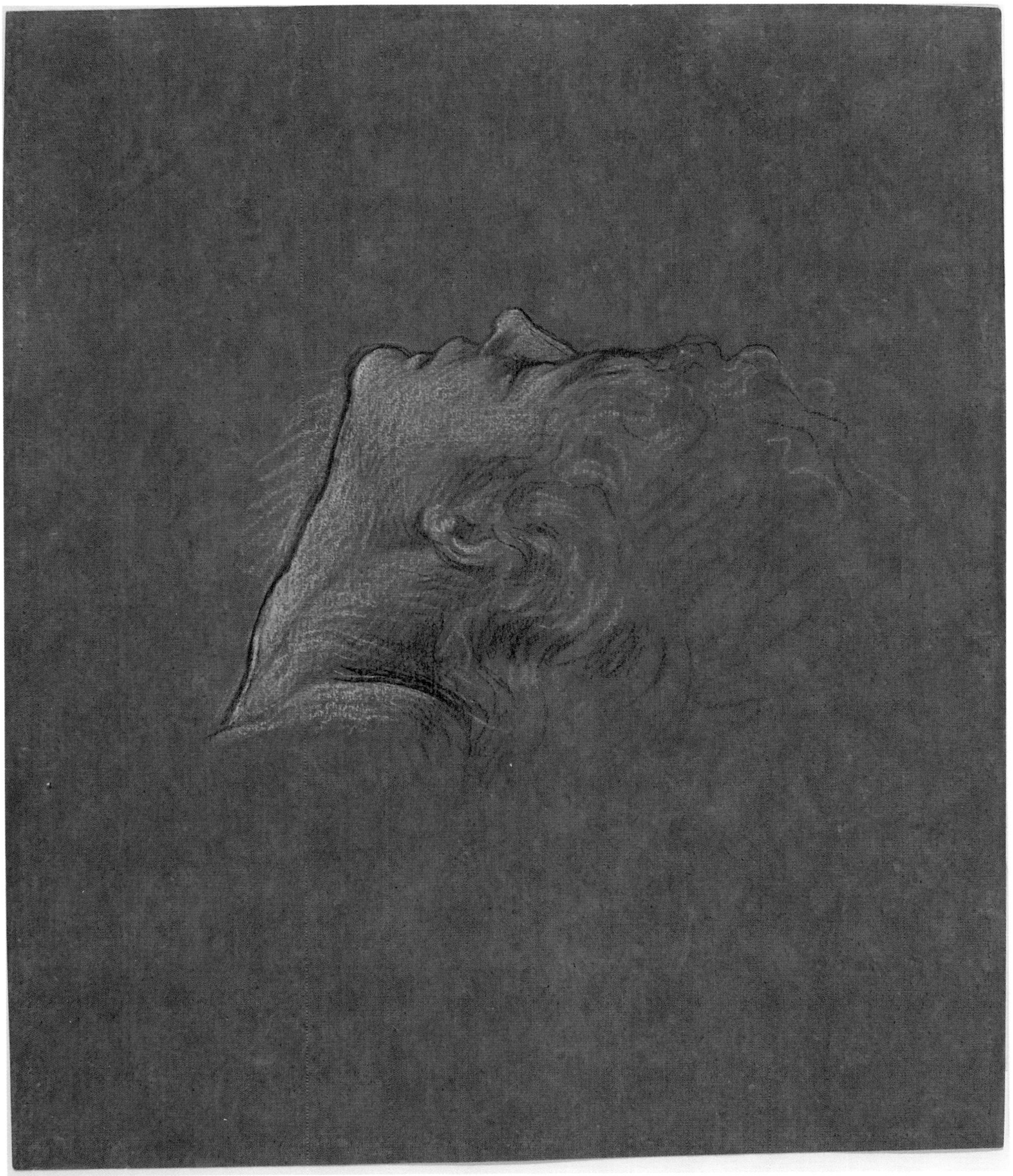

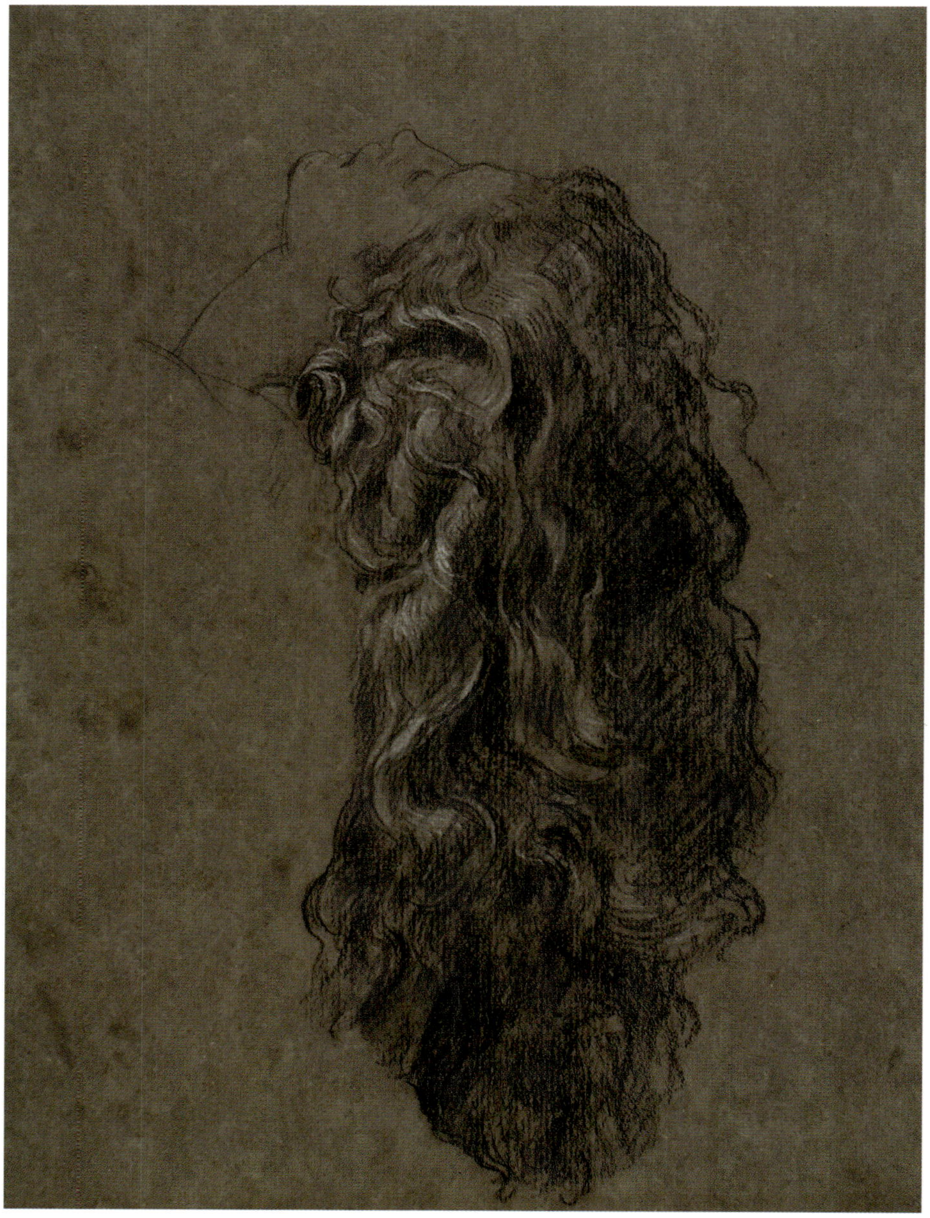

6.9

Study for 'Clytie': Hair, *c.*1895

Black and white chalk on grey-brown paper
365 x 275 mm
LHO/D/0713

INSCRIPTIONS
Stamped, lower left, 'LLC' encircled.

PROVENANCE
Bequeathed by the artist to his sisters, Mrs Augusta Matthews and Mrs Alexandra Orr; from whom purchased by the FAS in 1896; purchased by the LHC by 1897, transferred to RBK in 1926 (now RBKC).

BIBLIOGRAPHICAL REFERENCES
Cockerell 1898, pl. xxxix; Corkran 1904, ill. opp. p.162; Staley 1906, p. 213; Ormond 1975b, p. 173 (listed under cat. no. 396).

EXHIBITION HISTORY
LONDON 1896, no. 235; **LONDON 1897**, no. 24 ('Drawings for Clytie'); **LONDON 1900**, no. 27b; **LONDON 1969**, no. 52.

6.10

Study for 'Clytie': Composition, *c.*1895

Black and white chalk on grey-brown paper
183 x 161 mm
The British Museum (1897, 0512.25)

INSCRIPTIONS
Stamped, lower left, 'LLC' encircled.

PROVENANCE
Bequeathed by the artist to his sisters, Mrs Augusta Matthews and Mrs Alexandra Orr; from whom purchased by the FAS in 1896; from whom purchased by the British Museum in 1897.

BIBLIOGRAPHICAL REFERENCES
Staley 1906, p. 225; Ormond 1975b, p. 173 (listed under cat. no. 396); Newall 1990, p. 128, fig. 88.

EXHIBITION HISTORY
LONDON (RA) 1897, cat. no. 288; **LONDON 1901**, no. B 276.

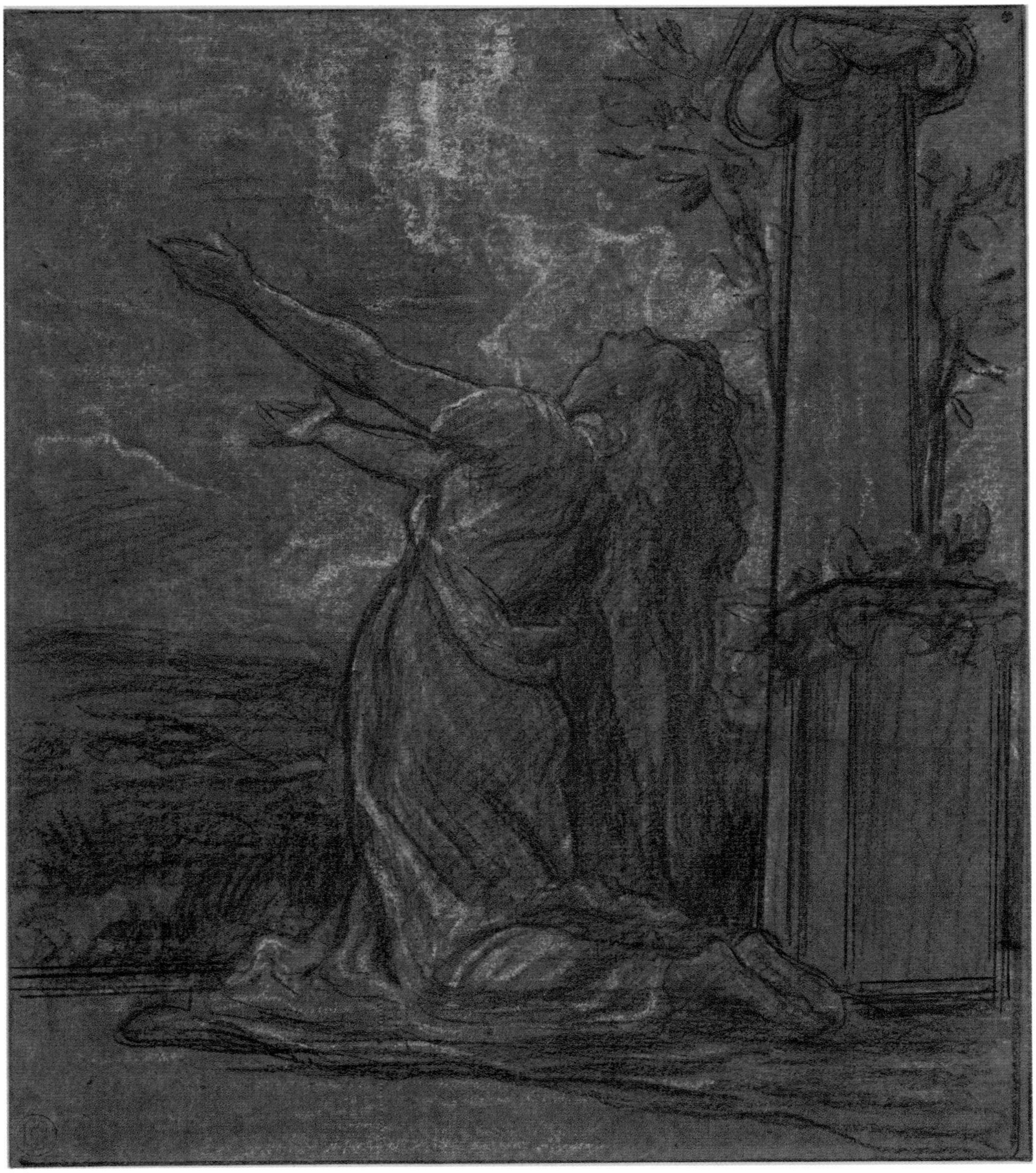

NOTES

1. Letter from Frederic, Lord Leighton to J.H. Nunn, dated 27 July 1894, Leighton House Archives, ref. no. LH/1/5/178.
2. Marion Harry Spielmann, 'The Late Lord Leighton P.R.A.', *Graphic*, 1 February 1896, p. 134.
3. Anon., 'Lord Leighton', *St James's Budget*, no. 810, vol. xxxii, 31 January 1896, p.8
4. Letter from Leighton to George Frederic Watts, 2 June 1895, Algiers, Leighton House Archives, ref. no. LH/1/1/74; letter from Leighton to Mary Watts, 2 November 1895, Paris, Leighton House Archives, ref. no. LH/1/1/80.
5. Barrington, 1906, vol. II, p. 263.
6. Richmond 1896, p. 465.
7. Corkran 1904, p. 162.
8. Letter from Leighton to Mary Watts, 2 November 1895, Paris, Leighton House Archives, ref. no. LH/1/1/80.
9. A.G. Temple, *Leighton House: Brief Notice of the Work of the Late Lord Leighton, as Illustrated by the Studies now Permanently on View at the Leighton House*, London, 1900, p. 20.
10. Staley 1906, p. 159.
11. Barrington 1906, pp 262–63.
12. Staley 1906, p. 158.
13. Simon 1996, pp 27–29; Simon Toll, *Herbert Draper 1863–1920: A Life Study*, Antique Collector's Club, 2003, pp 74–75.
14. Wilfred Meynell, 'The Pictures in the Royal Exchange', *Windsor Magazine*, May 1904, p. 702.
15. Wilfred Meynell, 'The Pictures in the Royal Exchange', *Windsor Magazine*, May 1904, p. 700.
16. *ibid.*
17. *ibid.*
18. Letter from Leighton to Enriqueta Rylands (dictated), dated 5 August 1895, The John Rylands University Library, Manchester. Ref. no. Rylands English Ms 380/1235.
19. Copy of a letter from Enriqueta Rylands to Leighton, 7 August 1895, John Rylands Library Archive, ref. no. JRL/5/2/1/5, The John Rylands University Library, The University of Manchester.
20. Cassidy, John, 'The Late Mrs Rylands: Doubts as to Bequests', *Manchester City News*, 22 February 1908.
21. Cockerell 1898.
22. Ormond 1975b, p. 58.
23. Anon., 'Lord Leighton', *St James's Budget*, no. 810, vol. xxxii, 31 January 1896, p. 6.
24. Comyns Carr 1908, p. 99.
25. Anon., 'Lord Leighton', *St James's Budget*, no. 810, vol. xxxii, 31 January 1896, p. 8.
26. Barrington 1906, vol. II, p. 378.

HANDLIST OF THE LEIGHTON DRAWINGS COLLECTION

The following list is organised by subject and then in reference number order. Drawings relating to finished works are commonly dated to circa the year before the work was first exhibited or known to have been completed. There are some exceptions to this rule. For example, a single sheet may include studies for several paintings and in this instance, the sheet is dated to the year before the exhibition of the earliest work. In some cases, such as *And the Sea Gave Up the Dead Which Were in It*, *The Arts of Industry as Applied to War*, *The Arts of Industry as Applied to Peace*, *Captive Andromache* and Illustrations for the Dalziels' *Bible Gallery*, preparatory drawings are known to have been made a considerable time before the related finished work and are dated accordingly. Further discussion of the dating of these studies is given in relevant catalogue entries.

Rather than assigning speculative dates, drawings which cannot be identified with any certainty and which do not appear to relate to any known painting are dated to the period of time when Leighton was working almost exclusively on a particular paper type. However, the on-line catalogue of the collection may include tentative links between studies and finished works that suggest more precise datings.

The on-line catalogue of the Leighton Drawings Collection is at:
www.rbkc.gov.uk/leightonhousemuseum/drawings

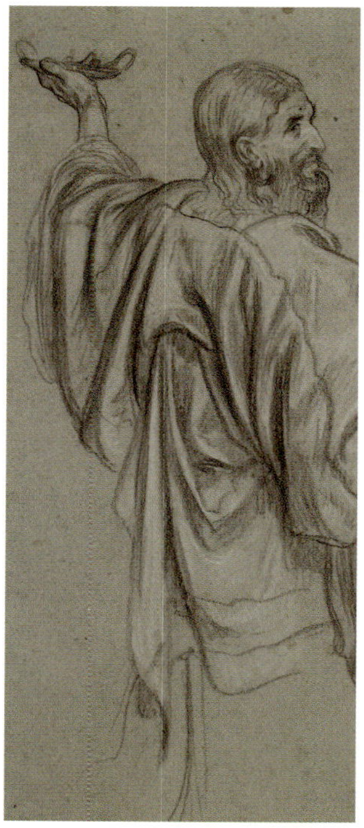

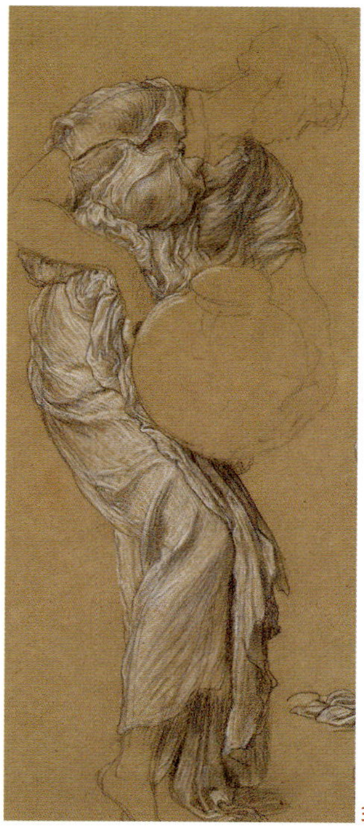

31 and 32.

cat. ill. **31.** Detail of ***Study for 'The Star of Bethlehem': Male Figure with Lamp***, *c.*1861. Black and white chalk on blue paper, LHO/D/0751.

cat. ill. **32.** Detail of ***Study for 'Captive Andromache': Drapery for Female Figures***, *c.*1887. Black and white chalk on brown paper, LHO/D/0683.

ARCHITECTURAL STUDIES

Ca' D'Oro, Venice, 1856
Graphite and watercolour on white paper
273 x 301 mm
LHO/D/0428

Santa Maria della Salute, Venice, 1850–60
Graphite on white paper
26 x 426 mm
LHO/D/0921

Architectural Ornament, 1852–55
Graphite on white paper
296 x 234 mm
LHO/D/0966

Cardinal of Portugal's Chapel in San Miniato, Including Study after a Fresco by Alesso Baldovinetti, Florence, Italy, 1852
Watercolour on white paper
394 x 296mm
LHO/D/0968

House, Possibly in Austria, 1845–52
Graphite on white paper
132 x 224 mm
LHO/D/1034

BOTANICAL STUDIES

Cyclamen Flowers, Tivoli, 1856
Graphite on white paper
162 x 95 mm
LHO/D/0978
(fig. 5)

Crocus, Boboli Gardens, Florence, 1856
Graphite on white paper
162 x 97 mm
LHO/D/0979

Aloes, *c.*1854
Graphite on white paper
95 x 163 mm
LHO/D/0980

Thistle and a Shrub, *c.*1856
Graphite on white paper
162 x 97 mm
LHO/D/0981

Bramble, *c.*1856
Graphite on white paper
97 x 162 mm
LHO/D/0982

Foliage with Flower, 1890–96
Silverpoint on white paper
130 x 92 mm
LHO/D/0983

Foliage, 1850–60
Graphite on white paper
135 x 85 mm
LHO/D/0984

Foliage, 1867
Graphite on white paper
165 x 114 mm
LHO/D/0985

Foliage with Flower, 1890–96
Silverpoint on white paper
161 x 95 mm
LHO/D/0986

Foliage with Flower, 1890–96
Silverpoint on white paper
147 x 94 mm
LHO/D/0987

Foliage, 1850–60
Graphite on white paper
134 x 86 mm
LHO/D/0988

Foliage and Female Figure with Child, 1870–75
Graphite on white paper
122 x 73 mm
LHO/D/0989

Foliage, Possibly Related to 'Cymon and Iphigenia', *c.*1883
Graphite on white paper
162 x 95 mm
LHO/D/0990

Foliage, Related to 'Cymon and Iphigenia', *c.*1883
Graphite on white paper
162 x 91 mm
LHO/D/0991

Foliage, Possibly Related to 'Cymon and Iphigenia', *c.*1883
Graphite on white paper
149 x 94 mm
LHO/D/0992

Foliage, Possibly Related to 'Cymon and Iphigenia', *c.*1883
Graphite on white paper
91 x 162 mm
LHO/D/0993

Foliage, Related to 'Cymon and Iphigenia', *c.*1883
Graphite on white paper
89 x 162 mm
LHO/D/0994

Branch of a Fig Tree, Probably Capri, 1871
Graphite on white paper
139 x 222 mm
LHO/D/0995

Foliage, Possibly Related to 'Cymon and Iphigenia', *c.*1883
Graphite on white paper
90 x 162 mm
LHO/D/0996

Jasmine in Flower, *c.*1859
Graphite on white paper
197 x 274 mm
LHO/D/0997

Branches of a Bay Tree, 1867
Graphite on white paper
206 x 154 mm
LHO/D/0998

Asphodel Buds and Flowers, Lindos, 1867
Graphite on white paper
210 x 166 mm
LHO/D/0999

Branches of a Bay Tree, 1867
Graphite on white paper
209 x 155 mm
LHO/D/1001

Foliage, Related to 'Cymon and Iphigenia', *c.*1883
Graphite on white paper
148 x 230 mm
LHO/D/1002

Foliage, Related to 'Cymon and Iphigenia', *c.*1883
Graphite on white paper
140 x 229 mm
LHO/D/1003

Foliage with Flowers, 1850–60
Graphite on white paper
220 x 280 mm
LHO/D/1004

Branch of a Fig Tree, Capri, 1871
Graphite on buff paper
140 x 220 mm
LHO/D/1007

Rhododendron Buds, *c.*1856
Graphite on tracing paper
87 x 62 mm
LHO/D/1008

Mountain Laurel Buds and Blossoms, *c.*1856
Graphite on tracing paper
106 x 66 mm
LHO/D/1009

Oleander and Tuberose, 1852–55
Graphite, watercolour and white bodycolour on blue paper
266 x 287 mm
LHO/D/1010

Doves and a Rose Bush, 1850–60
Graphite on white paper
274 x 200 mm
LHO/D/1011

Trumpet Vine in Flower, 1855–60
Graphite on white paper
175 x 243 mm
LHO/D/1012

Pumpkin Blossoms, 1856
Graphite on white paper
162 x 97 mm
LHO/D/1013

Pumpkin Blossoms, 1856
Graphite and white bodycolour on white paper
303 x 221 mm
LHO/D/1014

Branch of a Fig Tree, Probably Capri, 1871
Graphite on white paper
136 x 219 mm
LHO/D/1015

Daffodils and Primroses, 1850–60
Graphite on white paper
280 x 216 mm
LHO/D/1016

Thistle, Tiber River, 1856
Graphite on white paper
236 x 221 mm
LHO/D/1017

Branch of a Fig Tree, 1890–96
Graphite on buff paper
181 x 152 mm
LHO/D/1018
(cat. ill. 33)

Tree, *c.*1855
Graphite and white bodycolour on brown paper
319 x 301 mm
LHO/D/1020

Orange Tree, Athens, 1867
Graphite on white paper
217 x 170 mm
LHO/D/1021

Branch of a Fig Tree, Probably Capri, 1871
Graphite on white paper
141 x 220 mm
LHO/D/1022

Branch of a Fig Tree, Probably Capri, 1871
Graphite on white paper
140 x 215 mm
LHO/D/1023

Branch of a Fig Tree, Probably Capri, 1871
Graphite on white paper
139 x 217 mm
LHO/D/1024

Branch of a Fig Tree, Probably Capri, 1871
Graphite on white paper
139 x 217 mm
LHO/D/1024 verso

Trunk of a Lemon Tree, 1873
Graphite on white paper
215 x 135 mm
LHO/D/1025

Trunk of a Lemon Tree, 1873
Graphite on white paper
220 x 135 mm
LHO/D/1026

Cypress Tree, 1854
Graphite on white paper
276 x 209 mm
LHO/D/1029

Foliage, Related to 'Cymon and Iphigenia', *c.*1883
Graphite on white paper
81 x 162 mm
LHO/D/1116

STUDIES AFTER OTHER ARTISTS

Study after a Painting by Jacopino del Conte, 1856
Graphite on white paper
226 x 199 mm
LHO/D/0465
(cat. no. 1.8)

Studies after a Painting by Giorgione, 1852
Graphite on white paper
170 x 234 mm
LHO/D/0928

Study after a Painting by Luca Signorelli, 1852–55
Graphite on white paper
174 x 129 mm
LHO/D/0929

Study after a Painting by Vittore Carpaccio, 1853
Graphite on white paper
147 x 152 mm
LHO/D/0930
(fig. 6)

Studies after a Painting by Vittore Carpaccio, 1853
Graphite on white paper
295 x 232 mm
LHO/D/0931

Study after a Fresco by Andrea di Firenze, 1853
Graphite on white paper
292 x 230 mm
LHO/D/0932

Study after a Painting by the Master of the Adimari Coffer, 1853
Graphite on white paper
235 x 300 mm
LHO/D/0933

Studies after Paintings by Vittore Carpaccio, 1853
Graphite on white paper
295 x 233 mm
LHO/D/0934

Studies after a Fresco by Andrea di Firenze, 1853
Graphite on white paper
296 x 233 mm
LHO/D/0935

Studies after a Painting by the Master of the Adimari Coffer, A Window, 1853
Graphite on white paper
300 x 235 mm
LHO/D/0936

Study after a Work by an Unidentified Italian Renaissance Artist, Possibly School of Paolo Veronese, 1845–52
Graphite on white paper
243 x 179 mm
LHO/D/0937

Study after a Painting by Vittore Carpaccio, 1853
Graphite on white paper
133 x 135 mm
LHO/D/0938

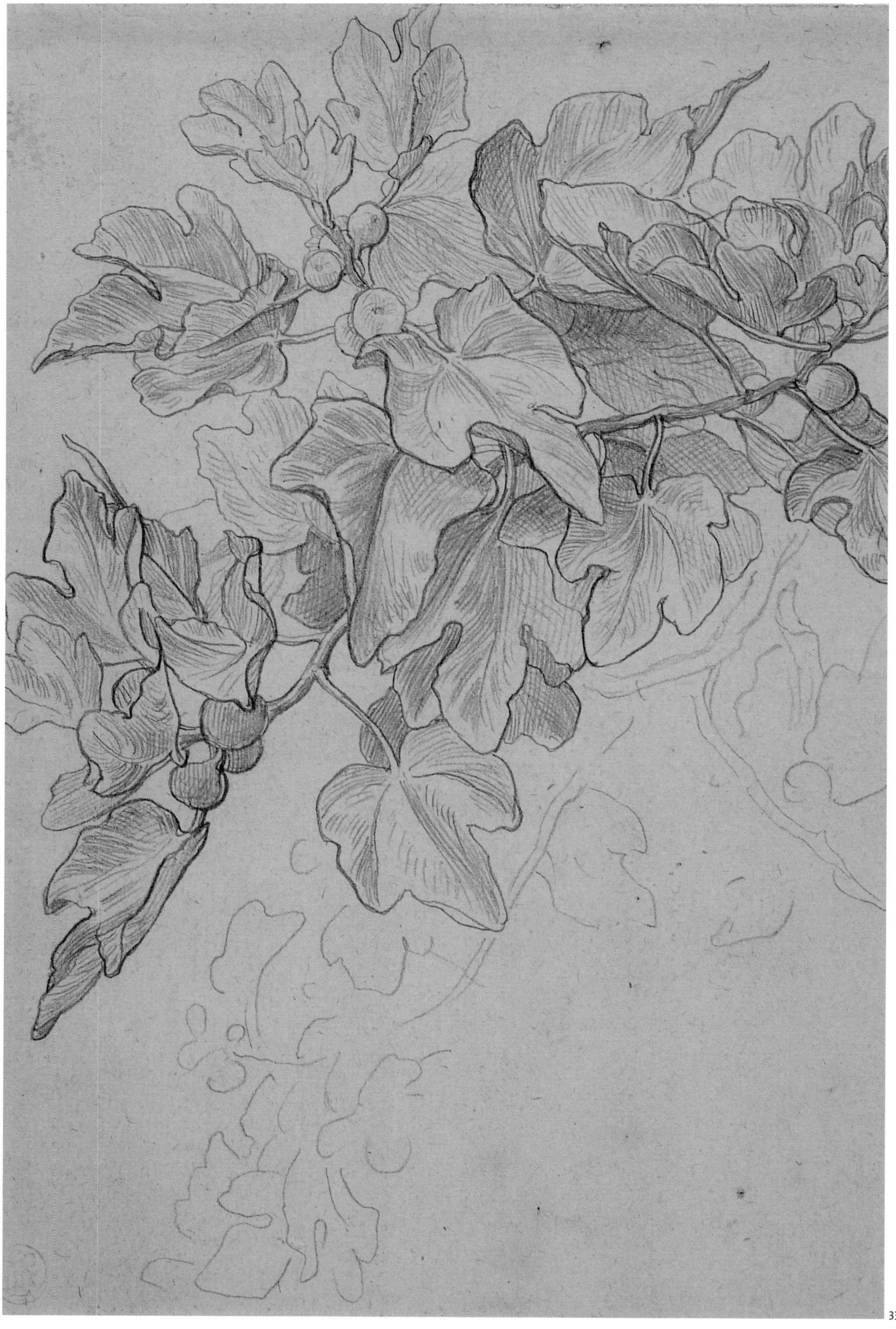

33.

Study after a Painting by Vittore Carpaccio, 1853
Graphite on white paper
220 x 291 mm
LHO/D/0939

Study after a Bust by Benedetto da Maiano, 1853
Graphite on white paper
298 x 233 mm
LHO/D/0940

Study after a Bust attributed to Antonio Pollaiolo, 1853
Graphite on white paper
292 x 234 mm
LHO/D/0941

Study after a Bust by Mino da Fiesole, 1854
Graphite on white paper
279 x 210 mm
LHO/D/0942

Study after a Bust by Benedetto da Maiano, 1854
Graphite on white paper
260 x 210 mm
LHO/D/0943

Study after a Bust by Antonio Rossellino, 1854
Graphite on white paper
279 x 210 mm
LHO/D/0944

Study after a Fresco attributed to Giotto, 1852–55
Graphite and watercolour on white paper
213 x 163 mm
LHO/D/0952

Study after a Work by an Unidentified Italian Renaissance Painter, 1852–55
Graphite on tracing paper
147 x 78 mm
LHO/D/0964

Study after a Painting by Eduard Jakob von Steinle, 1845–52
Graphite on white paper
470 x 318 mm
LHO/D/0967

Study after a Painting by Simone and Lippo Memmi, 1852–55
Graphite on white paper
189 x 243 mm
LHO/D/1142

Study after a Painting by Hans Holbein, 1856
Graphite on white paper
177 x 139 mm
LHO/D/1143

Study after a Fresco by Raphael (Raffaello Sanzio), 1852–55
Graphite and watercolour on white paper
238 x 348 mm
LHO/D/2180

LANDSCAPE STUDIES

View of Rocks and Water in Scotland, 1891
Black chalk and watercolour on blue paper
317 x 428 mm
LHO/D/0431

Island of Ischia, Italy, *c.*1859
Graphite, watercolour and white bodycolour on white paper
291 x 464 mm
LHO/D/0439

Rocky Landscape, 1890–96
Graphite on buff paper
155 x 182 mm
LHO/D/0906

Athens, Greece , 1867
Graphite on buff paper
170 x 215 mm
LHO/D/0907

Brescia Hills, Italy, *c.*1856
Graphite on white paper
99 x 160 mm
LHO/D/0908

Bay of Salamis, Greece, 1867
Graphite on white paper
171 x 216 mm
LHO/D/0909

Landscape, Probably in Greece, 1867
Graphite on white paper
171 x 216 mm
LHO/D/0909 verso

Landscape with Mountains, 1865–75
Graphite on white paper
93 x 161 mm
LHO/D/0910

Rocky Landscape, 1890–96
Graphite on buff paper
151 x 182 mm
LHO/D/0911

Rocky Landscape, 1890–96
Graphite on buff paper
153 x 174 mm
LHO/D/0912

Cervara, Italy, 1856
Graphite on white paper
287 x 437 mm
LHO/D/0913

House and Vine, Possibly Italy, 1850–60
Graphite on white paper
228 x 189 mm
LHO/D/0919

View of Subiaco, Italy, *c.*1853
Graphite on white paper
136 x 212 mm
LHO/D/0920

Landscape with Mulberry Trees and Ladders, 1850
Graphite and brown watercolour on white paper
269 x 411 mm
LHO/D/1027

View of Cypress Trees, Florence, 1854
Graphite, brown watercolour and white bodycolour on buff paper
408 x 266 mm
LHO/D/1028
(cat. no. 1.6)

STUDIES RELATING TO SPECIFIC JOURNEYS

Studies Made in Algiers, 1857

Male and Female Figures, Male Heads
Graphite on white paper
253 x 187 mm
LHO/D/0972

Male Heads
Graphite on white paper
275 x 203 mm
LHO/D/0973

Male and Female Figures
Graphite on white paper
272 x 203 mm
LHO/D/0974

Male and Female Figures
Graphite on white paper
275 x 202 mm
LHO/D/0976

Female Figures
Graphite on white paper
270 x 202 mm
LHO/D/0977

Studies Made in Capri, 1859

Houses in Capri, 1859
Graphite on white paper
271 x 200 mm
LHO/D/0914
(cat. no. 2.1)

Capri, 1859
Graphite on white paper
200 x 274 mm
LHO/D/0915
(cat. no. 2.4)

Capri, 1859
Graphite on white paper
201 x 273 mm
LHO/D/0916
(cat. no. 2.2)

Landscape with Buildings, Capri, 1859
Graphite on white paper
201 x 273 mm
LHO/D/0917
(cat. no. 2.3)

House in Capri, 1859
Graphite on white paper
202 x 276 mm
LHO/D/0918

Female Head, Capri, 1859
Graphite on white paper
274 x 201 mm
LHO/D/0958

Mallow Plant, Capri, 1859
Graphite on white paper
202 x 277 mm
LHO/D/1000

Maize, Capri, 1859
Graphite on white paper
276 x 202 mm
LHO/D/1005
(cat. no. 2.6)

Branches of a Fig Tree, Capri, 1859
Graphite on white paper
270 x 200 mm
LHO/D/1019
(cat. no. 2.5)

Studies Made in Egypt, 1868

Male Head, Luxor
Graphite on white paper
218 x 173 mm
LHO/D/0970

Male Head, Luxor
Graphite on white paper
212 x 172 mm
LHO/D/0971

Male Head, Luxor
Graphite on white paper
213 x 172 mm
LHO/D/0975
(cat. no. 3.3)

STUDIES OF HEADS

Male Head, *c.*1856–77
Black and white chalk on blue paper
297 x 226 mm
LHO/D/0757

Portrait of Dorothy Dene, *c.*1880
Black and white chalk on brown paper
293 x 200 mm
LHO/D/0758
(cat. no. 5.1)

cat. ill. 33. ***Study of the Branch of a Fig Tree***, 1890–96. Graphite on buff paper, LHO/D/1018.

Portrait of John Scott Cowell, 1854
Graphite on white paper
176 x 139 mm
LHO/D/0879

Male Head, Probably of Walter Pennington Creyke, 1855
Graphite on white paper
296 x 222 mm
LHO/D/0880
(cat. no. 1.7)

Female Head, Probably Dorothy Dene, 1877–92
Black and white chalk on brown paper
234 x 198 mm
LHO/D/0886

Female Head, 1856–77
Black and white chalk on blue paper
322 x 241 mm
LHO/D/0894

Female Head, *c.*1870
Black and white chalk on blue paper
317 x 233 mm
LHO/D/0895
(cat. no. 3.4)

Female Head, 1891–96
Black and white chalk on grey-brown paper
218 x 219 mm
LHO/D/0897

Female Head, 1891–96
Black and white chalk on grey-brown paper
368 x 282 mm
LHO/D/0898

Portrait of Charles Augustus Howell, *c.*1866
Black and white chalk on blue paper
224 x 214 mm
LHO/D/0905

Female Head, 1856
Graphite on white paper
280 x 218 mm
LHO/D/0947

Female Head Traced from LHO/D/0947, 1856
Graphite on white paper
280 x 218 mm
LHO/D/0947 verso

Female Head, 1856
Graphite on white paper
290 x 225 mm
LHO/D/0948

Male Head with a Hood representing Girolamo Savonarola, 1853
Graphite on white paper
291 x 227 mm
LHO/D/0949

Male Head with a Hat, 1854
Graphite on tracing paper
155 x 125 mm
LHO/D/0951

Female Head, 1856
Graphite on tracing paper
195 x 160 mm
LHO/D/0953

Female Head, 1856
Graphite on white paper
290 x 221 mm
LHO/D/0954

Female Head, 1852–55
Graphite on white paper
296 x 234 mm
LHO/D/0955

Female Head, 1853
Graphite on white paper
296 x 355 mm
LHO/D/0957

Female Head, 1852–55
Graphite on white paper
274 x 201 mm
LHO/D/0960

Head of Dorothy Dene, 1881
Graphite on white paper
228 x 174 mm
LHO/D/1039
(cat. no. 5.2)

EARLY DESIGNS AND RELATED STUDIES

Composition Showing a Female Figure and a Fireplace, *c.*1849
Watercolour on white paper
102 x 75 mm
LHO/D/0426

Street in Boulogne, 1847
Watercolour on white paper
104 x 75 mm
LHO/D/0427

Composition Showing Nymphs Dancing on a Sea Shore, 1855
Watercolour on white paper
72 x 187 mm
LHO/D/0430

Farmyard, 1849
Watercolour on white paper
92 x 129 mm
LHO/D/0432

***Giotto as a Shepherd Boy*, 1849**
Graphite and grey watercolour on white paper
302 x 276 mm
LHO/D/0454
(cat. no. 1.1)

Study for 'Giotto as a Shepherd Boy': Composition, 1849
Graphite and brown pastel on white paper
287 x 235 mm
LHO/D/0455

Study for 'Preparing for a Festa': Composition, *c.*1851
Graphite, black chalk and white bodycolour on white paper
561 x 389 mm
LHO/D/0832
(cat. no. 1.2)

Composition Showing Musicians and Dancing Figures, *c.*1851
Graphite and white bodycolour on paper
216 x 343 mm
LHO/D/0833

Composition Showing Male Figures with Shields and Weapons, and a Horse, 1856–77
Black and white chalk on blue paper
293 x 418 mm
LHO/D/0836

Study for 'Madonna and Child with St John': Composition, *c.*1851
Graphite, black chalk and white bodycolour on white paper
478 x 340 mm
LHO/D/0837

***Madonna and Child with St John*, *c.*1851**
Graphite, brown watercolour, and white bodycolour on white paper
467 x 410 mm
LHO/D/0838

Composition Showing a Jester, a Male Figure and a Bird, 1845–52
Oil on white paper
230 x 286 mm
LHO/D/0864

Composition Showing Soldiers Invading a Town, 1845–52
Graphite and black ink on white paper
444 x 345 mm
LHO/D/0865

Composition Showing Soldiers and Demons at a Shrine, *c.*1845
Graphite and brown watercolour on white paper
398 x 524 mm
LHO/D/0866

***Buffalmacco the Painter*, 1852**
Black chalk, white bodycolour and brown watercolour on white paper
602 x 274 mm
LHO/D/0867

Study for an Unidentified Composition Showing Horses, Children, Dolphins and Neptune, 1850–60
Graphite on tracing paper
166 x 305 mm
LHO/D/0868

Composition Showing a Female Figure, a Baby and Fruit, 1850–60
Black chalk and white bodycolour on white paper
222 x 177 mm
LHO/D/0869

Composition Showing a Male and Female Figure, a Baby and a Grape Vine, 1850–60
Graphite on tracing paper
104 x 155 mm
LHO/D/0870

Composition Showing Male Figures, 1845–52
Graphite on white paper
507 x 415 mm
LHO/D/0871

Composition Showing St Nicholas, Female Figures, Children, and a Boat, 1845–52
Graphite on white paper
298 x 195 mm
LHO/D/0874

Humorous Composition Showing a Male Figure and Boys, 1845–52
Black watercolour on buff paper
198 x 150 mm
LHO/D/0875

Female Figure and Baby, 1850–60
Graphite on tracing paper
129 x 89 mm
LHO/D/0963

Composition Showing a Monk Dividing Two Enemies, 1852
Graphite on white paper
290 x 220 mm
LHO/D/0969

Study for 'Preparing for a Festa': Painted Frame, *c.*1851
Graphite and red chalk on tracing paper
108 x 157 mm
LHO/D/1110

Study for 'Preparing for a Festa': Painted Frame, *c.*1851
Graphite and red chalk on tracing paper
125 x 140 mm
LHO/D/1111

Study for 'Preparing for a Festa': Painted Frame, *c.*1851
Graphite and red chalk on tracing paper
131 x 97 mm
LHO/D/1112

Study for 'A Midsummer Night's Dream': Composition, 1850
Graphite and watercolour on white paper
726 x 437 mm
LHO/D/1120

PREPARATORY STUDIES FOR PAINTINGS

Studies for 'Actaea, Nymph of the Shore', *c.*1867

Female Figure
Black and white chalk on blue paper
184 x 288 mm
LHO/D/0792

Female Figures
Black and white chalk on blue paper
245 x 277 mm
LHO/D/0816

Female Figures
Black and white chalk on blue paper
441 x 282 mm
LHO/D/0791

Studies for 'After Vespers', *c.*1871

Composition
Black and white chalk on blue paper
240 x 173 mm
LHO/D/0519

Studies for 'And the Sea Gave up the Dead Which Were in It', *c.*1877–84

Composition, *c.*1877
Black and white chalk on blue paper
137 x 133 mm
LHO/D/0600

Composition, 1882–84
Black and white chalk on brown paper
147 x 146 mm
LHO/D/0601

Male Figures, *c.*1877
Black chalk on blue paper
134 x 130 mm
LHO/D/0602

Composition, Figures, 1877–78
Graphite on white paper
115 x 179 mm
LHO/D/0603

Male Figures, 1877–82
Black and white chalk on brown paper
324 x 288 mm
LHO/D/0604

Drapery, 1882
Black and white chalk on brown paper
314 x 217 mm
LHO/D/0605

Male and Female Figures, 1882–84
Black and white chalk and brown watercolour on brown paper
226 x 226 mm
LHO/D/0606

Male Figures, 1877–82
Black and white chalk on brown paper
226 x 220 mm
LHO/D/0607

Male Figure, Male Arms, 1877–82
Black and white chalk
on brown paper
330 x 227 mm
LHO/D/0608

Male Figure, Male Legs, Male Feet, 1882
Black and white chalk
on brown paper
315 x 223 mm
LHO/D/0609

Male Figures, 1877–82
Black and white chalk
on brown paper
227 x 314 mm
LHO/D/0610

Male Figures, Male Leg, 1877–82
Black and white chalk
on brown paper
306 x 218 mm
LHO/D/0611

Male Figures, 1882–84
Black and white chalk
on brown paper
226 x 317 mm
LHO/D/0612

Male Figures, 1877–82
Black and white chalk
on brown paper
228 x 320 mm
LHO/D/0613

Male Figures, 1882–84
Black and white chalk
on brown paper
226 x 301 mm
LHO/D/0614

Male Figure, 1877–82
Black and white chalk
on brown paper
321 x 220 mm
LHO/D/0615
(cat. no. 5.5)

Male Figure, Hands, 1877–82
Black and white chalk
on brown paper
311 x 229 mm
LHO/D/0616

Male Heads, 1877–82
Black and white chalk
on brown paper
320 x 231 mm
LHO/D/0617

Female Figure, 1882–84
Black and white chalk
on brown paper
328 x 217 mm
LHO/D/0618

Study for 'And the Sea Gave up the Dead Which Were in It', later used for 'Perseus and Andromeda': Female Figure, *c.*1877
Black and white chalk
on blue paper
329 x 246 mm
LHO/D/0693
(cat. no. 4.1)

Female Figure, Female Arm, 1882–84
Black and white chalk
on brown paper
303 x 227 mm
LHO/D/0845

Male Figure, 1882–84
Black and white chalk
on brown paper
371 x 289 mm
LHO/D/1103

Studies for 'Antique Juggling Girl', *c.*1871–72

Composition, *c.*1872
Oil on blue paper
130 x 95 mm
LHO/D/0370

Studies for 'Antique Juggling Girl', 'The Courtyard of a House at Damascus' and 'Summer Moon': Female Figures, *c.*1871
Black and white chalk
on blue paper
319 x 235 mm
LHO/D/0520

Female Figure, *c.*1872
Black and white chalk
on blue paper
296 x 210 mm
LHO/D/0562

Studies for 'Antique Juggling Girl' and 'Clytemnestra': Compositions, *c.*1872
Black and white chalk
on blue paper
186 x 246 mm
LHO/D/0563

Studies for 'At the Fountain', *c.*1891

Composition
Black and white chalk
on brown paper
270 x 217 mm
LHO/D/0805

Studies for 'Augusta, Lady Hoare', *c.*1857

Composition
Black and white chalk
on white paper
341 x 248 mm
LHO/D/0902

Studies for 'Bacchante', *c.*1891

Drapery for Female Figure
Black and white chalk
on brown paper
484 x 333 mm
LHO/D/0622

Composition, Head of Deer
Black and white chalk
on brown paper
258 x 232 mm
LHO/D/0714

Studies for 'The Bath of Psyche', *c.*1889

Female Figure
Black and white chalk
on brown paper
564 x 367 mm
LHO/D/0686

Female Figure, Female Hands
Black and white chalk
on grey-brown paper
292 x 369 mm
LHO/D/0687

Female Figure
Black and white chalk
on brown paper
325 x 229 mm
LHO/D/0784

Curtain
Black and white chalk
on brown paper
412 x 298 mm
LHO/D/0826

Female Head
Black and white chalk
on brown paper
236 x 199 mm
LHO/D/0828

Studies for 'Bianca', *c.*1861

Studies for 'Bianca' and 'Orpheus and Eurydice': Orpheus and Eurydice, Hand of Orpheus, Composition, Figure
Black and white chalk
on blue paper
289 x 441 mm
LHO/D/0478

Studies for 'A Boy Saving a Baby from the Clutches of an Eagle', *c.*1850

Composition, Head of Eagle
Graphite and watercolour
on white paper
165 x 175 mm
LHO/D/0456

Alternative Composition, Boy with Scythe
Graphite and watercolour
on white paper
165 x 175 mm
LHO/D/0456 verso

Studies for 'The Bracelet', *c.*1893

Female Figures
Black and white chalk
on grey-brown paper
281 x 368 mm
LHO/D/0736

Studies for 'Fatidica', 'The Spirit of the Summit', 'Summer Slumber' and 'The Bracelet': Compositions
Black and white chalk
on grey-brown paper
280 x 368 mm
LHO/D/0741

Girl, Female Figure with Girl
Black and white chalk
on grey-brown paper
368 x 280 mm
LHO/D/0840

Composition
Black and white chalk
on brown paper
198 x 89 mm
LHO/D/1107

Studies for 'Captive Andromache', *c.*1870–87

Studies for 'Captive Andromache' and 'Hercules Wrestling with Death for the Body of Alcestis': Compositions, Male and Female Figures, *c.*1870
Black and white chalk
on blue paper
324 x 245 mm
LHO/D/0516

Composition, *c.*1887
Graphite on tracing paper
199 x 414 mm
LHO/D/0663

Female Figures with Pitchers, *c.*1870
Black and white chalk
on blue paper
227 x 300 mm
LHO/D/0665

Female Figures with Pitchers, *c.*1885
Black and white chalk
on brown paper
280 x 370 mm
LHO/D/0666

Female Figures with Pitchers, Female Arms, *c.*1887
Black and white chalk
on blue paper
245 x 322 mm
LHO/D/0667

Female Figures with Pitchers, *c.*1870
Black and white chalk
on blue paper
318 x 235 mm
LHO/D/0668

Female Figure with Pitcher, *c.*1887
Black and white chalk
on brown paper
363 x 277 mm
LHO/D/0670

Female Figures with Pitchers, *c.*1887
Black and white chalk
on brown paper
275 x 359 mm
LHO/D/0671

Female Figures with Pitchers, *c.*1887
Black and white chalk
on brown paper
274 x 365 mm
LHO/D/0672

Drapery for Female Figure, *c.*1887
Black and white chalk on brown paper
552 x 373 mm
LHO/D/0673

Drapery for Female Figure, *c.*1887
Black and white chalk
on brown paper
556 x 367 mm
LHO/D/0674

Drapery for Female Figure, *c.*1887
Black and white chalk
on brown paper
559 x 370 mm
LHO/D/0675

Seated Female Figure, Female Figure with Baby, Baby, *c.*1887
Black and white chalk
on brown paper
272 x 370 mm
LHO/D/0676

Drapery for Seated Female Figure, *c.*1887
Black and white chalk
on brown paper
556 x 369 mm
LHO/D/0677
(cat. no. 5.9)

Drapery for Mother, *c.*1887
Black and white chalk
on brown paper
559 x 370 mm
LHO/D/0678

Male and Female Figures, Baby, *c.*1887
Black and white chalk
on brown paper
281 x 369 mm
LHO/D/0679

Male Figures, *c.*1870
Black and white chalk
on blue paper
223 x 288 mm
LHO/D/0680

Drapery for Male Figure, *c.*1887
Black and white chalk
on brown paper
556 x 369 mm
LHO/D/0681

Male Figure, *c.*1887
Black chalk on brown paper
556 x 369 mm
LHO/D/0681 verso

Drapery for Female Figure, *c.*1887
Black and white chalk on brown paper
556 x 372 mm
LHO/D/0682

Drapery for Female Figures, Drapery, *c.*1887
Black and white chalk
on brown paper
524 x 370 mm
LHO/D/0683
(cat. ill. 32)

Girl with Basket, *c.*1887
Black and white chalk
on brown paper
280 x 365 mm
LHO/D/0808

Female Figures with Baskets, Female Head, *c.*1870
Black and white chalk
on blue paper
236 x 318 mm
LHO/D/0811

Drapery for Female Figures, *c.*1870
Black and white chalk
on blue paper
243 x 316 mm
LHO/D/0813

Studies for 'Cimabue's Celebrated Madonna is Carried in Procession through the Streets of Florence; in front of the Madonna, and crowned with laurels, walks Cimabue himself, with his pupil Giotto; behind it Arnolfo Di Lapo, Gaddo Gaddi, Andrea Tafi, Niccola Pisano, Buffalmacco, and Simone Memmi; in the corner Dante', 1853–54

Composition, *c.*1854
Graphite and white bodycolour
on tracing paper
191 x 435 mm
LHO/D/0457

Female Figure at Window with Blue Scarf, *c.*1854
Graphite, blue watercolour and
white bodycolour on white paper
296 x 256 mm
LHO/D/0458

Head of Dante, 1853
Graphite on white paper
333 x 226 mm
LHO/D/0476

Drapery for Male and Female Figures, Hand, *c.*1854
Black chalk and white bodycolour
on white paper
475 x 338 mm
LHO/D/0831

Drapery for Female Figure, *c.*1854
Black chalk and white bodycolour
on white paper
475 x 338 mm
LHO/D/0831 verso

Musician Tuning a Violin, Male Figure, *c.*1854
Graphite, grey watercolour
and white bodycolour
on white paper
313 x 233 mm
LHO/D/0876

Male Head, 1853
Graphite on white paper
296 x 234 mm
LHO/D/0945

Female Head, 1853
Graphite on tracing paper
221 x 181 mm
LHO/D/0956

Male Figure on Horseback, 1854
Graphite on white paper
331 x 230 mm
LHO/D/0961

Hands, 1854
Graphite on white paper
290 x 230 mm
LHO/D/0965
(cat. no. 1.5)

Vine, Head of Boy with Wreath, Architectural Details, *c.*1854
Graphite and white bodycolour
on buff paper
295 x 442 mm
LHO/D/1006

Female Head, 1853
Graphite on white paper
226 x 182 mm
LHO/D/1036

Male Head, 1853
Graphite on white paper
275 x 224 mm
LHO/D/2177
(cat. no. 1.3)

Male Head, 1853
Graphite on white paper
226 x 182 mm
LHO/D/2178
(cat. no. 1.4)

Studies for 'Cleobolus Instructing his Daughter Cleoboline', *c.*1870

Head of Cleoboline
Black and white chalk on blue paper
244 x 224 mm
LHO/D/0891

Studies for 'Clytemnestra from the Battlements of Argos Watches for the Beacon Fires which are to Announce the Return of Agamemnon', *c.*1872–73

Head of Clytemnestra, *c.*1873
Black and white chalk
on blue paper
189 x 166 mm
LHO/D/0495

Studies for 'Antique Juggling Girl' and 'Clytemnestra': Compositions, *c.*1872
Black and white chalk
on blue paper
186 x 246 mm
LHO/D/0563

Composition, *c.*1873
Black and white chalk
on blue paper
192 x 120 mm
LHO/D/0564

Arms and Shoulders, Composition, *c.*1873
Black and white chalk
on blue paper
244 x 328 mm
LHO/D/0565

Female Figure, *c.*1873
Black and white chalk
on blue paper
215 x 320 mm
LHO/D/0566

Arms, *c.*1873
Black and white chalk
on blue paper
315 x 234 mm
LHO/D/0567

Female Figure, *c.*1873
Black and white chalk
on blue paper
225 x 313 mm
LHO/D/0568

Studies for 'Clytie', *c.*1891–95

Female Figure, *c.*1895
Black and white chalk
on brown paper
365 x 277 mm
LHO/D/0706
(cat. no. 6.7)

Female Head, *c.*1895
Black and white chalk
on brown paper
264 x 225 mm
LHO/D/0707
(cat. no. 6.8)

Female Head, *c.*1895
Black and white chalk
on grey-brown paper
360 x 265 mm
LHO/D/0710

Female Head, *c.*1895
Black and white chalk
on grey-brown paper
265 x 227 mm
LHO/D/0711

Female Head, Female Hand, *c.*1895
Black and white chalk
on grey-brown paper
364 x 281 mm
LHO/D/0712

Hair, *c.*1895
Black and white chalk
on grey-brown paper
365 x 275 mm
LHO/D/0713
(fig. 9, cat. no. 6.9)

Early Poses, *c.*1891
Black and white chalk
on brown paper
236 x 325 mm
LHO/D/0762

Studies for 'A Condottiere', *c.*1871

Composition
Black and white chalk
on blue paper
207 x 135 mm
LHO/D/0521

Studies for 'The Courtyard of a House at Damascus', *c.*1871

Studies for 'Antique Juggling Girl', 'The Courtyard of a House at Damascus' and 'Summer Moon': Female Figures
Black and white chalk
on blue paper
319 x 235 mm
LHO/D/0520

Studies for 'Cupid and Dove', *c.*1860–70

Alternative Composition
Black and white chalk
on blue paper
158 x 138 mm
LHO/D/0656

Studies for 'Cupid and Dove' and 'Phryne at Eleusis': Cupid, Composition, Figures
Black and white chalk
on blue paper
245 x 318 mm
LHO/D/0657

Studies for 'Cymon and Iphigenia', *c.*1880–83

Composition, *c.*1883
Black and white chalk
on brown paper
301 x 486 mm
LHO/D/0635

Male Figures, *c.*1883
Black and white chalk
on brown paper
232 x 330 mm
LHO/D/0636

Female Figures, *c.*1883
Black and white chalk
on brown paper
245 x 323 mm
LHO/D/0637

Female Figures, *c.*1883
Black and white chalk
on brown paper
321 x 238 mm
LHO/D/0638

Drapery for Sleeping Female Figure, *c.*1883
Black and white chalk
on brown paper
346 x 522 mm
LHO/D/0640

Sleeping Female Figures, *c.*1883
Black and white chalk
on brown paper
235 x 328 mm
LHO/D/0641

Iphigenia, Female Figure, *c.*1883
Black and white chalk
on brown paper
230 x 330 mm
LHO/D/0642

Iphigenia, *c.*1883
Black and white chalk
on brown paper
331 x 237 mm
LHO/D/0643

Iphigenia, *c.*1883
Black and white chalk
on brown paper
218 x 310 mm
LHO/D/0644

Iphigenia, *c.*1883
Black and white chalk
on brown paper
244 x 320 mm
LHO/D/0645

Studies for 'Cymon and Iphigenia' and 'Idyll': Male and Female Figures, *c.*1880
Black and white chalk
on brown paper
322 x 237 mm
LHO/D/0702

Sleeping Female Figures, *c.*1883
Black and white chalk
on brown paper
165 x 323 mm
LHO/D/0815

Drapery for Iphigenia, Pillow, *c.*1883
Black and white chalk
on brown paper
369 x 561 mm
LHO/D/0830
(cat. no. 5.6)

Studies for 'Daedalus and Icarus', *c.*1868

Composition
Black and white chalk
on blue paper
242 x 205 mm
LHO/D/0497

Icarus
Black and white chalk
on blue paper
320 x 223 mm
LHO/D/0498

Arm of Icarus, Male Figure
Black and white chalk on blue paper
321 x 240 mm
LHO/D/0499

Daedalus, Icarus, Head of Daedalus, Hands
Graphite on white paper
282 x 425 mm
LHO/D/0501

Drapery
Black and white chalk
on blue paper
220 x 288 mm
LHO/D/0823

Studies for 'The Dance', *c.*1882

Female Figures, Male Figure with Child
Black and white chalk on brown paper
251 x 323 mm
LHO/D/0619

Drapery for Girl
Black and white chalk on brown paper
330 x 257 mm
LHO/D/0620
(cat. no. 5.3)

Female Figures
Black and white chalk on brown paper
227 x 317 mm
LHO/D/0621

Drapery
Black and white chalk on brown paper
279 x 374 mm
LHO/D/0623

Male Figure, Drapery for Female Figure
Black and white chalk on brown paper
285 x 346 mm
LHO/D/0624

Studies for 'The Dance' and 'Music': Seated Female Figures, Hands
Black and white chalk on brown paper
231 x 318 mm
LHO/D/0629

Female Figure with Tambourine
Black and white chalk on grey-brown paper
370 x 268 mm
LHO/D/0794

Male and Female Figures, Girls
Black and white chalk on blue paper
240 x 330 mm
LHO/D/0797

Standing Female Figures
Black and white chalk on brown paper
331 x 219 mm
LHO/D/1748

Reclining Female Figures
Black and white chalk on brown paper
165 x 308 mm
LHO/D/1749

Studies for 'Dante in Exile (Dante at Verona)', *c.*1862–63

Composition, Female Figures, Child, Foot of Child, *c.*1863
Black and white chalk on blue paper
280 x 439 mm
LHO/D/0477

Drapery for Male and Female Figures, Male Figures, Feet, *c.*1863
Black and white chalk on blue paper
252 x 295 mm
LHO/D/0766

Studies for 'Dante in Exile' and for Illustrations to Dalziels' 'Bible Gallery': 'Death of the First Born', 'Eliezer and Rebekah', Male and Female Figures, Male Legs, Male Hands, 1862–63
Black and white chalk on blue paper
293 x 448 mm
LHO/D/0782

Studies for 'The Daphnephoria', *c.*1873–75

Figures, *c.*1875
Black and white chalk on blue paper
246 x 325 mm
LHO/D/0571

Female Figures and Children, *c.*1875
Black and white chalk on blue paper
240 x 315 mm
LHO/D/0572

Female Figure, *c.*1875
Black and white chalk on blue paper
282 x 135 mm
LHO/D/0573

Female Figure, *c.*1875
Black chalk on blue paper
390 x 419 mm
LHO/D/0574

Female Figure, *c.*1875
Black and white chalk on blue paper
277 x 184 mm
LHO/D/0575

Male and Female Figures, *c.*1875
Black and white chalk on blue paper
242 x 325 mm
LHO/D/0576

Male and Female Figures, *c.*1875
Black chalk on blue paper
249 x 323 mm
LHO/D/0577

Female Figure, *c.*1875
Black and white chalk on blue paper
285 x 185 mm
LHO/D/0578

Studies for 'The Daphnephoria' and 'Moorish Garden; A Dream of Granada': Girls, *c.*1873
Black and white chalk on blue paper
244 x 321 mm
LHO/D/0579
(cat. no 3.8)

Drapery for Male Figures, *c.*1875
Black and white chalk on blue paper
290 x 226 mm
LHO/D/1137

Studies for 'David' ('Oh that I had the wings of a dove! For then I would fly away and be at rest'), 1863–68

Composition
Black and white chalk on blue paper
128 x 162 mm
LHO/D/0480

Male Figure, Male Feet
Black and white chalk on blue paper
146 x 193 mm
LHO/D/0481

Male Head, Male Hand
Black and white chalk on blue paper
227 x 100 mm
LHO/D/0482

Male Hand
Black and white chalk on blue paper
63 x 134 mm
LHO/D/0483

Studies for 'David' and for Illustrations to Dalziels' 'Bible Gallery': Abraham and the Angel', 'Samson at the Mill', Abraham, Angel, Samson, Male Figure, Female Figure, 1863–64
Black and white chalk on blue paper
285 x 443 mm
LHO/D/0765

Studies for 'Day-Dreams', *c.*1881

Studies for 'Day-Dreams' and 'Phryne at Eleusis': Head of Phryne, Female Figure
Black and white chalk on brown paper
323 x 247 mm
LHO/D/0803

Studies for Decorative Panels for No.44 Belgrave Square, London, *c.*1869

Male Figure
Black and white chalk on blue paper
248 x 154 mm
LHO/D/1035

Studies for Decorative Panels for Longford Hall, Stretford, 1895–96

Female Figures
Black and white chalk on grey-brown paper
283 x 366 mm
LHO/D/0783

Female Figures
Black and white chalk on grey-brown paper
279 x 371 mm
LHO/D/0787
(cat. no 6.5)

Rough Compositions within Architectural Setting
Black and white chalk on grey-brown paper
280 x 368 mm
LHO/D/0846
(cat. no 6.4)

Studies for 'Eastern Slinger Scaring Birds in the Harvest Time - Moonrise', *c.*1874

Male and Female Figures
Black and white chalk on blue paper
242 x 285 mm
LHO/D/0569

Male Figures
Black and white chalk on blue paper
322 x 243 mm
LHO/D/0570

Studies for 'Electra at the Tomb of Agamemnon', *c.*1868

Studies for 'Electra at the Tomb of Agamemnon': Composition
Black and white chalk on blue paper
214 x 116 mm
LHO/D/0502

Studies for 'Elijah in the Wilderness', *c.*1877

Wings of Angel
Black and white chalk on brown paper
235 x 280 mm
LHO/D/0517

Elijah
Black and white chalk on blue paper
214 x 313 mm
LHO/D/0585
(cat. no 4.4)

Elijah
Black and white chalk on blue paper
202 x 280 mm
LHO/D/0586
(cat. no 4.2)

Elijah
Black and white chalk on blue paper
210 x 281 mm
LHO/D/0587
(cat. no 4.3)

Elijah
Black and white chalk on blue paper
224 x 283 mm
LHO/D/0588
(cat. no 4.5)

Studies for 'Elijah in the Wilderness' and 'Nausicaa': Female Figure, Angel, Composition
Black and white chalk on blue paper
295 x 225 mm
LHO/D/0589
(cat. no 4.6)

Angel, Male Figure
Black and white chalk on blue paper
220 x 276 mm
LHO/D/0590

Angel
Black and white chalk on brown paper
235 x 265 mm
LHO/D/0591
(cat. no 4.7)

Studies for 'Elijah in the Wilderness', 'Greek Girls Playing at Ball' and 'Return of Persephone': Compositions, Male and Female Figures
Black and white chalk on blue paper
215 x 279 mm
LHO/D/0806

Studies for 'Elisha Raising the Son of the Shunammite', *c.*1880

Elisha, Boy
Black and white chalk on brown paper
310 x 233 mm
LHO/D/0593

Elisha, Boy, Composition
Black and white chalk on brown paper
329 x 231 mm
LHO/D/0594

Elisha, Boy
Black and white chalk on brown paper
229 x 317 mm
LHO/D/0595

Studies for 'Farewell!', *c.*1892

Drapery for Female Figure
Black and white chalk on grey-brown paper
369 x 228 mm
LHO/D/0717

Drapery for Female Figure
Black and white chalk on grey-brown paper
560 x 324 mm
LHO/D/0718

Studies for 'Fatidica', *c.*1893

Studies for 'Fatidica' and 'The Marquand Ceiling': Seated Female Figures
Black and white chalk on brown paper
217 x 323 mm
LHO/D/0648

Female Figures
Black and white chalk
on grey-brown paper
267 x 366 mm
LHO/D/0649

Composition
Black and white chalk
on grey-brown paper
226 x 317 mm
LHO/D/0732

Female Figure
Black and white chalk
on grey-brown paper
281 x 367 mm
LHO/D/0735

Studies for 'Fatidica', 'The Spirit of the Summit', 'Summer Slumber' and 'The Bracelet': Compositions
Black and white chalk
on grey-brown paper
28 x 368 mm
LHO/D/0741

Studies for 'Flaming June', *c.*1891–94

Studies for 'Flaming June' and 'The Garden of the Hesperides': Female Figures, *c.*1891
Black and white chalk
on brown paper
304 x 233 mm
LHO/D/0704

Female Figure, *c.*1894
Black and white chalk
on grey-brown paper
367 x 281 mm
LHO/D/0742
(cat. no 6.2)

Female Figures, *c.*1894
Black and white chalk
on grey-brown paper
367 x 278 mm
LHO/D/0743
(cat. no 6.1)

Female Figure, Male Figure, *c.*1894
Black and white chalk
on brown paper
234 x 321 mm
LHO/D/0745

Studies for 'The Garden of the Hesperides', *c.*1891

Female Figures with Snake
Black and white chalk
on grey-brown paper
284 x 370 mm
LHO/D/0699

Female Figure
Black and white chalk
on grey-brown paper
242 x 318 mm
LHO/D/0700

Studies for 'Flaming June' and 'The Garden of the Hesperides': Female Figures
Black and white chalk on brown paper
304 x 233 mm
LHO/D/0704

Female Figures with Serpent, Female Figures
Black and white chalk
on brown paper
280 x 371 mm
LHO/D/0705

Studies for 'The Garden of Hesperides': Sketch, head of a young woman, profile
Black and white chalk
on grey-brown paper
368 x 278 mm
LHO/D/0801

Female Figure
Black and white chalk
on grey-brown paper
206 x 267 mm
LHO/D/1106

Studies for 'A Girl Feeding Peacocks', *c.*1862

Composition
Graphite on tracing paper
504 x 364 mm
LHO/D/0474

Female Figure with Peacock
Black and white chalk
on blue paper
215 x 147 mm
LHO/D/0650

Studies for 'Golden Hours', *c.*1863

Studies for an Illustration for Dalziels' 'Bible Gallery', 'Golden Hours', and 'Orpheus and Eurydice': 'Eliezer and Rebekah', Compositions
Black and white chalk
on blue paper
290 x 301 mm
LHO/D/0487

Studies for 'Greek Girl Dancing (Spanish Dancing Girl: Cadiz in the Old Times)', *c.*1866

Composition
Graphite on tracing paper
152 x 194 mm
LHO/D/0494

Female Figure, Female Feet
Black and white chalk
on blue paper
224 x 214 mm
LHO/D/0905 verso

Studies for 'Greek Girls Picking up Pebbles by the Sea', *c.*1870

Female Figures
Black and white chalk
on blue paper
242 x 325 mm
LHO/D/0518

Studies for 'Greek Girls Playing at Ball', *c.*1888

Female Figures, Drapery, Pitchers, *c.*1888
Black and white chalk
on brown paper
370 x 280 mm
LHO/D/0684

Studies for 'Elijah in the Wilderness', 'Greek Girls Playing at Ball' and 'Return of Persephone': Compositions, Male and Female Figures, *c.*1877
Black and white chalk
on blue paper
215 x 279 mm
LHO/D/0806

Studies for 'Head of a Girl', *c.*1893

Female Head
Black and white chalk
on grey-brown paper
340 x 275 mm
LHO/D/0893

Studies for 'Helen of Troy' ('Thus as she spoke, in Helen's breast arose, fond recollections of her former lord'), *c.*1864

Female Figures
Black and white chalk
on blue paper
292 x 443 mm
LHO/D/0485

Studies for 'Helios and Rhodos', *c.*1868

Legs of Helios, Foot of Helios
Graphite on white paper
290 x 220 mm
LHO/D/0503

Torso of Rhodos, Arm of Rhodos
Graphite on white paper
213 x 272 mm
LHO/D/0504

Helios, Leg of Helios
Graphite on white paper
289 x 219 mm
LHO/D/0505

Heads of Helios and Rhodos
Graphite on white paper
278 x 211 mm
LHO/D/0506

Helios and Rhodos
Graphite on white paper
281 x 212 mm
LHO/D/0507

Helios and Rhodos
Graphite on white paper
290 x 218 mm
LHO/D/0508

Helios
Graphite on white paper
291 x 219 mm
LHO/D/0509

Rhodos
Graphite on white paper
289 x 217 mm
LHO/D/0510

Studies for 'Hercules Wrestling with Death for the Body of Alcestis', *c.*1870

Composition
Graphite on tracing paper
135 x 280 mm
LHO/D/0511

Hercules and Death, Hercules
Black and white chalk
on blue paper
234 x 281 mm
LHO/D/0512

Hercules and Death, Hercules
Black and white chalk
on blue paper
225 x 272 mm
LHO/D/0513

Alcestis
Black and white chalk
on blue paper
178 x 278 mm
LHO/D/0514

Alcestis
Black and white chalk
on blue paper
279 x 206 mm
LHO/D/0515

Studies for 'Captive Andromache' and 'Hercules Wrestling with Death for the Body of Alcestis': Compositions, Male and Female Figures
Black and white chalk
on blue paper
324 x 245 mm
LHO/D/0516

Alcestis
Black and white chalk
on blue paper
246 x 325 mm
LHO/D/0789

Drapery for Death
Black and white chalk
on blue paper
405 x 284 mm
LHO/D/0824
(cat. no 3.5)

Studies for 'Hit', *c.*1892

Male Figure with Boy
Black and white chalk
on brown paper
238 x 329 mm
LHO/D/0719

Studies for 'Idyll', *c.*1880

Studies for 'Idyll' and 'Summer Slumber': Female Figures
Black and white chalk
on brown paper
236 x 320 mm
LHO/D/0701

Studies for 'Cymon and Iphigenia' and 'Idyll': Male and Female Figures
Black and white chalk
on brown paper
322 x 237 mm
LHO/D/0702

Male Figures Playing Pipe, Female Figures
Black and white chalk
on brown paper
234 x 322 mm
LHO/D/0771

Female Figures
Black and white chalk
on brown paper
212 x 321 mm
LHO/D/1113

Studies for 'Invocation', *c.*1888

Female Figure
Black and white chalk
on brown paper
223 x 287 mm
LHO/D/0829

Studies for 'Iostephane', *c.*1879

Female Figures
Black and white chalk
on brown paper
238 x 332 mm
LHO/D/0715

Studies for 'The Jealousy of Simoetha the Sorceress', *c.*1883–85

Studies for 'The Jealousy of Simoetha the Sorceress' and 'The Marquand Ceiling': Mnemosyne, Female Figures, *c.*1885
Black and white chalk
on brown paper
225 x 303 mm
LHO/D/0734

Studies for 'The Jealousy of Simoetha the Sorceress' and 'Sun-Gleams': Female Figures, Female Head, Hands, *c.*1883
Black and white chalk
on brown paper
227 x 317 mm
LHO/D/0812

Studies for 'Jezebel and Ahab, having caused Naboth to be put to death, go down to take possession of his vineyard: they are met at the entrance by Elijah the Tishbite. "Hast thou killed, and also taken possession?"', *c.*1862

Head of Jezebel
Black chalk on blue paper
320 x 242 mm
LHO/D/0475
(cat. no 3.2)

Studies for 'Lachrymae', c.1894

Female Head
Black and white chalk
on grey-brown paper
263 x 227 mm
LHO/D/0708

Composition
Black and white chalk
on grey-brown paper
212 x 108 mm
LHO/D/0716

Studies for 'The Last Watch of Hero', c.1886

Composition
Black and white chalk
and oil on brown paper
165 x 101 mm
LHO/D/0661

Composition
Black and white chalk
on brown paper
291 x 214 mm
LHO/D/0662

Studies for 'Leander Drowned', c.1886

Composition
Black chalk and oil
on brown paper
46 x 134 mm
LHO/D/0661A

Studies for 'Lieder Ohne Worte', c.1860

Composition
Black and white chalk
on blue paper
595 x 385 mm
LHO/D/0834
(cat no. 3.1)

Composition
Graphite on tracing paper
572 x 369 mm
LHO/D/0835

Male Head (John Hanson Walker)
Graphite on white paper
173 x 140 mm
LHO/D/0959

Studies for 'The Marquand Ceiling', c.1885

Seated Female Figure
Red chalk on white paper
256 x 180 mm
LHO/D/0646

Seated Female Figure,
Female Head
Black and white chalk
on brown paper
262 x 369 mm
LHO/D/0647

Studies for 'Fatidica' and 'The Marquand Ceiling':
Seated Female Figures
Black and white chalk
on brown paper
217 x 323 mm
LHO/D/0648

Composition of Right Hand Panel
Black and white chalk
on brown paper
357 x 259 mm
LHO/D/0652
(cat. no. 5.8)

Boy
Black and white chalk
on brown paper
289 x 362 mm
LHO/D/0653

Terpsichore, Erato and Cherub
Black and white chalk
on brown paper
227 x 308 mm
LHO/D/0654

Composition of Left Hand Panel
Black and white chalk
on brown paper
367 x 254 mm
LHO/D/0655
(cat. no. 5.7)

Cherubs
Black and white chalk
on blue paper
305 x 242 mm
LHO/D/0658

Studies for 'The Jealousy of Simoetha the Sorceress' and 'The Marquand Ceiling':
Mnemosyne, Female Figures
Black and white chalk
on brown paper
225 x 303 mm
LHO/D/0734

Wreaths, Drapery for
Female Figure
Black and white chalk
on brown paper
496 x 323 mm
LHO/D/0821

Wreaths, Drapery
Black and white chalk
on brown paper
489 x 326 mm
LHO/D/0822

Studies for 'Melittion', c.1881

Drapery for Female Figure
Black and white chalk
on brown paper
324 x 233 mm
LHO/D/0809

Drapery for Female Figure
Black and white chalk
on brown paper
360 x 275 mm
LHO/D/0810
(cat. ill. 34)

Studies for 'Memories', c.1882

Composition
Black and white chalk
on brown paper
275 x 243 mm
LHO/D/0625

Studies for 'Michelangelo Nursing his Dying Servant', c.1861

Composition
Black and white cha k
on blue paper
336 x 281 mm
LHO/D/0466

Composition
Black and white chalk
on blue paper
166 x 143 mm
LHO/D/0467
(fig. 7)

Composition
Graphite on tracing paper
180 x 139 mm
LHO/D/0468

Head of Servant
Black and white chalk
on blue paper
429 x 292 mm
LHO/D/0469

Head of Servant
Black and white chalk
on blue paper
439 x 286 mm
LHO/D/0470

Servant, Hand of Servant
Black and white chalk
on blue paper
375 x 282 mm
LHO/D/0471

Hands of Michelangelo
Black and white chalk
on blue paper
420 x 248 mm
LHO/D/0472

Drapery for Servant
Black and white chalk
on blue paper
420 x 245 mm
LHO/D/0473

Hands of Servant
Black and white chalk
on blue paper
290 x 265 mm
LHO/D/0825

Hands of Servant
Black and white chalk
on blue paper
400 x 235 mm
LHO/D/0839

Studies for 'Miss Ruth Stewart Hodgson', c.1877

Composition
Black and white chalk
on brown paper
327 x 232 mm
LHO/D/0900

Studies for 'Moorish Garden; A Dream of Granada', c.1873

Studies for 'The Daphnephoria' and 'Moorish Garden; A Dream of Granada': Girls
Black and white chalk
on blue paper
244 x 321 mm
LHO/D/0579

Studies for 'Moorish Garden; A Dream of Granada' and 'Phryne at Eleusis': Phryne, Girl
Black and white chalk on blue paper
240 x 323 mm
LHO/D/0597

Studies for 'Mrs Charles Magniac', c.1863

Composition
Black and white chalk
on blue paper
333 x 290 mm
LHO/D/0888

Studies for 'Mrs Stephen Ralli', c.1880

Composition
Black and white chalk
on brown paper
327 x 236 mm
LHO/D/0901

Studies for 'Mrs Williams', c.1877–92

Female Head
Black and white chalk
on brown paper
261 x 224 mm
LHO/D/0887

Studies for 'Music', c.1884

Male and Female Figures
Black and white chalk
on brown paper
368 x 274 mm
LHO/D/0627

Drapery for Seated Female Figure
Black and white chalk
on brown paper
261 x 222 mm
LHO/D/0628

Studies for 'The Dance' and 'Music': Seated Female Figures, Hands, c.1882
Black and white chalk
on brown paper
231 x 318 mm
LHO/D/0629

Female Figure
Black and white chalk
on brown paper
213 x 301 mm
LHO/D/0630

Female Figure
Black and white chalk
on brown paper
315 x 230 mm
LHO/D/0631

Male Figure
Black and white chalk
on brown paper
227 x 315 mm
LHO/D/0632

Male and Female Figures
Black and white chalk
on brown paper
237 x 321 mm
LHO/D/0633

Male and Female Figures
Black and white chalk
on brown paper
288 x 369 mm
LHO/D/0634

Drapery for Female Figures
Black and white chalk
on brown paper
318 x 227 mm
LHO/D/0804

Female Figure with Lyre,
Male Figure
Black and white chalk
on brown paper
246 x 339 mm
LHO/D/1747

Female Arm
Black and white chalk
on brown paper
246 x 339 mm
LHO/D/1747 verso

Composition
Graphite and white bodycolour
on tracing paper
87 x 456 mm
LHO/D/3003
(cat. no. 5.4)

Studies for 'Nausicaa', c.1877

Female Figure
Black and white chalk
on blue paper
218 x 292 mm
LHO/D/0581
(cat. no. 4.9)

Studies for 'Nausicaa' and 'Winding the Skein':
Composition, Female Figures
Black and white chalk
on blue paper
290 x 222 mm
LHO/D/0582
(cat. no. 4.8)

Studies for 'Elijah in the Wilderness' and 'Nausicaa': Female Figure,
Angel, Composition
Black and white chalk
on blue paper
295 x 225 mm
LHO/D/0589

Studies for 'Orpheus and Eurydice' ('But give them me - the mouth, the eyes, the brows'), c.1861–63

Studies for 'Bianca' and 'Orpheus and Eurydice': Orpheus and Eurydice, Hand of Orpheus,
Composition, Figure, c.1861
Black and white chalk
on blue paper
289 x 441 mm
LHO/D/0478

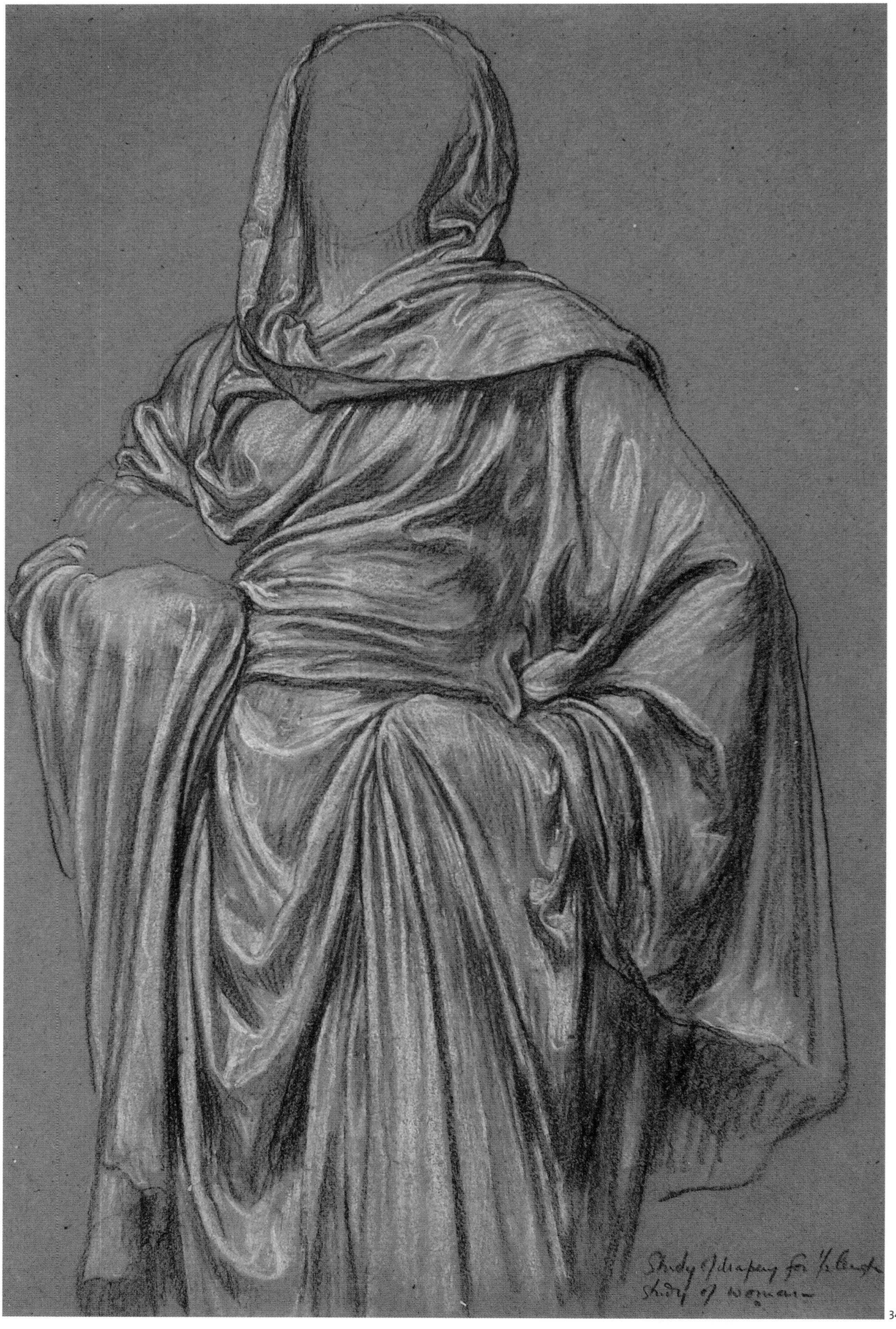

34.

cat. ill. 34. *Study for 'Melittion': Drapery for Female Figure*, c.1881. Black and white chalk on brown paper, LHO/D/0810.

Composition *c.*1863
Black and white chalk
on blue paper
297 x 137 mm
LHO/D/0479

Studies for an Illustration to Dalziels' 'Bible Gallery', 'Golden Hours', and 'Orpheus and Eurydice': 'Eliezer and Rebekah', Compositions, *c.*1863
Black and white chalk
on blue paper
290 x 301 mm
LHO/D/0487

Studies for 'The Painter's Honeymoon', *c.*1865

Composition, Male and Female Figures, Hands
Black and white chalk
on blue paper
297 x 445 mm
LHO/D/0486

Studies for 'Paolo and Francesca' ('Ma solo un punto fu quel che ci vinse'), *c.*1860

Paolo, Legs of Paolo
Black and white chalk
on blue paper
427 x 279 mm
LHO/D/0462

Composition
Graphite on tracing paper
484 x 363 mm
LHO/D/0463

Studies for 'Pastoral', *c.*1866

Composition
Graphite on tracing paper
170 x 83 mm
LHO/D/0496

Studies for 'Perseus and Andromeda', *c.*1877–90

Wings of Pegasus, Female Figure *c.*1890
Black chalk on
grey-brown paper
366 x 274 mm
LHO/D/0500

Andromeda *c.*1890
Black and white chalk
on brown paper
372 x 287 mm
LHO/D/0669

Studies for 'And the Sea Gave up the Dead', later 'Perseus and Andromeda': Female Figure, *c.*1877–79
Black and white chalk
on blue paper
329 x 246 mm
LHO/D/0693

Studies for 'Perseus on Pegasus Hastening to the Rescue of Andromeda', *c.*1895

Composition
Black and white chalk
on grey-brown paper
368 x 277 mm
LHO/D/0691

Composition, Perseus and Pegasus
Black and white chalk
on grey-brown paper
367 x 283 mm
LHO/D/0692

Perseus
Black chalk on
grey-brown paper
276 x 358 mm
LHO/D/0773

Composition
Black and white chalk
on grey-brown paper
368 x 258 mm
LHO/D/0802

Studies for 'Phoenicians Bartering with Ancient Britons', *c.*1894

Composition
Graphite on tracing paper
461 x 291 mm
LHO/D/0746

Drapery for Female Figure
Black and white chalk
on grey-brown paper
365 x 280 mm
LHO/D/0747
(cat. no. 6.3)

Male Figure
Black and white chalk
on grey-brown paper
365 x 280 mm
LHO/D/0747 verso

Drapery for Female Figures and Arms
Black and white chalk
on grey-brown paper
281 x 367 mm
LHO/D/0748

Male and Female Figures
Black and white chalk
on grey-brown paper
284 x 369 mm
LHO/D/0749

Male Figures
Black and white chalk
on grey-brown paper
283 x 369 mm
LHO/D/0750

Drapery for Male Figure
Black and white chalk
on grey-brown paper
367 x 282 mm
LHO/D/0752

Drapery for Male Figures
Black and white chalk
on grey-brown paper
368 x 448 mm
LHO/D/0753

Female Figure
Black chalk on grey-brown paper
368 x 448 mm
LHO/D/0753 verso

Male Figure
Black and white chalk
on grey-brown paper
368 x 284 mm
LHO/D/0754

Male Figures, Feet, Hands
Black and white chalk
on grey-brown paper
369 x 280 mm
LHO/D/0755

Male Figure, Male Head
Black and white chalk
on grey-brown paper
370 x 279 mm
LHO/D/0756

Male Head
Black and white chalk
on blue paper
382 x 296 mm
LHO/D/0774

Female Figure
Black and white chalk
on grey-brown paper
365 x 276 mm
LHO/D/0785

Male Figure
Black and white chalk
on grey-brown paper
340 x 225 mm
LHO/D/3001

Studies for 'Phryne at Eleusis', *c.*1873–81

Compositions, Figures, *c.*1881
Black and white chalk
on blue paper
165 x 235 mm
LHO/D/0596

Studies for 'Moorish Garden; A Dream of Granada' and 'Phryne at Eleusis': Phryne, Girl, *c.*1873
Black and white chalk
on blue paper
240 x 323 mm
LHO/D/0597

Studies for 'Cupid and Dove' and 'Phryne at Eleusis': Cupid, Composition, *c.*1873
Black and white chalk
on blue paper
245 x 318 mm
LHO/D/0657

Drapery for Female Figure, *c.*1881
Black and white chalk
on brown paper
476 x 225 mm
LHO/D/0685

Studies for 'Day-Dreams' and 'Phryne at Eleusis': Head of Phryne, Female Figure, *c.*1881
Black and white chalk
on brown paper
323 x 247 mm
LHO/D/0803

Studies for 'The Reconciliation of the Montagues and the Capulets over the Dead Bodies of Romeo and Juliet', 1854

Head of Paris
Graphite on white paper
284 x 220 mm
LHO/D/0878

Male Head
Graphite on white paper
292 x 220 mm
LHO/D/0946

Studies for 'Return of Persephone', *c.*1890

Composition
Black and white chalk
on brown paper
269 x 209 mm
LHO/D/0694

Hermes and Persephone, Hands and Drapery for Hermes
Black and white chalk
on brown paper
361 x 280 mm
LHO/D/0695

Persephone
Black and white chalk
on brown paper
37 x 289 mm
LHO/D/0696

Demeter, Persephone
Black and white chalk
on brown paper
261 x 369 mm
LHO/D/0697

Drapery for Demeter
Black and white chalk
on brown paper
558 x 369 mm
LHO/D/0698
(fig. 8)

Head of Demeter
Black and white chalk
on grey-brown paper
241 x 226 mm
LHO/D/0709

Drapery for Hermes
Black and white chalk
on grey-brown paper
367 x 287 mm
LHO/D/0775

Studies for 'Elijah in the Wilderness', 'Greek Girls Playing at Ball' and 'Return of Persephone': Compositions, Male and Female Figures, *c.*1877
Black and white chalk
on blue paper
215 x 279 mm
LHO/D/0806

Head of Persephone
Black and white chalk
on brown paper
240 x 240 mm
LHO/D/0820

Studies for 'Rizpah', *c.*1892

Composition
Black and white chalk
on brown paper
181 x 173 mm
LHO/D/0720

Composition
Graphite on
tracing paper
125 x 90 mm
LHO/D/0721

Rizpah and Male Figure, Male Feet
Black and white chalk
on grey-brown paper
277 x 368 mm
LHO/D/0722

Rizpah, Male Figures
Black and white chalk
on brown paper
272 x 359 mm
LHO/D/0723

Male Figure
Black and white chalk
on brown paper
273 x 360 mm
LHO/D/0724

Male Figure
Black and white chalk
on brown paper
368 x 270 mm
LHO/D/0725

Rizpah, Male Figures
Black and white chalk
on blue paper
230 x 299 mm
LHO/D/0726

Head of Rizpah
Black and white chalk
on brown paper
258 x 180 mm
LHO/D/0727

Drapery for Male Figure
Black and white chalk
on grey-brown paper
359 x 268 mm
LHO/D/0728

Drapery and Pitcher
Black and white chalk
on grey-brown paper
268 x 367 mm
LHO/D/0729

Drapery
Black and white chalk
on brown paper
199 x 163 mm
LHO/D/0827

Studies for 'Salomé Dancing', *c.*1864

Composition, Salomé, Hands of Salomé
Black and white chalk
on blue paper
325 x 481 mm
LHO/D/0459

Studies for 'Samson and Delilah', *c.*1858

Samson
Black chalk on white paper
467 x 293 mm
LHO/D/0460
(cat. no. 1.9)

Leg of Samson, Male Head
Black chalk and white bodycolour
on buff paper
471 x 290 mm
LHO/D/0461

Samson and Male Figure
Black chalk on buff paper
290 x 471 mm
LHO/D/0461 verso

Drapery and Legs of Delilah
Black and white chalk
on blue paper
474 x 304 mm
LHO/D/0842

Studies for 'Sibyl', *c.*1888

Composition
Black and white chalk
on brown paper
217 x 136 mm
LHO/D/0733

Drapery for Female Figure
Black and white chalk
on brown paper
556 x 370 mm
LHO/D/0841
(cat. no. 5.10)

Studies for 'Sisters', *c.*1861

Composition
Black and white chalk
on buff paper
82 x 40 mm
LHO/D/0799L

Studies for 'Sister's Kiss', *c.*1879

Female Figure and Girl
Black and white chalk
on blue paper
224 x 290 mm
LHO/D/0592

Studies for 'Solitude', *c.*1889

Female Figure
Black and white chalk
on brown paper
326 x 236 mm
LHO/D/0793

Studies for 'The Spirit of the Summit', *c.*1893

Female Figures
Black and white chalk
on brown paper
274 x 369 mm
LHO/D/0730

Female Figures
Black and white chalk
on grey-brown paper
277 x 368 mm
LHO/D/0731

Studies for 'Fatidica', 'The Spirit of the Summit', 'Summer Slumber' and 'The Bracelet': Compositions
Black and white chalk
on grey-brown paper
280 x 368 mm
LHO/D/0741

Studies for 'The Star of Bethlehem. One of the Magi, from the terrace of his house, stands looking at the star in the east. The lower part of the picture indicates a revel, which he may be supposed to have just left', *c.*1861

Composition
Watercolour on white paper
115 x 50 mm
LHO/D/0429

Composition
Black and white chalk
on blue paper
234 x 137 mm
LHO/D/0464

Male Figure with Lamp
Black and white chalk
on blue paper
444 x 296 mm
LHO/D/0751
(cat. ill. 31)

Studies for 'Summer Moon', *c.*1871

Studies for 'Antique Juggling Girl', 'The Courtyard of a House at Damascus' and 'Summer Moon': Female Figures
Black and white chalk
on blue paper
319 x 235 mm
LHO/D/0520

Studies for 'Summer Slumber', *c.*1880–93

Statue with Pitcher, *c.*1893
Black and white chalk
on grey-brown paper
302 x 285 mm
LHO/D/0664

Studies for 'Idyll' and 'Summer Slumber': Female Figures, *c.*1880
Black and white chalk
on brown paper
236 x 320 mm
LHO/D/0701

Sleeping Female Figure, *c.*1893
Black and white chalk
on grey-brown paper
258 x 357 mm
LHO/D/0737

Sleeping Female Figure, *c.*1893
Black and white chalk
on grey-brown paper
172 x 282 mm
LHO/D/0738

Sleeping Female Figure, *c.*1893
Black and white chalk
on grey-brown paper
281 x 369 mm
LHO/D/0739

Composition, *c.*1893
Black and white chalk
on grey-brown paper
214 x 268 mm
LHO/D/0740

Studies for 'Fatidica', 'The Spirit of the Summit', 'Summer Slumber' and 'The Bracelet': Compositions, *c.*1893
Black and white chalk
on grey-brown paper
280 x 368 mm
LHO/D/0741

Sleeping Female Figure, *c.*1893
Black chalk on grey-brown paper
284 x 369 mm
LHO/D/0749 verso

Male Figures, *c.*1893
Black and white chalk
on grey-brown paper
281 x 368 mm
LHO/D/0772

Cat, Female Head, *c.*1893
Black and white chalk
on grey-brown paper
341 x 243 mm
LHO/D/0800

Studies for 'Sun-Gleams', *c.*1883

Studies for 'The Jealousy of Simoetha the Sorceress' and 'Sun-Gleams': Female Figures, Female Head, Hands
Black and white chalk
on brown paper
227 x 317 mm
LHO/D/0812

Studies for 'The Syracusan Bride leading Wild Beasts in Procession to the Temple of Diana', *c.*1865

Composition
Graphite on tracing paper
141 x 444 mm
LHO/D/0488

Male and Female Figures
Black chalk on blue paper
325 x 482 mm
LHO/D/0489

Lion, Tiger
Graphite on buff paper
234 x 151 mm
LHO/D/0872

Studies for 'Tragic Poetess', *c.*1889

Composition
Black and white chalk
on brown paper
323 x 231 mm
LHO/D/0688

Female Figure with Chair
Black and white chalk
on brown paper
565 x 366 mm
LHO/D/0689

Drapery
Black and white chalk
on grey-brown paper
368 x 277 mm
LHO/D/0690

Female Figure
Black and white chalk
on brown paper
300 x 238 mm
LHO/D/0781

Studies for 'The Triumph of Music', *c.*1855

Drapery for Orpheus
Black and white chalk
on blue paper
400 x 278 mm
LHO/D/1138

Studies for 'Venus and Cupid', 1856

Architectural Detail
Graphite and watercolour
on white paper
306 x 108 mm
LHO/D/0873

Studies for 'The Vestal', *c.*1882

Composition
Black and white chalk
on brown paper
297 x 222 mm
LHO/D/1038

Studies for 'Wedded', *c.*1881

Composition
Black and white chalk
on blue paper
136 x 245 mm
LHO/D/0598

Male and Female Figures
Black and white chalk
on blue paper
315 x 241 mm
LHO/D/0599

Studies for 'Winding the Skein', *c.*1877

Studies for 'Nausicaa' and 'Winding the Skein': Composition, Female Figures
Black and white chalk
on blue paper
290 x 222 mm
LHO/D/0582

Composition
Black and white chalk
on brown paper
212 x 299 mm
LHO/D/0583
(cat. no. 4.10)

Female Figures
Black and white chalk
on blue paper
184 x 255 mm
LHO/D/0584

Studies for 'The Wise and Foolish Virgins', *c.*1863

Drapery for Female Figure
Black and white chalk
on blue paper
420 x 272 mm
LHO/D/0490

Female Head and Hands
Black and white chalk
on blue paper
435 x 292 mm
LHO/D/0491

Female Figure, Female Arms, Female Hand
Black and white chalk
on blue paper
432 x 283 mm
LHO/D/0492

Head of Christ, Hand of Christ
Black chalk on blue paper
430 x 278 mm
LHO/D/0493

Female Hands
Black and white chalk
on blue paper
430 x 278 mm
LHO/D/0493 verso

Female Head
Graphite on tracing paper
181 x 155 mm
LHO/D/0881

PREPARATORY STUDIES FOR FRESCOES, MOSAICS ETC.

Studies for 'The Arts of Industry as Applied to Peace' (Fresco), *c.*1872–85

Composition, Figures, *c.*1872
Black and white chalk
on blue paper
231 x 315 mm
LHO/D/0554
(cat. no. 3.7)

Composition, Female Figures, *c.*1872
Black and white chalk
on blue paper
317 x 232 mm
LHO/D/0555

Males Figures, *c.*1872
Black and white chalk
on blue paper
237 x 308 mm
LHO/D/0556

Male Figures, *c.*1872
Black and white chalk
on blue paper
243 x 327 mm
LHO/D/0557

Male Figures, *c.*1872
Black and white chalk
on blue paper
240 x 307 mm
LHO/D/0558

Male Figures, *c.*1872
Black and white chalk
on blue paper
233 x 310 mm
LHO/D/0559

Male Figures, *c.*1872
Black and white chalk
on blue paper
237 x 324 mm
LHO/D/0560

Female Figures, *c.*1872
Black and white chalk
on blue paper
233 x 321 mm
LHO/D/0561

Relief, *c.*1872
Black and white chalk
on blue paper
161 x 125 mm
LHO/D/0660

Female Figures, Part of Composition, *c.*1885
Black and white chalk
on brown paper
280 x 370 mm
LHO/D/0666 verso

Drapery for Female Figures, *c.*1872
Black and white chalk
on blue paper
247 x 334 mm
LHO/D/0795

Female Figures, *c.*1872
Black and white chalk
on blue paper
243 x 324 mm
LHO/D/0798

Left Side of Composition, *c.*1872
Black chalk on blue paper
140 x 125 mm
LHO/D/1121 verso

Relief, *c.*1872
Black and white chalk
on blue paper
158 x 158 mm
LHO/D/1122

Right Side of Composition, *c.*1872
Black chalk on blue paper
158 x 158 mm
LHO/D/1122 verso

Studies for 'The Arts of Industry as Applied to War' (Fresco), *c.*1871–79

Male Figures, *c.*1871
Black and white chalk
on blue paper
233 x 318 mm
LHO/D/0522

Male Figures, *c.*1871
Black and white chalk
on blue paper
238 x 323 mm
LHO/D/0523

Male Figures, *c.*1871
Black and white chalk
on blue paper
232 x 310 mm
LHO/D/0524

Male Figures, *c.*1871
Black and white chalk
on blue paper
230 x 309 mm
LHO/D/0525

Male and Female Figures, *c.*1871
Black and white chalk
on blue paper
242 x 329 mm
LHO/D/0526

Male and Female Figures, *c.*1871
Black and white chalk
on blue paper
315 x 236 mm
LHO/D/0527

Drapery for Male Figures, *c.*1871
Black and white chalk
on blue paper
236 x 299 mm
LHO/D/0528

Drapery for Female Figure, Female Figure, *c.*1871
Black and white chalk
on blue paper
330 x 242 mm
LHO/D/0529

Drapery for Male Figure, *c.*1871
Black and white chalk
on blue paper
319 x 232 mm
LHO/D/0530

Drapery for Male Figure, *c.*1871
Black and white chalk
on blue paper
234 x 300 mm
LHO/D/0531

Drapery for Male Figure, *c.*1871
Black and white chalk
on blue paper
232 x 309 mm
LHO/D/0532

Male Figure, Drapery for Male Figure, *c.*1871
Black and white chalk
on blue paper
225 x 302 mm
LHO/D/0533

Drapery for Male Figure, *c.*1871
Black and white chalk on blue paper
316 x 225 mm
LHO/D/0534

Male and Female Figures, *c.*1871
Black and white chalk
on blue paper
238 x 314 mm
LHO/D/0536

Drapery, *c.*1871
Black and white chalk
on blue paper
234 x 310 mm
LHO/D/0537

Drapery, *c.*1871
Black and white chalk
on blue paper
234 x 310 mm
LHO/D/0537 verso

Drapery for Male Figure, *c.*1871
Black and white chalk
on blue paper
316 x 233 mm
LHO/D/0538

Drapery for Male Figure , *c.*1871
Black and white chalk
on blue paper
319 x 238 mm
LHO/D/0539

Drapery for Female Figures , *c.*1871
Black and white chalk
on blue paper
235 x 313 mm
LHO/D/0540

Costume, *c.*1871
Black and white chalk
on blue paper
319 x 243 mm
LHO/D/0541

Costume for Male Figure, *c.*1871
Black and white chalk
on blue paper
229 x 300 mm
LHO/D/0542

Male Figure, Drapery, *c.*1871
Black and white chalk
on blue paper
234 x 300 mm
LHO/D/0543

Drapery for Male Figure, *c.*1871
Black and white chalk
on blue paper
313 x 231 mm
LHO/D/0544

Drapery for Female Figure, *c.*1871
Black and white chalk
on blue paper
329 x 240 mm
LHO/D/0545
(cat. no. 3.6)

Male Figure, *c.*1871
Black and white chalk
on blue paper
227 x 298 mm
LHO/D/0546

Drapery for Male Figure, *c.*1871
Black and white chalk
on blue paper
230 x 304 mm
LHO/D/0547

Drapery, Female Figure, *c.*1871
Black and white chalk
on blue paper
236 x 313 mm
LHO/D/0548

Female Figure, *c.*1871
Black and white chalk
on blue paper
231 x 316 mm
LHO/D/0549

Male Figures, *c.*1879
Black and white chalk
on brown paper
228 x 306 mm
LHO/D/0550

Male Figures, Boy, *c.*1871
Black and white chalk
on blue paper
239 x 319 mm
LHO/D/0551

Male Figures, *c.*1879
Black and white chalk
on brown paper
231 x 312 mm
LHO/D/0552

Male Figure, *c.*1871
Black and white chalk
on blue paper
245 x 323 mm
LHO/D/0553

Male Figure, *c.*1879
Black and white chalk
on brown paper
293 x 214 mm
LHO/D/0770

Drapery for Male Figures, *c.*1871
Black and white chalk
on blue paper
236 x 320 mm
LHO/D/0776

Male Figure, Banner, *c.*1871
Black and white chalk
on blue paper
300 x 228 mm
LHO/D/0843

Composition, Figures, *c.*1871
Black and white chalk
on blue paper
231 x 306 mm
LHO/D/1115

Studies for 'The Arts, Welcomed by the Lord of the Castle, Greet the Spring' (Fresco), *c.*1850

Composition
Graphite on white paper
287 x 387 mm
LHO/D/0858

Studies for 'Cimabue' (Mosaic), *c.*1864

Cimabue
Black and white chalk
on blue paper
295 x 444 mm
LHO/D/0764

Studies for 'The Echoes of Hellas' (Tableau Vivant), *c.*1882

Part of Composition
Black and white chalk
on brown paper
344 x 271 mm
LHO/D/0807

Studies for a Jubilee Medal for Queen Victoria, *c.*1886

Male Figure
Black and white chalk
on grey-brown paper
362 x 280 mm
LHO/D/0769

Figure of Industry
Black and white chalk
on brown paper
338 x 279 mm
LHO/D/0847

Studies for 'Nicola Pisano' (Mosaic), *c.*1863

Male Figure, Hand with Sculpture, Feet
Black anc white chalk
on blue paper
287 x 408 mm
LHO/D/0763

Studies for the Tomb of Elizabeth Barrett Browning

Elevations, Female Figure, 1856–77
Black and white chalk
on blue paper
169 x 234 mm
LHO/D/0759 verso

PREPARATORY STUDIES FOR ILLUSTRATIONS

Studies for Illustrations to 'Buch der Lieder', *c.*1850

Study for an Illustration to 'Buch der Lieder': Composition
Graphite, white bodycolour
and grey watercolour
on white paper
207 x 277 mm
LHO/D/0862

Study for an Illustration to 'Buch der Lieder': Male and Female Figures
Graphite and watercolour
on white paper
234 x 300 mm
LHO/D/0863

Studies for Illustrations to Dalziels' 'Bible Gallery', 1863–64

'Death of the First Born', Composition
Graphite on tracing paper
97 x 94 mm
LHO/D/0484

Studies for an Illustration to Dalziels' 'Bible Gallery', 'Golden Hours', and 'Orpheus and Eurydice': 'Eliezer and Rebekah', Compositions
Black and white chalk
on blue paper
290 x 301 mm
LHO/D/0487

Studies for 'David' and for Illustrations to Dalziels' 'Bible Gallery': Abraham and the Angel', 'Samson at the Mill', Abraham, Angel, Samson, Male Figure, Female Figure, 1863–64
Black and white chalk
on blue paper
285 x 443 mm
LHO/D/0765

Studies for 'Dante in Exile' and for Illustrations to Dalziels' 'Bible Gallery': 'Death of the First Born', 'Eliezer and Rebekah', Male and Female Figures, Male Legs, Male Hands
Black and white chalk
on blue paper
293 x 448 mm
LHO/D/0782

'Eliezer and Rebekah', Composition
Graphite and brown
watercolour on white paper
175 x 149 mm
LHO/D/0850

'Samson at the Mill', Composition
Black and white chalk
on blue paper
238 x 235 mm
LHO/D/0851

'Samson Carrying Away the Gates of Gaza', Composition
Black and white chalk
on blue paper
241 x 327 mm
LHO/D/0852

'Samson Slaying the Lion': Composition
Black and white chalk
on blue paper
240 x 260 mm
LHO/D/0853

'The Escape of the Spies': Composition
Black and white chalk
on blue paper
216 x 233 mm
LHO/D/0854

'Death of the First Born', Composition
Graphite on tracing paper
84 x 73 mm
LHO/D/0855

'The Return of the Prodigal Son', Composition
Graphite on tracing paper
129 x 110 mm
LHO/D/0856

Studies for the Illustration 'Dead Christ', 1845–52

Composition
Graphite on white paper
68 x 135 mm
LHO/D/0860

Composition
Graphite, black chalk
and white bodycolour
on white paper
119 x 185 mm
LHO/D/0861

Studies for an Illustration to 'A Musical Instrument', *c.*1859

'The Great God Pan', Composition
Black chalk and white
bodycolour on blue paper
181 x 103 mm
LHO/D/0857

Studies for Illustrations to 'Romola', *c.*1862

'Monna Brigida's Conversion', Male Figures
Black and white chalk
on blue paper
256 x 350 mm
LHO/D/0777

Studies for Illustrations to 'A Week in a French Country House', *c.*1866

'Drifting', Seated Boy
Black and white chalk
on blue paper
243 x 323 mm
LHO/D/0780

'Drifting', Composition
Black and white chalk
on blue paper
166 x 219 mm
LHO/D/1030

'An Evening in a French Country House', Interior Including a Fireplace
Black and white chalk
on blue paper
167 x 200 mm
LHO/D/1031

'An Evening in a French Country House', Rough Composition
Black and white chalk
on blue paper
41 x 66 mm
LHO/D/1108

UNIDENTIFIED PREPARATORY STUDIES

Figure, *c.*1857
Black chalk on white paper
460 x 293 mm
LHO/D/0460 verso

Drapery, 1856–77
Black and white chalk
on blue paper
236 x 309 mm
LHO/D/0535

Study for an Unidentified Portrait of Female Figure: Composition, *c.*1872
Black and white chalk
on blue paper
237 x 324 mm
LHO/D/0560 verso

Male Figure with Lyre, and Male Figure with Tripod, 1891–96
Black and white chalk
on grey-brown paper
277 x 367 mm
LHO/D/0580

Female Figure, *c.*1881
Black and white chalk
on blue paper
240 x 323 mm
LHO/D/0597 verso

Female Figures, 1891–96
Black and white chalk
on grey-brown paper
366 x 282 mm
LHO/D/0626

Reclining Female Figures, 1891–96
Black and white chalk
on grey-brown paper
262 x 357 mm
LHO/D/0639

Female Figure with a Lyre and Chair, 1856–77
Graphite and black and
white chalk on blue paper
211 x 179 mm
LHO/D/0651

Study for an Unidentified Composition, Probably for a Decorative Scheme, 1886
Black and white chalk
on blue paper
150 x 239 mm
LHO/D/0659

Female Figure and Female Head, 1891–96
Black and white chalk
on grey-brown paper
229 x 238 mm
LHO/D/0703

Female Figure, 1891–96
Black and white chalk
on grey-brown paper
268 x 367 mm
LHO/D/0729 verso

Female Figure, 1891–96
Black and white chalk
on grey-brown paper
280 x 371 mm
LHO/D/0744

Study for a Project relating to the Subject of 'Alexander Entering the House of Darius': Composition, 1856–77
Black and white chalk
on blue paper
169 x 234 mm
LHO/D/0759

Study for a Project relating to the Subject of 'Alexander Entering the House of Darius': Female Figures, Children, 1856–77
Black and white chalk
on blue paper
231 x 324 mm
LHO/D/0760

Study for a Project relating to the Subject of 'Alexander Entering the House of Darius': Female Head, Hands, 1856–77
Black and white chalk
on blue paper
275 x 281 mm
LHO/D/0761

Male and Female Figures, Female Head, Male Hands, Male Feet, 1856–77
Black and white chalk
on blue paper
321 x 322 mm
LHO/D/0767

Male Figure, 1856–77
Black and white chalk
on blue paper
433 x 292 mm
LHO/D/0768

Male Figure, 1856–77
Graphite on blue paper
300 x 406 mm
LHO/D/0779

Girl, Legs, Arm, 1856–77
Black and white chalk
on blue paper
445 x 295 mm
LHO/D/0786

Seated Female Figure, 1895–96
Black and white chalk
on grey-brown paper
279 x 371 mm
LHO/D/0787 verso

Female Figure, 1856–77
Black and white chalk
on blue paper
452 x 300 mm
LHO/D/0788

Female Figures, Female Hands, 1891–96
Black and white chalk
on grey-brown paper
365 x 278 mm
LHO/D/0790

Female Figure, 1891–96
Black and white chalk
on grey-brown paper
292 x 243 mm
LHO/D/0796

Composition Showing a Mother and Child and a Female Figure, 1856–77
Black and white chalk
on blue paper
67 x 49 mm
LHO/D/0799R

Female Figures Descending Steps, 1877–92
Black and white chalk
on brown paper
240 x 336 mm
LHO/D/0814

Female Figures in a Doorway, 1877–92
Black and white chalk
on brown paper
240 x 336 mm
LHO/D/0814 verso

Female Figures with a Bow, 1877–92
Black and white chalk
on brown paper
231 x 298 mm
LHO/D/0817

Female Figure and Girl, Female Figure, 1856–77
Black and white chalk
on blue paper
245 x 330 mm
LHO/D/0818

Female Head, Probably Dorothy Dene or One of Her Sisters, 1891–96
Black and white chalk
on grey-brown paper
323 x 280 mm
LHO/D/0819

Female Figure, 1895–96
Black and white chalk
on grey-brown paper
280 x 368 mm
LHO/D/0846 verso

Female Figures Descending Steps, 1877–92
Black and white chalk
on brown paper
185 x 283 mm
LHO/D/0849

Female Head in Contemporary Dress, Probably Dorothy Dene or One of Her Sisters, 1891–96
Black and white chalk
on grey-brown paper
255 x 199 mm
LHO/D/0889

Female Head in Contemporary Dress, Probably Dorothy Dene or One of Her Sisters, 1877–92
Black and white chalk
on brown paper
261 x 191 mm
LHO/D/0890

Female Figure, 1891–96
Black and white chalk
on grey-brown paper
359 x 273 mm
LHO/D/0892

Girl, 1891–96
Black and white chalk on
grey-brown paper
370 x 278 mm
LHO/D/0899

Study for a Portrait, 1856–77
Black and white chalk
on blue paper
355 x 293 mm
LHO/D/0903

Girl, 1850–60
Black chalk and white bodycolour
on grey paper
404 x 324 mm
LHO/D/0904

Female Figure and Girl, 1850–60
Black chalk and white bodycolour
on grey paper
404 x 324 mm
LHO/D/0904 verso

Girl, 1893
Black and white chalk
on grey-brown paper
363 x 275 mm
LHO/D/1037

Drapery, 1856–77
Black and white chalk
on blue paper
303 x 230 mm
LHO/D/1109

Female Hands, 1845–52
Black chalk and white bodycolour
on buff paper
179 x 157 mm
LHO/D/1117

Foot and Toes, 1850–60
Black chalk and
white bodycolour
on buff paper
206 x 221 mm
LHO/D/1118

Foot, 1850–60
Black chalk on buff paper
180 x 156 mm
LHO/D/1119

Study for an Unidentified Composition Showing a Cherub and a Lyre, *c.*1872
Black and white chalk
on blue paper
140 x 125 mm
LHO/D/1121

MISCELLANEOUS STUDIES (INCL. STUDIES OF ANIMALS, COSTUME ETC.)

Shepherd, 1845–52
Graphite and watercolour
on white paper
359 x 250 mm
LHO/D/0433

Female Figure, 1852
Graphite and watercolour
on white paper
359 x 254 mm
LHO/D/0434

Male Figure with Arm Raised, 1855–65
Black on white chalk
on mauve paper
312 x 236 mm
LHO/D/0848

Lower Half of Seated Female Figure Seen in LHO/D/0853 verso, 1863–64
Black and white chalk on blue paper
241 x 327 mm
LHO/D/0852 verso

Seated Female Figure, 1863–64
240 x 260 mm
Black and white chalk on blue paper
LHO/D/0853 verso

Dog, 1845–52
Black chalk on white paper
119 x 185 mm
LHO/D/0861 verso

Sleeping Baby, 1850
Graphite on white paper
180 x 234 mm
LHO/D/0877

Study for an Unidentified Portrait of a Seated Female Figure with a Fan, 1850–60
Graphite on white paper
415 x 306 mm
LHO/D/0882

Seated Male Figure in Contemporary Dress, 1845–52
Graphite on white paper
237 x 209 mm
LHO/D/0883

Drapery, 1845–52
Graphite on white paper
237 x 209 mm
LHO/D/0883 verso

Male Figure in Contemporary Dress with a Chair, 1845–52
Graphite on white paper
283 x 217 mm
LHO/D/0884

Male Figure in Contemporary Dress, 1845–52
Graphite on white paper
285 x 219 mm
LHO/D/0885

Portrait of a Female Figure, Probably Dorothy Dene or One of Her Sisters, 1879–96
Silverpoint on white paper
283 x 231 mm
LHO/D/0896

Farmhouse and Cows, Chickens, Cows, Ducks and Donkeys, 1845–52
Graphite on white paper
230 x 285 mm
LHO/D/0922

Female Figure in Traditional Italian Costume, 1852–55
Graphite on white paper
298 x 235 mm
LHO/D/0923

Female Figure in Traditional Italian Costume, 1852–55
Graphite on white paper
297 x 234 mm
LHO/D/0924

'Saltner' from Meran, Italy, 1845
Graphite on white paper
216 x 217 mm
LHO/D/0925

'Saltner' from Meran, Italy, 1845
Graphite on tracing paper
311 x 236 mm
LHO/D/0926

Female Figure, 1852
Graphite on white paper
428 x 289 mm
LHO/D/0927

Male Head, 1856
Graphite on white paper
277 x 205 mm
LHO/D/0950

Female Figure, 1852–55
Graphite on white paper
297 x 235 mm
LHO/D/0962

Dog and Mule's Head, 1845–52
Graphite on white paper
73 x 131 mm
LHO/D/1032

Male and Female Figures, Possibly in Austrian Costume, 1845–52
Graphite on white paper
125 x 201 mm
LHO/D/1033

LEIGHTON SKETCHBOOKS AND ALBUMS

Sketchbook Including Figures, Caricatures and Studies for a Composition, *c.*1845
Graphite, watercolour and ink
on white paper
225 x 138 x 14 mm
LHO/D/1135

Sketchbook Including Landscapes, Figures and Notes, 1895
Graphite on white paper
85 x 121 x 10 mm
LHO/D/1136

Album of Drawings, Formerly Belonging to Adelaide Sartoris, 1854–59
Various media
204 x 282 x 46 mm
LHO/D/1139

SKETCHBOOKS FORMERLY BELONGING TO LEIGHTON

Sketchbook Including Landscapes and Architecture in Italy, 1852–55
Graphite and watercolour
on white paper
430 x 272 x 17 mm
LHO/D/0437

Sketchbook Including Costume Studies, Compositions and Landscapes, 1845–65
Graphite and watercolour
on blue and white paper
306 x 422 x 26 mm
LHO/D/0438

BIBLIOGRAPHY, EXHIBITIONS & EXHIBITION CATALOGUES

Aitchison 1896. George Aitchison: 'Lord Leighton P.R.A.: Some Reminiscences', *Journal of the Royal Institute of British Architects*, 3rd series, 1896, pp 264–65.

Anon. 1874a. Anon., 'Exhibition of Works in Black and White, Dudley Gallery', *Athenaeum*, 27 June 1874, p. 867

Anon. 1874b. Anon., 'Black and White Exhibition', *Art Journal*, 1874, p. 232

Anon. 1880. Anon., 'The Grosvenor Gallery. – Winter Exhibition. (First Notice)', *Athenaeum*, 3 January 1880, p. 24

Anon. 1894. Anon: 'The Study of a Lemon Tree', *Studio: An Illustrated Magazine of Fine and Applied Art*, 1894, vol. III, pp 24–27.

Anon. 1896a. Anon: 'Millais and Leighton by one who knew them both', *St James' Budget*, 17 August 1896.

Anon. 1896b. Anon: 'Lord Leighton's Studies', *The Times*, 14 December 1896, p. 4.

Anon. 1898. Anon: *The Times*, 28 June 1898, p. 9.

Anon. 1900. Anon: 'Lord Leighton's House', *The Times*, 17 November 1900, p. 9.

Anon. 1901. Anon: *The Times*, Friday 27 December 1901.

Anon. 1902. Anon: 'The Leighton House Muddle', *The Sovereign*, 30 October 1902.

Ash 1995. Russell Ash: *Lord Leighton*, Pavilion Books, London, 1995.

Barringer & Prettejohn 1999. Tim Barringer and Elizabeth Prettejohn (editors): *Frederic Leighton Antiquity, Renaissance, Modernity*, Yale University Press, New Haven and London, 1999.

Barrington 1896. Emilie Barrington: 'Lord Leighton's Sketches', *National Review*, December 1896. Reprinted in *A Collection of Essays on Lord Leighton and his Works with Illustrated Catalogue of the Contents of Leighton House*, privately published, London, 1900–01 (one known copy, held at Leighton House Museum).

Barrington 1897. Emilie Barrington: 'Lord Leighton's Sketches', *The Times*, 22 March 1897, p. 8.

Barrington 1906. Mrs Russell Barrington (Emilie Barrington): *The Life, Letters and Work of Frederic, Lord Leighton*, George Allen, London, 1906.

Barrow 1999. Rosemary Barrow: 'Drapery, Sculpture and the Praxitelean Ideal', in **Barringer & Prettejohn 1999**, pp 54–55.

CAMBRIDGE, MINNEAPOLIS, CHICAGO, KANSAS CITY 1968. *Drawings from the David Daniels Collection*, Minneapolis Institute of Arts, USA, 22 February – 21 April 1968; Art Institute of Chicago, USA, 03 May – 23 June 1968; Nelson Gallery and Atkins Museum, Kansas City, USA, 11 July – 29 September 1968; Fogg Art Museum, USA, 16 October – 25 November 1968. Exh. cat. by Mary Lee Bennett and Agnes Mongan, Cambridge (Mass.), 1968.

Caldwell Hutchinson 1893. G.W. Caldwell Hutchinson: *Some Hints on Learning to Draw*, Macmillan & Co., London, 1893.

CHRISTIES'S 1896. *The Collection of Lord Leighton, P.R.A.: Drawings by Different Artists*, Christie's, London, 14 July 1896.

Cockerell 1896. Samuel Pepys Cockerell: 'Lord Leighton's Drawings', *The Nineteenth Century*, 40, November, 1896, pp 809–15.

Cockerell 1898. Samuel Pepys Cockerell (Foreword): *Drawings and Studies by the Late Lord Leighton of Stretton, P.R.A.*, The Fine Art Society, 1898.

Comyns Carr 1908. Joseph Comyns Carr: *Some Eminent Victorians: Personal Recollections in the World of Art and Letters*, Duckworth & Co., London, 1908.

Cook 1903–12. E.T. Cook and A. Wedderburn: *The Works of Ruskin*, London, 1903–12, vol. XXXIII.

Corkran 1904. Alice Corkran: *Frederic Leighton*, Methuen & Co., London, 1904

Costa 1897. Giovanni Costa: 'Notes on Lord Leighton', *Cornhill Magazine*, 2 March 1897, pp 373–84.

Denis 1999. Rafael Cardoso Denis: 'From Burlington House to the Peckham Road: Leighton and Art and Design Education', in **Barringer & Prettejohn 1999**, pp 247–66.

Denis 2000. Rafael Cardoso Denis and Colin Trodd (editors): *Art and the Academy in the Nineteenth Century*, Manchester University Press, 2000.

DUBLIN 1907. *Irish International Exhibition*, Dublin, 1907.

Ironside 1948. Robin Ironside and John Gere, *Pre-Raphaelite Painters*, Phaidon, London, 1948.

LONDON 1859–60. Exhibition at the Hogarth Club, London, 1859–60.

LONDON 1874. *Black and White Exhibition*, Dudley Gallery, London, 1874.

LONDON 1880. Exhibition at the Grosvenor Gallery, London.

LONDON 1896. *Collection of Studies for Pictures, Designs and Sketches by the Late Lord Leighton, P.R.A.*, Fine Art Society, London, December 1896 to 1897. Exh. cat. foreword by Samuel Pepys Cockerell, London, 1896.

LONDON 1897. *Drawings by the late Lord Leighton Preserved for the Nation*, Leighton House, London, 1897. Exh. cat., 1897 (one known copy, at Leighton House Museum).

LONDON 1897 (RA). *Exhibition of Works by the Late Lord Leighton of Stretton President of the Royal Academy: Winter Exhibition*, Royal Academy of Arts, London, 4 January – 13 March 1897. Exh. cat., London, 1897.

LONDON 1900. A display at Leighton House Museum of the drawings collection, opening on 9 April 1900 and believed to have remained in place, with minor alterations, until at least 1936. Exh. cat. by Mrs Russell Barrington: 'Catalogue: Lord Leighton's House and What it Contains', 1900. Reprinted as part of *A Collection of Essays on Lord Leighton and his Works with Illustrated Catalogue of the Contents of Leighton House*, privately published, London, 1900–01 (one known copy, held at Leighton House Museum).

LONDON 1901. *Drawings and Sketches by Old Masters and Deceased Artists of the English School, Principally Acquired Between 1895 and 1901*, The British Museum, London, 1901. Exh. cat., London, 1901.

LONDON 1969. *High Victorian Art: An Exhibition in Conjunction with the Tate Gallery, the Victoria and Albert Museum and the York Art Gallery*, Leighton House, London, 1969. Exh. cat: John R.H. Yeoman (Foreword), William Gaunt (Introduction).

LONDON 1996. *Frederic Leighton 1830–1896*, Royal Academy of Arts, London, 15 February – 21 April 1996. Exh. cat. by Stephen Jones, Leonée Ormond, Richard Ormond, Christopher Newall and Benedict Read, London, 1996.

LONDON 2003. *The Canvas of Many Feet: Frederic Leighton in Rome, 1852–55*, Leighton House Museum, 7 November 2003 – 1 February 2004.

LONDON 2004. *Pre-Raphaelite Vision: Truth to Nature*, exhibition catalogue, Tate Britain and other venues, London, 2004. Exh. cat. by Christopher Newall and Allen Staley, London, 2004,

LONDON 2005. *The Leighton Drawings Project: A Preview*, Leighton House Museum, London, 19 September – 9 December 2005.

MANCHESTER (UK), MINNEAPOLIS, NEW YORK 1978–79. *Victorian High Renaissance*, Manchester Art Gallery, 1 September – 15 October 1978; Minneapolis Institute of Arts, U.S.A., 19 November 1978 – 7 January 1979; Brooklyn Museum, New York, U.S.A., 10 February – 8 April 1979. Exh. cat. by Richard Dorment et al, Minneapolis, 1978.

Meynell 1884. Alice Meynell: 'Cymon and Iphigenia', *Art Journal*, May 1884, pp 130–31.

Monkhouse 1882. Cosmo Monkhouse: 'Some English Artists and their Studios', *The Century*, May – October 1882, pp 553–58.

Morse 1987. Belinda Morse: *John Hanson Walker: The Life and Times of a Victorian Artist*, Alan Sutton Publishing, 1987.

Murray-Fennell 2003. Michael Murray-Fennell: 'The Canvas of Many Feet – multiplicity and simplicity in Frederic Leighton's Cimabue's Celebrated Madonna', MA dissertation, Royal Holloway, University of London, 2003.

Newall 1990. Christopher Newall: *The Art of Lord Leighton*, Phaidon Press Ltd., London, 1990.

NEW YORK 2005. *English Romantic Art 1850–1920*, Shepherd & Derom Galleries, New York, 20 September – 22 October 2005.

Ormond 1975a. Ormond, Richard: *Leighton's Frescoes in the Victoria and Albert Museum*, W. & J. Mackay, Chatham, 1975.

Ormond 1975b. Leonée and Richard Ormond: *Lord Leighton*, Yale University Press, London, 1975.

OXFORD 1894. Display at the Taylorian Institute, Oxford, from 1894.

Poynter 1897. E.J. Poynter: 'Lecture 3: Systems of Art Education' (2 October 1871), in *Ten Lectures on Art*, 1897.

Prettejohn 1996. Elizabeth Prettejohn: 'Painting indoors: Leighton and his studio', *Apollo*, February 1996, pp 17–21.

Prettejohn 2000a. Elizabeth Prettejohn: *The Art of the Pre-Raphaelites*, Tate Publishing, London, 2000.

Prettejohn 2000b. Elizabeth Prettejohn: 'Leighton: The Aesthete as Academic', in Denis 2000, pp 33–52.

Prinsep 1897. Valentine Prinsep and Samuel Cockerell: 'The Lord Leighton Memorial', *The Times*, 15 June 1897, p. 5.

Richmond 1896. W.B. Richmond: 'Lord Leighton and His Art', *The Nineteenth Century*, January – June 1896, pp 465–76.

Richmond 1900. W.B. Richmond: 'Leighton, Millais and William Morris', lecture delivered to the students of the RA, in *A Collection of Essays on Lord Leighton and his Works with Illustrated Catalogue of the Contents of Leighton House*, privately published, London, 1900–01 (one known copy, held at Leighton House Museum), pp 108–29.

Robbins 2005. Daniel Robbins and Reena Suleman: *Leighton House Museum*, The Royal Borough of Kensington and Chelsea, London, 2005.

Rhys 1895. Ernest Rhys (prefatory essay by F.G. Stephens): *Sir Frederic Leighton, Bart., P.R.A.: An Illustrated Chronicle*, George Bell and Sons, London, 1895.

Rhys 1900. Ernest Rhys: *Frederic Lord Leighton, Late President of the Royal Academy of Arts: An Illustrated Record of his Life and Work*, George Bell and Sons, London, 1900.

Ruskin 1843. John Ruskin: *Modern Painters: Their Superiority in the Art of Landscape Painting to all the Ancient Masters Proved by Examples of the True, the Beautiful, and the Intellectual from the Works of Modern Artists, especially Those of J.M.W. Turner Esq., R.A.*, vol. I, Smith Elder and Co., London, 1843.

Simon 1996. Robin Simon (editor): 'Lord Leighton 1830–1896 and Leighton House: A Centenary Celebration', *Apollo*, London, 1996.

Spielmann 1888. Marion Harry Spielmann: 'Painters in Their Studios, I. – Sir Frederick Leighton, P.R.A.', *Graphic*, 2 June 1888, pp 588–90.

Spielmann 1889. Marion Harry Spielmann: 'Current Art: the Royal Academy', *Magazine of Art*, 1889, pp 224–27.

Spielmann 1892. Marion Harry Spielmann, 'Greek Girls Playing Ball', *Graphic*, May 28 1892, p. 637.

Spielmann 1896. Marion Harry Spielmann: 'The Late Lord Leighton', *Magazine of Art*, 1896, pp 198–216.

Staley 1973. Allen Staley: *The Pre-Raphaelite Landscape*, Clarendon Press, Oxford, 1973.

Staley 1906. Edgcumbe Staley: *Lord Leighton of Stretton, P.R.A.*, The Walter Scott Publishing Company, London, 1906.

Towndrow 1939. Kenneth Romney Towndrow: *Alfred Stevens: Architectural Sculptor, Painter and Designer*, Constable and Co. Ltd., London, 1939.

Yellow Book 1894. *The Yellow Book*, vol. I, April 1894, ill. p. 133.

Vasari, 2005. Giorgio Vasari, Marilyn Aronberg Lavin (editor), Jonathan Foster (translator): *Lives of the Artists*, Dover Publications, New York, 2005.

Williams 1889. Annie Williams: 'Expression in Drapery', *Magazine of Art*, 1889, pp 61–63.

YORK, LONDON, NOTTINGHAM 1999. *The Artist's Model: From Etty to Spencer*, York City Art Gallery, 29 May – 11 July 1999; Kenwood House, London, 23 July – 26 September 1999; Djanogly Gallery, Nottingham, 16 October – 12 December 1999. Exh. cat. by Martin Postle and William Vaughan, London, 1999.

INDEX

Q

R

S

T

U

V

W